MW00611451

Praise for *Sister in Law*:

'Harriet Wistrich is a total inspiration. Her work to secure
justice for women has been groundbreaking. She's a game changer.
A brilliant lawyer – a brilliant book!'
**Baroness Helena Kennedy of the Shaws KC,
author of *Misjustice***

'Justice needs both warriors and champions and in Harriet Wistrich
she found both. *Sister in Law* is compelling, inspiring, horrifying and
humbling in equal measure. Everybody should read it.'
**Dame Professor Sue Black, author of
All That Remains and *Written in Bone***

'Harriet Wistrich is a heroine. Here is her story: 30 years of
feminist and human rights activism, legal creativity, and tenacity.'
Beatrix Campbell, author of *Secrets and Silence*

'Harriet Wistrich is one of our most courageous and
outspoken lawyers and has written a remarkable, impressive and
revelatory book. *Sister in Law* should be read by everyone involved in
the criminal justice system, everyone interested in how women are
treated in our courts and everyone who wants to know what is really
going on in Britain today in terms of crime and punishment.'
Duncan Campbell, author of *Underworld*

'A must-read for anyone interested in social activism and law,
this is an incredible record of a unique career. Harriet Wistrich's work
on behalf of abused women who have also been failed by the state is
inspirational. She is one of the feminist pioneers of our age.'
**Susanna Rustin, author of
*Sexed: A History of British Feminism***

www.penguin.co.uk

'For decades, Harriet Wistrich has been bravely standing up for women who have been abused, imprisoned and denied their rights. This stirring account of her impressive work will remind readers that the fight for justice is far from over, and inspire all of us who still hope to build a more equal and safer world.'
Natasha Walter, author of *Living Dolls* and
Before the Light Fades

'Complex, heartbreaking cases from Harriet's stellar career as a feminist lawyer, turned into a vital, compelling, enraging narrative about how the justice system must change to protect women and girls. Extraordinary. Everyone should read it.'
Anna Mazzola, lawyer and novelist

'This page-turning account shows how a determined, innovative, feminist lawyer can squeeze improved outcomes for women from a creaking, patriarchal legal system.'
Rahila Gupta, author of *Enslaved*

Sister in Law

*Fighting for Justice in a System
Designed by Men*

HARRIET WISTRICH

torva

TRANSWORLD PUBLISHERS
Penguin Random House, One Embassy Gardens,
8 Viaduct Gardens, London SW11 7BW
www.penguin.co.uk

Transworld is part of the Penguin Random House group of companies
whose addresses can be found at global.penguinrandomhouse.com

Penguin
Random House
UK

First published in Great Britain in 2024 by Torva
an imprint of Transworld Publishers

A CIP catalogue record for this book
is available from the British Library.

ISBN 9781911709268

Typeset in 12/15.5pt Minion Pro by Jouve (UK), Milton Keynes
Printed and bound in Great Britain by Clays Ltd, Elcograf S.p.A.

The authorized representative in the EEA is Penguin Random House Ireland,
Morrison Chambers, 32 Nassau Street, Dublin D02 YH68.

Penguin Random House is committed to a sustainable
future for our business, our readers and our planet. This book
is made from Forest Stewardship Council® certified paper.

MIX
Paper | Supporting
responsible forestry
FSC® C018179

1

In memory of Emma Humphreys and in honour
of all those who have told their painful stories to
raise awareness and create change.

In memory of my parents, Enid and Ernest, for their
love and support and for fostering in me a feminist spirit,
an open-minded and political approach to the world
and a strong sense of justice. I wish you were still here.

And in memory of my much-loved and
missed rebel cousin, Joanne.

Contents

Introduction

ON THE EVENING OF 7 October 1992, seven-year-old Nikki Allan disappeared from her home on the Wear Garth estate in Sunderland. The following morning, after locals joined the police search for the missing child, her battered body was found in a derelict warehouse close to the estate. A post-mortem examination revealed that in addition to being bludgeoned with a brick, she had been stabbed thirty-seven times in the chest and abdomen.

The police launched a major investigation to find Nikki's killer. Nine days later, they arrested a local man, George Heron, who had moved to the area only a few months previously and was described by neighbours as a loner. After three days of questioning, he confessed to the crime and was charged with her murder. Nikki's mother, Sharon Henderson, alongside other members of her family and local community, attended his trial in 1993 in the expectation of seeing this 'monster' convicted and sentenced to a lengthy term of imprisonment. When he was acquitted by the jury, the judge having ruled that the police used oppressive methods to secure his confession, there was uproar in the court. Many thought Heron had got away with murder on a technicality, a view the police tacitly confirmed when they stated they were not looking for anyone else in connection with Nikki's death.

Left to struggle alone with her grief and despair, Sharon Henderson was in freefall. Not only had she lost her precious daughter in the most horrific circumstances, she believed the man who had killed Nikki had got off scot-free. Rumours began to circulate that Sharon, an uneducated single mother of four small children who had herself mainly grown up in care, had neglected Nikki, and that this had in some way contributed to the targeting of her little girl. Among the false stories doing the rounds was a tale that, shortly before her disappearance, Nikki had been seen begging outside a pub. These rumours, it transpired decades later, probably emanated from the police. Somehow, Sharon survived and, over time, and in the face of police resistance, began an extraordinary campaign to get justice for Nikki. It was to take her thirty years.

In May 2023, I was standing beside Sharon on the steps of Newcastle Crown Court as she spoke to a bank of reporters and photographers after another man, David Boyd, was convicted of Nikki's murder. Boyd had lived three doors away from Nikki's grandfather's home, where the seven-year-old had last been seen by her family, and he had previous convictions for sexual offences against children. Although, finally, justice had been delivered for her daughter, the battle was not over for Sharon. Now she wanted Northumbria Police to be held to account for their past failings and had asked me to assist her.

By this time, I had been a practising solicitor for twenty-six years. In the early 1990s, when Sharon Henderson's ordeal began, switching to a career in the law was an idea I was just beginning to contemplate, motivated by a desire to help women who, like Sharon, were being failed in myriad ways by a criminal justice system often not fit for purpose.

In the days when I made my decision to study for the law, outdated and discriminatory attitudes to women still pervaded both its statutes and its application. Rape within marriage, for example, had only just been acknowledged as a crime. The police had long tended towards a non-interventionist approach to 'domestics' and a new Home Office policy of 'positive action' would take a while to be widely exercised. Harassment, stalking, forced marriage and honour-based violence were not defined or recognized as separate offences in law.

In courtrooms across the country, judges considered rape victims to be complicit for wearing short skirts. One famously warned a jury that 'women and small children are prone to tell lies'. Men who killed their female partners and relied on the defence of provocation were often spared jail by sympathetic judges. Teenage girls from disadvantaged and abusive backgrounds, groomed and pimped into street prostitution, were regularly arrested and labelled 'common prostitutes'. There were no legally enforceable duties on the state to prevent violence against women, to protect victims from foreseeable harm or to investigate and prosecute serious crimes. There was no entitlement to an independent and transparent inquiry into deaths caused by the state which could examine the role of state bodies in contributing to those deaths.

In the course of the thirty-year period this book spans, important legislative and policy reforms have changed the legal landscape, perhaps most notably the Human Rights Act 1998, the Sexual Offences Act 2003, the Equality Act 2010, the Modern Slavery Act 2015 and, most recently, the Domestic Abuse Act 2021. Specialist units were created within police forces to investigate sexual violence and domestic abuse. The Crown Prosecution Service (CPS) appointed dedicated rape and serious sexual offences prosecutors and promulgated guidance on rape myths and stereotypes.

However, as the stories in these pages reveal, there remains a great deal of room for improvement in the law and legislative and policy reforms have limited meaning in any event if they rely on enforcement by those who have little understanding, commitment or reason to implement them. This is where litigation can make an impact and drive change, not just for the individuals involved in the cases but for innumerable others affected by the laws and systems they seek to challenge.

Throughout my legal career, I have fought the corner of people from all backgrounds who have been let down by the justice system:

survivors of male violence or abuse, or of the actions of the state; sometimes the bereaved families of those who did not survive seeking justice in their name. Increasingly, I came to specialize in acting for women whose lives, like Sharon Henderson's, have been irrevocably damaged as a result.

This book examines, through the lens of my own role as lawyer, a selection of just some key cases where my clients have become involved in litigation that has led to wider change – cases that demonstrate the inequities in the treatment of women throughout our system, from police to government, the CPS to our immigration services. Together we have found ways to counter antiquated laws, to navigate byzantine and archaic systems and to challenge state actors in the long struggle for justice. In the process, we have shaken the status quo; sometimes, we have succeeded in reshaping the law as well as public attitudes.

I am grateful to the brave women and men whose stories feature here for allowing me to write about the experiences they shared with me during our legal campaigns. All were spurred on by a thirst for justice and showed huge courage and tenacity. Some of the women who have waived their right to anonymity in order to speak out publicly are referred to by their real names, others by the pseudonyms used in their cases or created for the purposes of this book. Some details are not discussed, for legal reasons or out of respect for the privacy of the litigants.

In all of the cases explored, the law is that pertaining at the time in England and Wales (there may be, or have been, differences in Scotland, which has its own system, and variations in Northern Ireland).

As will quickly become apparent, I am not the type of lawyer who loves the law for its own sake but the kind who looks for ways around the law when it gets in the way of justice. To help my clients to achieve a fair outcome, I take my lead from them. I believe in and encourage a collaborative approach, working closely as a team with my colleagues and the barristers I instruct, and with campaigners or support groups, where they exist. I draw on the skills and insights of researchers and academics, and use the media where we feel publicity may be beneficial in amplifying the issues or putting pressure on the authorities.

This journey through the maze of our legal system is a bumpy and unpredictable ride, sometimes gruelling, sometimes mired in slow and convoluted processes. Not every battle ends in victory – but we always make a mark.

1

From Campaigner to Lawyer

ON A HOT SUMMER'S DAY in July 1991, as a thirty-one-year-old feminist activist, I joined a group of women protesting outside the Royal Courts of Justice in London. We were there to voice our opposition to the murder conviction of Sara Thornton, who was serving a mandatory life sentence for killing her violent, alcoholic husband. Inside, Sara's appeal lawyers were arguing that her conviction should be reduced to manslaughter on the grounds of provocation.

Our ad hoc campaign had been sparked by a friend in Leeds, Sandra McNeill, who had asked my partner Julie and me if we could mobilize support for Sara Thornton on the day of the appeal. In those pre-internet years, this consisted largely of rounding up our feminist mates by word of mouth or on the home phone. I worked for a film training organization at a women's centre on Kingsway, just down the road from the Royal Courts, and rallied women in the building to join us. We brought placards and banners demanding 'Free Sara Thornton' and 'Justice for Battered Women Who Kill' and handed out leaflets to passers-by and the steady stream of lawyers hurrying to and from the courtrooms – this sprawling gothic edifice houses over a hundred of them, for every conceivable type of dispute from the Family Division to Chancery to the Criminal Appeal Courts.

The leaflets we had put together set out the reasons for our

assertion that Sara Thornton's conviction was a miscarriage of justice. We included examples of cases where lenient sentences had been
handed down to men for killing their wives after they claimed to
have been driven to it by 'provocative' behaviour and compared
them with the discriminatory treatment in the courts of women like
Sara, who killed in response to their husbands' repeated physical
assaults. Sara had stabbed her abusive husband once, after a threatening altercation, and then immediately called an ambulance. At her
original trial, she had pleaded guilty to manslaughter on the grounds
of diminished responsibility. When sentencing Sara, the judge had
told her that after the confrontation with her husband she could
have 'walked out or gone upstairs'. His remarks stood in stark con-
trast to the ready acceptance of some of the reasons offered by men
for lashing out in anger at their wives.

The law as it relates to murder differs from other criminal offences
because murder is the only charge where a partial as well as a full
defence may be applicable. A full defence might be that the killing
was an accident; where there was no intention to kill or injure, it
might be self-defence, provided it was the outcome of a proportionate and immediate response to the threat faced.

A partial defence does not absolve the defendant of guilt, but it
does reflect a lower level of culpability. If accepted by the jury, it will
reduce a murder conviction to one of manslaughter. The partial
defence of provocation is said to date back to the sixteenth century,
when it was available to men who killed as a result of their honour or
dignity being 'insulted'. It was from here that it took the shape of a
defence available to those who killed in 'justifiable anger'. It relied
upon the immediacy of the retaliation and the absence of premedita-
tion. For it to be admissible there had to be evidence that the
defendant had killed 'in the heat of the moment', reacting in a way in
which any 'reasonable man' might understandably react.

The interpretation of this defence was, we were arguing, biased towards a male response. Women who lived with domestic violence under the constant threat of assault or rape were more likely to act out of fright or desperation than to strike out in retaliation to an 'insult' – the classic hot-blooded reaction that male defendants so often successfully relied on. On the face of it, 'provocation' was a more accurate description of what these women had suffered and it should have worked in their favour, but because of the way the law had evolved, their responses did not always fit with how the defence was framed. This was, we believed, a law designed for men who kill in anger, not for women who kill out of fear.

Until 1965, when capital punishment in the UK was suspended, prior to being permanently abolished in 1969, if a person was convicted of murder, they were likely to face the death penalty. The last woman to be executed in the UK was Ruth Ellis, who was hanged at Holloway prison in 1955 after being found guilty of the murder of her boyfriend, David Blakely. The child of an abusive father, she had been the victim of abusive relationships all her life. Not long before Ruth shot him, Blakely had beaten her up so badly that she had suffered a miscarriage.

Campaigners sought clemency for Ruth and although they ultimately failed in her case, their efforts escalated the movement for the abolition of the death penalty. Two years after she was executed, two new partial defences to murder – diminished responsibility and killing due to suicide pact – were introduced in the Homicide Act 1957, which codified the common-law defence of provocation and restricted the use of capital punishment.

It was a chilling thought that, only about twenty-five years earlier, women like Sara Thornton would have faced the death penalty. As it was, their convictions for murder carried a mandatory life sentence, with the judge setting the minimum term to be served before the offender would be eligible for release on a life licence.

That day in 1991, the Court of Appeal dismissed the legal argument that women may experience a form of 'slow-burn' provocation. Sara Thornton's murder conviction stood.

Sandra McNeill, who had kick-started Sara's campaign, had for many years been doggedly compiling newspaper reports of the light sentences being handed down to men making use of the provocation defence. Thanks to Sandra, we had a growing dossier of case studies. So many male perpetrators of violence were successfully claiming that 'she provoked me because she wouldn't shut up' or 'she was having an affair' that we dubbed it the 'nagging and shagging' defence.

The point we were making about the way men and women were treated differently by the law couldn't have been illustrated much more plainly than it was just two days after the dismissal of Sara's appeal by a small newspaper report of the trial of one Joseph McGrail, who had successfully used the defence of provocation for kicking his wife Marion to death. The judge, on sentencing McGrail to just two years' imprisonment, commented that his wife 'would have tried the patience of a saint'. When we drew the attention of the press to the conspicuous disparity between the two cases, the story was picked up by the national media, which gave our campaign a massive boost.

As a result, despite losing her appeal, Sara returned to HMP Bullwood Hall in Essex encouraged by the increased media coverage of her case, and by the growing public support that sprang from it, determined to fight for a fresh one.

My partner, Julie Bindel, and I continued to meet up with a few of the group formed around Sara's battle. Julie and I had got together in the mid-1980s. She had left a 'sink school' in Darlington without qualifications and educated herself through feminist activism. My background was very different: I was from a middle-class, secular Jewish family in North London and had studied at Oxford University, where I, too, began to actively engage the feminist principles I'd grown up with. Both Julie and I were middle children sandwiched between two brothers. Both our families had encouraged us to be strong, independent women and both families were staunchly Labour – even if it came as a surprise to Julie's dad, when I eventually met him, that both my parents had been Labour councillors. He had assumed that all 'posh people' were Tories.

Julie and I certainly didn't agree on everything – we still don't – but we shared a commitment to political and feminist activism and a strong belief in the importance of analysis, debate and the communication of ideas. We had seen how campaigning around a single case had helped draw attention not only to what was happening to the woman at its centre but also to the wider context of a patriarchal society in which misogyny pervaded the criminal justice system and delivered outrageously unjust outcomes.

We decided to broaden the remit of the Free Sara Thornton campaign. Our aim was to create a clear identity for our group in taking up the cause of other individual women in similar situations, lending our support to other similar campaigns and to drive our fight for systemic change.

And so the Free Sara Thornton campaign became Justice for Women (JFW), an organization that continues, thirty years on, to support and advocate for women who have fought back against, or killed, violent men, to combat male abuse and brutality and to lobby for change in associated areas of law, policy and practice that discriminate against women.

Another woman whose campaign we were backing was also appealing a murder conviction for killing her cruel and controlling husband. Kiranjit Ahluwalia had endured a decade of rapes, beatings and a life under virtual house arrest at his hands. One night, after he burned her face with an iron, she made a desperate bid to escape. To prevent him from pursuing her, and to give him a taste of his own medicine, she set fire to his bedclothes. She had not intended to kill him, but he had died of his injuries ten days later.

Kiranjit's campaign was being led by Southall Black Sisters (SBS), a long-established, dynamic feminist activist group and domestic violence service that supports black and Asian women in West London and beyond. They would come to demos equipped with megaphones and sing made-up songs with excruciating rhymes that amplified the volume and exuberance of the protest and brought smiles to the faces of campaigners and onlookers alike.

SBS had been a little wary at first of this assortment of protesters who had rocked up seemingly from nowhere outside the Royal Courts of Justice. But as we began to get to know each other and work together, we forged a mutual respect.

The women's movement was emerging from a period of fragmentation in the 1980s which had seen political in-fighting between different factions on issues such as race. The alliance between JFW and SBS was important not only in practical ways but also symbolically: it marked the start of a transition we needed to make from a decade of internal strife to a more optimistic, action-orientated approach to feminism and feminist activism.

Many feminist organizations were suspicious of the press, often with very good cause. So much reporting on violence against women was imbued with the worst sort of victim-blaming peppered with salacious detail. 'Women's libbers' were portrayed as ugly, angry women in dungarees. Women's groups tended to be anti-hierarchical and a lot of them operated as collectives. In some cases, this meant that any decision made or action taken had to be discussed and agreed by all the members, which effectively prevented any individual taking the lead or becoming a spokeswoman for a cause.

Cooperation between the media and feminist groups could therefore be tricky to navigate. As media interest in the issue of 'battered women who kill' snowballed, journalists began to come to JFW for comment. We quickly learned that we needed to take care with how such approaches were managed after Hannana Siddiqui of the SBS took Julie aside to complain that we were providing quotes directly to the media on the Kiranjit Ahluwalia case instead of referring reporters to SBS, who were organizing the campaign. As white women, we were very familiar with how the press would favour a male spokesperson over a female one and yet, back then, it simply hadn't occurred to us that they would discriminate in exactly the same way against the black women actually spearheading the action by automatically turning for comment to white women, as if we somehow had more authority to speak on the matter. We didn't make that mistake again.

Like most people at that time, none of us yet had access to email or a mobile phone, and social media, of course, was not even invented. From the campaigning perspective, then, if we wanted to make an impact, we had to trust individuals who could respond quickly to media requests in order to get the message out.

JFW used the address and phone number of the home I shared with Julie, and it wasn't unusual for us to get a call in the middle of dinner from someone asking to speak to our 'press officer', a role assumed by whichever one of us happened to answer the phone.

Increasingly, we were being asked to give broadcast interviews. While Julie was bold enough to take this in her stride, I was nervous and initially reluctant to get involved. Quite a few of our group refused point blank. The first TV interview I ever gave was about Sara Thornton's case after Julie persuaded me to go on one of the breakfast programmes. Experience had taught her that the knack with these short live interviews was to decide in advance on the three most important points to be made and ensure that you made them, whatever question was asked. It is a strategy that has stood me in good stead.

Kiranjit Ahluwalia's appeal was eventually listed for July 1992 before the lord chief justice, Peter Taylor. Her legal team developed arguments raised at Sara Thornton's appeal about the gender bias inherent in the defence of provocation. Although Kiranjit's appeal was allowed, it was not in respect of provocation but on a separate ground which relied on fresh psychiatric evidence to support the defence of diminished responsibility. A retrial was ordered.

Kiranjit's arraignment, where the defendant is invited to enter a plea, was fixed for 25 September 1992 at the Old Bailey. We had learned that the CPS was willing to accept the plea of guilty to manslaughter by reason of diminished responsibility, but we had no idea what sentence might be handed down by the court. Scores of supporters, including many survivors of domestic violence, gathered outside the Old Bailey to await the outcome of the sentencing hearing.

It was some hours before an excited murmur swept through the crowd: Kiranjit had been given three years and four months. This was the time she had already served: she was going to be released there and then. As the news circulated, she walked out of the court, arms aloft, flanked by Pragna Patel and Hannana Siddiqui of SBS. It was a ground-breaking victory for Kiranjit, for all those who had worked so hard in her fight for justice and for all women discriminated against by the law.

While the reduction of Kiranjit's conviction to manslaughter and the impact of the campaign to free Sara Thornton were important stepping stones, the systemic problems of blatant and pervasive bias remained. Was this due simply to the wider inequalities between the sexes embedded in a patriarchal culture, or was it also embedded in the laws themselves, which were designed around male behaviour and responses? How exactly could the law be modified to redress the balance?

At meetings with SBS and a feminist law charity, Rights of Women, we discussed where we should direct our campaign to reform the law. The subjective part of the provocation test required a defendant on a charge of murder to show that the provoking words or conduct had caused a 'sudden and temporary' loss of self-control. SBS took the view that the removal of the word 'sudden' from 'sudden and temporary' loss of control might accommodate the different and less immediate response of women subject to violence and abuse.

JFW were concerned that merely adjusting the wording would not prevent men from relying on the 'nagging and shagging' defence. Liz Kelly and Jill Radford, both feminist academics specializing in violence against women, and friends from our wider feminist networks proposed and drafted a new partial defence of 'self-preservation'. This would provide a partial defence to murder where the defendant (i) kills a partner or someone in a familial or familiar intimate relationship who (ii) has subjected them to abuse and intimidation to the extent that they (iii) honestly believe that they have reached a point at which there is no future, and no protection of safety from the abuse, and are convinced that they will not continue to live while the aggressor is alive.

Although our self-preservation defence never made it into law, the cases on which we were campaigning, and the question of whether legislation should be reformed, were being discussed by legal academics, criminologists and politicians, too. Several MPs contacted us to see if there was anything they could do to help. Jack Ashley and, later, Harry Cohen initiated debates in Parliament by tabling early-day motions and ten-minute-rule bills proposing reforms to the partial defence of provocation. The MPs' interventions weren't given enough of an airing to create new law, but they helped keep the issue of the discriminatory defence in the public eye.

It was only a couple of days after the release of Kiranjit Ahluwalia that a letter arrived at our home from Drake Hall open prison in Staffordshire, addressed simply to 'Julie Bindel, Justice for Women'. It was from a prisoner called Emma Humphreys. 'In Dec 85 I was convicted of murdering my boyfriend, Trevor Armitage, who was 33,' she wrote. 'I had met him six months previously when I was 16. I was a prostitute, he was a client. I was 17 at the time of the offence and I am now 24.'

Emma described the circumstances surrounding Armitage's death. Having moved in with him because she had nowhere else to live, she had suffered violence and abuse while working on the streets, including a traumatic gang rape, and at home, where she had been subjected to punishment rapes by Armitage.

'You might be wondering, "Why after so long fight your case?"' she concluded, explaining that it was only recently that she had gained the courage and confidence to talk to people about her background and about what had happened with Armitage. 'In my heart,' she said, 'I know I don't deserve this life sentence.'

Julie went to visit Emma in prison to find out more. It became clear from the story Emma told her that her conviction for murder was a miscarriage of justice. But in order to mobilize Justice for Women to press for an appeal, we had to find a solicitor who would agree to take on the case. With virtually no funding available for criminal appeal work, only someone dedicated to the cause was likely to be prepared to help. I approached Rohit Sanghvi, the solicitor who had assisted the SBS pro bono with establishing grounds for appeal for Kiranjit Ahluwalia. Rohit was up for it, but he warned that the process would be arduous, and that someone from JFW would need to do the legwork, starting with taking a detailed account from Emma.

I went to see Rohit to find out what this would entail. He told me that it was almost impossible to appeal a criminal conviction. The grounds on which a Court of Appeal will allow it are extremely limited and, unless there is fresh evidence, basically boil down to misdirections or errors by the judge at trial. In order to explore the possibilities, we would have to understand everything about Emma's life, about the relationship with Armitage and about the events leading up to his death, as well as Emma's arrest, how she was advised by her legal team and what had happened at trial. In putting together this narrative, it was important to go into more and more detail the closer you got to the moment the offence took place. Those last days and hours and minutes, including what was going on in Emma's mind in the seconds before she killed Armitage, could be the most critical. It would all have to be combed through by her lawyers.

Appalled by how this abused young woman had come to spend her entire adulthood to date in jail, and undeterred by the mountain to be climbed, I volunteered for the job.

I had no training in the law. At Oxford University – where I was somewhat surprised to be offered a place (I was a late bloomer academically) – I'd switched courses early on from history to politics, philosophy and economics.

After graduating, I'd wound up in Liverpool, where I had learned some film-making skills with the aim of communicating ideas through that medium.

The early 1980s and the launch of Channel 4 saw a burgeoning of the independent film sector, but by the time I moved back to London in 1987, funding was growing more and more difficult to come by. Five years on, I was employed as a training manager at WAVES (Women's Audio Visual Education Scheme), but it was a struggle to get film ideas commissioned and hard to escape the sense that who you knew seemed to count for more in the film and TV industries than talent, innovation and having something substantial to say.

What I did have was a deep-rooted desire to help change the world for the better, and Emma's cry for help had come at a point in my own life where I was feeling restless and looking for a new direction in which to channel it. Through my campaigning work, I'd had the occasional opportunity to sit in court, where I listened closely from the public gallery, fascinated by the legal arguments and following how judgments were reached, and I enjoyed discussing what I'd seen in the courtroom in our feminist groups as we debated how the law could be improved.

Julie and I had recently bought a house with a friend, Sarah Maguire, who had retrained in the law and was now a junior tenant at Tooks Court, a leading civil liberties chambers headed by the renowned QC Michael Mansfield. Aware of my frustration with the constant battles to secure funding in the film world, Sarah saw my interest in the legal side of our campaigns and had suggested that perhaps I should consider becoming a lawyer.

It had got me thinking. Could I retrain as a solicitor? The pressing need for more feminist lawyers in the justice system was plain. Here was a way of working very directly with individuals who had faced extreme adversity, of helping them from within the system to challenge the processes that had failed them. It was at this crossroads in my life that I stepped up to assist Rohit Sanghvi with the Emma Humphreys case. It felt like a perfect opening to dip my toe into the waters of campaign lawyering to see if it was for me.

A few years earlier, when my grandmother, Ewa, had been coming up to her ninetieth birthday, I had made a low-budget documentary, screened some time later at the Jewish Film Festival, telling the story of her extraordinary survival in Nazi-occupied Poland at the start of the Second World War, and I approached taking Emma's account in much the same fashion. I would explore her whole life, starting with her childhood and focusing initially on positive and neutral memories rather than more recent traumatic events, to reassure her and help her gradually to open up so that when the time came to talk about exactly what had happened on the night Armitage died, she would feel able to do so without fear or shame getting in the way. I was given permission by the prison to audio-record our meetings. It was important that Emma's statement remained faithful to her own vocabulary and articulation of her story through the necessary editing.

Emma was now being held just a couple of miles down the road from us, which made the logistics of my visits much easier: shortly after first writing to JFW, she had been shipped out of Drake Hall and transferred to Holloway as a result of being falsely accused of threatening another inmate with a knife. Although eventually cleared of the allegation, she was deeply upset by it.

It wasn't the first time I had set foot in a prison – Julie and I had been visiting Sara Thornton, who was on hunger strike in protest at the upholding of her conviction, at HMP Bullwood Hall in Essex. At Holloway, I appreciated the kindness of a sympathetic member of the in-house probation staff, who provided a room in the probation area for my meetings with Emma. As well as giving us privacy, it offered more comfortable seating, arranged for more relaxed conversation than was possible facing one another across a table in a public visiting area. We even had the luxury of a kettle to make tea and coffee. In a prison, small concessions like this can make a big difference.

I saw immediately that Emma had an eating disorder. She was painfully thin. There were scars up and down her arms from self-harming with a razor. As I would discover, both problems are common among women in prison and a strong indicator of abuse or neglect in childhood. Self-harm is fundamentally a maladaptive coping mechanism: focusing on the physical pain helps to distract the mind from being pulled down into horrible memories. Emma was bright, creative and had a wicked sense of humour. She could also be stroppy and difficult. I warmed to her quickly.

I returned to Holloway with my tape recorder every week for several months. Emma and I established a good rapport and it was clear that she not only wanted but needed to share her account and place it on record, however harrowing it was for her. I may have been new to this role but there was not much she had to tell me that shocked or even surprised me. Immersed as I was in feminist reading and thinking, over the years I had been confronted by many of the depravities of the hatred and violence inflicted by some men on women and children.

Her descriptions of her life as a 'street prostitute' were more of a revelation to me. Believing that it was important to grasp how she got there and the effect on her of these levels of degradation, I pressed her gently on various points to ensure accuracy and clarity and listened with a feminist understanding of victim-blaming and the impact this has on women generally, and specifically on anyone who has experienced sexual and physical abuse. This means never judging, except to challenge self-blame and guilt. And when the prison door was locked behind me, I was able to process what I had heard by talking it through with Julie and other JFW colleagues.

Emma was born in North Wales, the second of three girls. At some point the family returned to her mother's home town of Nottingham. Her father, John, and mother June separated when she was five. When Emma was ten, June married Al Somerville, a Canadian who worked on the oil rigs, and emigrated with him and her sisters to Edmonton, Alberta.

Al proved to be a sadistic husband. He was violent and controlling towards June, who resorted to alcohol and self-harm to get by. Growing up in this brooding environment was frightening and destabilizing for Emma, all the more so when her mother, to whom she had always been very close, apparently turned against her. She couldn't understand or explain why this happened, but with hindsight I suspect that Emma may herself have become a target for Al's abusive behaviour.

Whatever the case, from the age of twelve, the effects of her troubled childhood began to show themselves. It was then, scared to go home after school, that she first started to cut herself. She took to running away, hitching lifts from men who invariably sexually assaulted her. She was introduced to drink and drugs, used in child pornography and prostituted. When she was put into care, she ran away from that, too. She had one or two positive experiences with foster parents, but for the most part she was wayward and extremely vulnerable.

When Emma was about fifteen, her father managed to make contact. John had remarried and started a new family in Nottingham and she flew back to England to live with them. By that stage Emma was so out of control that the family relationship quickly broke down. She moved in with her maternal grandmother, but neither 'Nana', who set great store by respectability and keeping up appearances, nor her wild-child granddaughter was able to handle this arrangement, and before long Emma was begging to return to Canada. Her father and grandmother gratefully paid her fare.

Denied entry to the country over some immigration irregularity, she was soon on her way back to Nottingham. Feeling hemmed in and oppressed at her nana's house, she packed her bags again. It was a pattern that would repeat itself in the following months: for a while Emma would enjoy being taken care of, but then she and Nana would clash and Emma would take flight. Although she had nowhere else to go, experience had taught her that if needs must, it was never difficult to find a man who would give her a bed for the night in return for sex. In the early 1980s Nottingham was particularly notorious for street prostitution and she would join the women touting for business in the red-light district. It was here that she met Trevor Armitage, a thirty-three-year-old punter who took her home with him and called himself her boyfriend. In truth, he quickly assumed the role of her pimp. It would later emerge that he was known for his 'predilection for young girls' and had previous convictions for violence.

Emma appreciated having a roof over her head and comfortable surroundings for which the only rent she had to pay was to provide Trevor with sex on demand. He was soon declaring his love for her, and she began to believe she loved him, and yet he was still driving her to the red-light area in Forest Road at night to sell sex, collecting her after her 'shift' and 'taking care of her earnings' for her. The vice squad picked her up several times. Often she gave a false name. On one occasion the police brought her back to the house and questioned Emma and Trevor separately. They asked Emma if Trevor was her 'ponce', which she denied. Trevor later told her that the police had advised him to get rid of her because she was 'trouble'.

Trevor started to become very jealous and possessive, which Emma initially misread as a manifestation of his love for her. With the possessiveness came paranoia about other men she may be associating with outside 'work', which would erupt in violence. He watched her closely, regularly driving around her 'beat' and rifling through her personal things looking for evidence of 'infidelity'. When he was out and she was at home, he would ring her frequently to check up on her, singing Stevie Wonder's 'I Just Called To Say I Love You' down the phone.

Because Emma believed Trevor when he said he loved her, she began to feel confused by the contradictory demands of his jealousy, his own sexual requirements and his keenness for her to have sex with other men for money. Increasingly, to have sex with him she had to dissociate and go into 'prostitution mode'. If she said no, he would force her, telling her, 'Naughty girls must pay for what they have done wrong.' Rape and physical assaults became commonplace and she started to drink heavily to block it all out.

One night Emma was taken by a punter to an empty flat, where two more men appeared. One of them held the points of a pair of sharp scissors to her neck while they raped her in turn. She didn't resist, terrified that she would be stabbed or killed. She told Trevor about the attack but she was soon back out on the streets.

She could deal with selling sex to strangers by compartmentalizing it in a separate headspace. What she now struggled to handle was having sex with Trevor. In a situation where her tangled emotions were more engaged, and with a man she believed cared about her, the trauma of the gang rape came to the fore. She would acquiesce but immediately afterwards felt so sick she would vomit. Sometimes Trevor beat her and dragged her across the house by her hair or punched her in the head. Once he threatened to cut her face to 'make her ugly'.

Emma was unravelling. She began to get into more trouble with the police. One evening, after Trevor gave her a black eye, she booked into a hotel and got so drunk that she had a fight with the hotel manager and was arrested for soliciting and assault. Another arrest, this time for criminal damage to Trevor's house – he pressed charges – resulted in a court appearance and remand, initially to a bail hostel and then Risley prison after she breached the hostel rules. Three weeks later she was back in court to face the magistrates. Unwilling to relinquish control of his attractive teenage cash cow, Trevor turned up at the hearing and persuaded the court to release her into his 'care'.

While Emma was still convinced that Trevor loved her – maybe believed he was the only person who really did – she also dreaded returning to live with him. Her dread was completely justified. He beat her up, locked her in the house and went out. She was trapped. He had even nailed the windows shut. She phoned her mum in Canada, who said she would try to find someone to help her. When Trevor returned he removed the phone and locked it in his car.

The following day Trevor resumed driving Emma back to work in the red-light area. For a couple of nights she stayed out late, fearing what awaited her when she returned. She was repelling his sexual advances and the atmosphere was becoming unbearably tense. But, by now simply unable to cope on her own, return she did.

Another evening came. Trevor sent Emma out to 'work' and she 'did' one punter before asking a taxi driver to take her to a local pub. When Trevor walked in, she knew he would be angry that she wasn't out there earning money and that trouble was brewing. They moved on to another pub in the company of Trevor's sixteen-year-old son and a couple of friends. As they left, Trevor commented to the other men: 'We'll be all right for a gang bang tonight.' Nothing happened, but the sadistic threat unnerved and frightened Emma, so recently the victim of multiple rape, as it must surely have been calculated to do.

Later Trevor drove Emma back to his house. While he took his son home, desperate to do something to avoid the inevitable punishment rape, she decided she would cut her wrists, in order, she told me, to 'distract' Trevor, a tactic that had worked before. An experienced self-harmer, she knew how far she could cut to make herself bleed without endangering her life. She wanted to make the scene look dramatic so she took two knives from the kitchen, went upstairs, drew blood on both wrists and waited on the landing. When she heard him come in, she panicked. Feeling cornered, she feared now that he might use the knives on her, so she hid them under her legs as he came upstairs.

He walked past her, saying nothing, and went into the bedroom. When he came out wearing only his shirt and lay down beside her on the landing, Emma knew with utter certainty what he was going to do to her and she wanted it to stop. Without looking at him, she grabbed one of the knives and thrust it into his chest. Shocked at what she had done, at first she tried to reassure and comfort him but, realizing that the injury was serious, she ran out into the street and flagged down a passing car to summon help. By the time the police and ambulance arrived, it was too late.

Emma was arrested. The traumatized seventeen-year-old was simply unable to deal with the police questioning. 'I just felt that I couldn't explain it to the police,' she told me. 'It was everything, the whole mess. There was so much to tell and I didn't think the police had three weeks.' So she just responded with 'yes', 'no' or 'I don't remember'. She said that the police suggested possible answers to their own questions and that she found it easier to agree with these than to try to put into words what had actually happened. Although she had declined legal representation, the police called a duty solicitor, who was present when Emma was formally charged with murder.

Emma told me that she struggled to relate to her solicitor. It was extremely difficult for her to disclose to him details of the background to her relationship with Armitage. She felt, looking back, that he didn't push her to explore what led her to stab Trevor, instead developing her defence around the inaccurate police statement. She knew that to confirm this statement at her trial would be a lie. But if she said the account she had given to the police was not correct, she would have to go into the real reasons. She did not see how she could make anyone understand why having sex with the man she considered to be her boyfriend had become so awful for 'a prostitute'. She thought she would be disbelieved and mocked.

Emma told her solicitor that she didn't feel able to give evidence in court. He advised her that if she could, she would get a shorter sentence. She confided to me that he offered to get her a job on her release at his country club, where she could 'work as a prostitute'.

Emma recalled him voicing the view that she had 'psychopathic tendencies'. He arranged for her to be assessed by a psychiatrist in the hope that she would have a defence of diminished responsibility. But she was losing confidence in him and a friend found her another solicitor, who came to see her in prison. Emma felt he was more empathetic; that he didn't dismiss her as a 'hopeless alcoholic and a prostitute'. She thought she might be able to explain things to him. However, before he was due to visit again, the solicitor already acting for her turned up and said, 'Look, we have built a case and it's getting close to trial – you won't have time to start from scratch.' And so Emma just accepted her lot and stuck with the representation she had.

At her trial at Nottingham Crown Court, Emma was called into the witness box and confirmed her name. She said nothing more. She was so disturbed by the sight of the knives displayed as exhibits that she just couldn't speak. The judge allowed her QC time to talk to her and he tried to encourage her to 'fight for her life'. But, just as she was beginning to feel braver, he asked her a question that brought her straight back to square one: 'What were you more afraid of before you stabbed Trevor, a beating or the sex?'

'The sex,' she replied. And immediately she knew she could not go through with it. She stepped back into the witness box and simply confirmed that she relied on the account she had provided to the police. The jury were out for just two hours before returning a unanimous verdict: guilty of murder.

As Emma was still only seventeen, she was sentenced as a juvenile to be detained at Her Majesty's pleasure – an indefinite life sentence. She was sent first of all to the high-security HMP Durham, a notorious prison established at the beginning of the nineteenth century. It was predominantly a men's prison with a small separate women's unit.

After several months of weekly visits to Emma in Holloway, I had sixty pages of transcript, which I had edited into a coherent and chronological account. We had requested Emma's criminal file from her former solicitor. It was clear from the papers that little reference had been made in court to what she had suffered or what might have driven a vulnerable and abused child to kill.

Rohit was preparing to instruct a barrister and suggested some names, all men. Justice for Women felt it was important to have a woman on board. The two lawyers in the group, our housemate Sarah Maguire and Nan Mousley, both criminal defence experts, recommended Vera Baird, a tall, striking figure with flaming red hair who had practised in the north-east, taking on many political cases, notably during the miners' strike of the mid-1980s. Vera was provided with the papers and came with me to visit Emma in Holloway prison.

Vera spotted among the papers a document that could prove a real impediment to securing an appeal. Shortly after her conviction, Emma's lawyers had lodged a single ground of appeal, which concerned the judge's direction on provocation, arguing that the 'reasonable man' concept should be extended to 'the reasonable man with the mental characteristics of the defendant'. A judge at the criminal appeal court had considered on the papers and dismissed the application. This was not unusual: a majority of applications for leave to appeal are rejected. Emma had been summoned to the legal advice office in the prison, along with another recently convicted prisoner in the same boat. They were told they had the option of formally 'abandoning' their appeals. Emma, encouraged by her friend, signed the form. She was effectively signing away her rights.

In order to appeal her conviction now, we would have to seek to 'nullify' the abandonment by showing that Emma did not appreciate the significance of what she had signed. We would also need an extension of the time permitted to appeal the conviction. Normally, grounds of appeal must be lodged within twenty-eight days of a conviction. If they are not, the judge has to be persuaded that there are good reasons for the delay. By this point we were over eight years down the line with a client who had already waived her rights.

Vera drafted grounds of appeal together with applications for the abandonment to be treated as a nullity and for an extension of time. The grounds developed the argument made by Emma's original counsel: one was based on taking into account the mental characteristics of the 'reasonable man', the other the provocation to which she had been subjected in its entirety, not solely the final trigger. Eventually, a hearing took place in January 1995. A group of us from Justice for Women turned up at court, along with some journalists we'd alerted. In spite of the hurdles to be overcome, I felt Emma's case was so strong that I fully expected us to walk out with permission to go to a full appeal hearing. So I was shocked when the sceptical male lead judge looked down his nose through his glasses and said that the application on the abandonment issue came nowhere near an argument in support of a nullity.

That day we came very close to seeing the whole case thrown out. If it hadn't been for Vera's tenacity and courage, this could have been the end of the road for Emma. But Vera simply refused to sit down until she had persuaded the judges to allow us more time to obtain evidence that Emma would not have appreciated the significance of what she had signed. We were told to come back in a week with that evidence.

We got in touch with Emma's former solicitor, who wrote: 'I am quite sure Emma did not understand the nature of the appeal process. By that time, everyone had given up on Emma. What could one do for a girl who'd refused advice and wouldn't help herself?' More sympathetically, her former lead counsel, now a judge, wrote confirming that she would not have understood what she was signing. He added: 'I feel this was a classic example of the difficulties faced by defendants whose provocation (in the non-legal sense) consists of a long history of appalling violence and/or sexual abuse but who cannot point to a specific item of conduct giving rise to a sudden loss of self-control.'

The letter from the judge, which perhaps reflected a growing understanding in wider society in the decade since Emma's conviction of the nature and impact of violence and abuse, clearly impressed the court. They granted our applications and further suggested that we could benefit from the input of a lead counsel.

In discussing possible candidates for the role, we decided to stick to an all-female team. We felt this was symbolic. It would also help to gain Emma's trust after she had been so badly failed by her previous all-male line-up. Vera recommended Helen Grindrod QC, who had experience in both prosecution and defence. Vera had got to know Helen well while defending another complex case that Helen was prosecuting. They made a formidable duo.

I found working as a volunteer with Emma's legal team very fulfilling. The experience had convinced me that a legal career would offer a great opportunity to play a part in bringing about the political change I was striving for, as well as to fight on the ground for individuals ill-served by the justice system, and that I had the skills and the temperament for it. So I had decided to apply for a law conversion course at the University of Westminster, which I had started in the autumn of 1993. Simultaneously, I was continuing to learn on the job.

Now that we could be certain we were moving forward, Vera and Helen rolled up their sleeves to begin to develop their skeleton argument. The focus of the barristers' task was to forensically take apart the trial judge's summing-up to the jury, review previous case law on provocation and to find an argument to show how the judge had got it wrong. They were having to work round the evidence that had been before the original court in 1985, which meant the additional complication of relying on the statement Emma had made to the police at the time of her arrest.

JFW, meanwhile, set about building the campaign to reach maximum intensity by the time the appeal was listed. We gathered popular support with the two-pronged approach of mobilizing feminists across the country and reaching out to the national media. While the purpose of this campaign was first and foremost to highlight the miscarriage of justice in Emma's case, her story touched on a range of wider issues around violence against women and girls, including domestic violence, rape, prostitution, the law and women's treatment by the police and other criminal justice processes on which we were committed to raising awareness.

We had learned that the more effort we made to work with the media, and the better we packaged our case, the better the reporting would be. Wherever possible, we sought to retain as much control of the narrative as we could.

We were conscious that Emma's was a strong story and that journalists would be looking for exclusive angles and access to her if possible. It was therefore in their interests not to betray our trust.

Emma herself quickly appreciated that good media coverage would assist her campaign. She had followed the news stories about Sara and Kiranjit and was bright enough to recognize how going public had helped them. She knew she was not a murderer and she burningly wanted people to understand that. As she was locked up in Holloway, the extent to which she could contribute was limited, although far less limited than it would have been today, now that a prisoner's contact with the press is governed by very strict rules. Whatever rules there may have been then, we remained blissfully, if not wilfully, ignorant of them. We just wanted to highlight the injustice of Emma's case in any way we could. We sneaked in journalists on legal visits and recorded snatches of Emma's phone calls which could be broadcast on air.

Matters came to a head when Emma was allowed out on day release and we arranged for a documentary team from Yorkshire TV, who were making a programme featuring several cases of women who had killed their violent partners, to interview her.

Things did not go according to plan from the start, when Julie and I went to meet Emma outside the prison that morning as scheduled, only to find that she had also agreed to meet a man who had been writing to her in Holloway. It was obvious he was very creepy. In one of his letters, he had told her that a pet hate of his was chipped nail varnish and that he kept a bottle of nail varnish remover in his car. Unperturbed, Emma had arranged for him to drive her to King's Cross. When she insisted on getting into his car, Julie and I insisted we came, too. At King's Cross, Emma headed off, doubtless in pursuit of drugs, and Julie had words with her penpal, advising him in no uncertain terms that we knew what he was about and warning him not to put a foot wrong.

Emma assured us that she would get rid of him by lunchtime, ready to be filmed for the documentary. We were somewhat relieved when she turned up as promised. The crew followed her on a rather incongruous wander round a chemist's shop, accompanied by me, where she purchased a heap of make-up, and then we all went back to our house to record the interview. Unfortunately, most of it was unusable in the end because our dog, Peggy, just wouldn't stop barking.

When it was time for Emma to return to Holloway, the crew wanted to shoot some footage of her handing herself in at the gates. I was anxious about this, as the prison staff could not fail to notice the cameras. Sure enough, the next day we heard that Emma was in trouble. She was told that on any further temporary releases she would have to be accompanied by a prison officer. JFW were also read the riot act regarding any future direct contact between Emma and the media.

Emma's appeal was listed for 29 June 1995. It would be heard by three appeal court judges. By this time, the JFW organizing group consisted of about ten members. We had made the conscious decision not to formalize the status of JFW or to apply for funding: we didn't want to be beholden to any conditions or agendas on which financial support might potentially be reliant. But in the three and a half years since we had been established, we had opened a bank account for the unsolicited donations that had begun to arrive, which we would spend on campaigning material.

For Emma's appeal we produced glossy leaflets, posters, placards, T-shirts and coloured balloons. We also paid for some fly-posting in London. As the date got closer, it was exhilarating to see the message 'Free Emma Humphreys' suddenly appearing around the city on hoardings and railway bridges, and to know that thousands of others would be seeing it, too.

On the eve of the hearing, I agreed to pre-record an interview for BBC Radio 4's influential *Today* programme to be broadcast to its huge audience the following morning.

That same day, we were heartened to see *The Times* choosing to give Emma a voice by publishing a poem she had written addressed to the appeal court judges.

> You will never know the extent of abuse I have suffered, witnessed
>   and done to myself . . .
> I was twelve and running from hell,
> Straight into a life of hell.
> Five years later a man was dying in my arms.
> Over ten years later I will stand in front of you and bleed my heart
>   and mind for you just to try and grasp the realities, the effects
>   and the damage of an abused child/woman.
> It wasn't murder I did that night.
> And to try to change my conviction has been a harder fight than I
>   ever imagined.
> I ask you to look at the child of twelve in the school gym cutting her
>   wrists.
> I ask you to look at the child of seventeen in the dock accused of
>   murder . . .
> A life with only memories of hell.
> Please release me into the care of people I needed so many years ago.

As 29 June dawned, a huge crowd of women gathered outside the Royal Courts of Justice with our placards and balloons. I went to the cells to see Emma. With me was Linda Regan, who worked at the Child and Women's Abuse Studies Unit. Linda had kindly offered to provide counselling support to Emma in the lead-up to the appeal.

Emma was very volatile and there had been some worrying episodes of self-harm in prison. She was extremely anxious and, during those two days of argument, there were times when she couldn't bear to sit in the courtroom. When she could not, Linda would sit with her in the cells.

Inside, the court was packed with supporters in the public gallery and journalists on the press bench. I sat behind Vera Baird and Helen Grindrod and kept a note of the proceedings.

The three berobed and bewigged male judges duly appeared and Helen rose to set out the circumstances of the offence and present the two grounds of appeal that had been settled upon. Both, as we have seen, concerned the defence of provocation and deficiencies in the original trial judge's summing-up to the jury. The first centred on a very technical argument, which had been the subject of much previously litigated case law, on the matter of what 'relevant characteristics' could be ascribed to modify the 'reasonable man' test. Put another way, we said that the jury should have been asked to consider a two-stage test: first, whether the defendant had been provoked to lose her self-control, and second, would a 'reasonable man' of the same sex, age and other relevant characteristics as the defendant have lost his self-control in the face of the same provocation? A series of legal authorities were referenced as the complex process of dancing on the head of a pin played itself out.

From Justice for Women's perspective, the second ground of appeal was much more meaningful. This focused on the failure of the trial judge to sum up the cumulative acts of provocation over the history of Emma's relationship with Armitage.

Emma was a prime example of how, in women, a temporary loss of control could be caused by a long build-up of physical, emotional and sexual abuse and coercion. Without a full understanding of this history, her actions on that night made little sense.

As luck would have it, one of the judges, Mr Justice Kay, had recently heard another appeal case in which the trial judge had been criticized for failing to sum up the strands of provocative conduct that together resulted in a killing. In fact, in that case, *R v. Stewart*, the defendant was male, but the judgment was to prove decisive in assisting our cumulative provocation argument, enabling the Court of Appeal judges to rule that there were similar failings in Emma's case.

In criminal appeals where there is no jury, it is often possible to get an idea of whether the judges are being persuaded by the arguments from the sort of questions they ask counsel on both sides. After two days, we had a strong sense that they were persuaded by ours. But we had to wait a little longer to find out. They told us they needed time to consider the case carefully and would hand down their judgment the following week.

On 7 July, a large crowd of supporters once again assembled outside the Royal Courts of Justice as the judgment was read out inside the Court of Appeal. Having to sit through what can seem like an interminable summary of the facts and arguments from both sides, trying to guess whether you have won or lost, can be nerve-wracking. So much depended on the outcome of this appeal that my hands were shaking as I tried to transcribe what was being said. For me, the culmination of three years' painstaking and critical work. For all of us at Justice for Women, the legal team and Emma's supporters, three years of commitment and campaigning. But most of all, of course, for Emma, whose freedom and exoneration of premeditated murder hung in the balance.

Finally, the judge delivering the verdict reached his conclusion. We had done it. We had won our appeal on both grounds. I exhaled deeply, only now aware that I had been holding my breath. Emma was sentenced to the term she had already served, which meant she would walk out of the court a free woman.

Linda and I rushed off to fetch Emma from the cells, where she had been taken to collect her belongings. At the entrance to the Royal Courts of Justice, we were met by a bank of photographers, flashing cameras, euphoric supporters and cheering crowds. The sight of our balloons being released into the sky provided a nice image of freedom for the TV news. Battling our way into a taxi, we sped over to Conway Hall, where a press conference had been pre-arranged and Emma, dazed but elated, spoke to the media. Before the party we had organized that evening for Emma and her supporters, we took her back to our house for a spell of peace, quiet and calm. She had been incarcerated for a decade and the traumatized teenager who had gone into prison was now a twenty-seven-year-old woman. Dealing with life outside was going to demand a massive adjustment.

Emma's victory was front-page news the following morning. In the struggle for the fair treatment of women who kill their abusers, it was a crucial step forward. In winning the appeal on both grounds, we had succeeded in establishing an important legal precedent: that when the defence of provocation is being considered, the history of cumulative provocative conduct by the deceased could and should be taken into account, not just the final act.

Sara Thornton had yet to win her fight, but, by the end of July, she would be free on bail pending a further appeal that had been granted by the home secretary, Michael Howard, a few weeks before Emma's appeal was heard. In December, Sara's lawyers would successfully argue that her psychiatric condition, including the effect on her mental health of the abuse she had suffered over a prolonged period, should have been considered when judging her reaction to the provocative conduct of her husband. Her conviction was quashed and a retrial ordered for the following year. In 1996 she was finally found guilty of the lesser charge of manslaughter and released as a result of time served.

By the summer Emma Humphreys walked free, I had been working on her case for over two and a half years and had completed my law conversion course and the one-year legal practice course that would enable me to qualify as a solicitor. I had just finished my exams for the legal practice qualification and was awaiting the results. Had I still been entertaining any doubts about embarking on my new career, or the opportunity it would give me to challenge discrimination from within the system, they were swept away.

2

Jean Charles de Menezes and
the Politics of Policing

IT IS 7 JULY 2005, the tenth anniversary of Emma Humphreys' landmark victory at the Court of Appeal, and I have been a fully qualified solicitor for eight years.

On passing my legal practice exams shortly after Emma's release, I needed to find a job as a trainee. I had applied to several legal aid practices that represented people who found themselves at the sharp end of the justice system (beyond some family law firms handling domestic violence cases, there were none specializing in women's issues). So much of the work undertaken by solicitors is related to property or commercial litigation and, while I was required to train in these areas, I had no intention of completing my two years' grind as a law student to end up in conveyancing or probate. It wasn't what I wanted to be a lawyer for.

I was given my first job by Winstanley Burgess, a mixed legal aid practice with a reputation as a leading specialist in immigration and asylum law, which occupied offices in two tall terraced houses on City Road in Islington. Here I cut my teeth as a trainee solicitor in the 'actions against the police' department, where I learned how to bring civil proceedings against state institutions.

I am thinking of Emma, and of how it all began a decade before, on my morning Tube journey to the firm where I have been working for the past three years. The offices of Birnberg Peirce and Partners are in a terraced house in a busy side street in the middle of Camden Market. I am the first one in, apart from the inimitable Hoppy, our receptionist. He asks me if I have heard that there has been an explosion on the Tube at King's Cross, just a couple of stops away.

Before long, the whole world has heard. On the day that would quickly become known as 7/7, fifty-two people were killed and over 700 injured in attacks by suicide bombers on three different London Underground trains, followed less than an hour later by a blast that ripped the roof off a double-decker bus in Tavistock Square. The four bombers, who also died, had pledged their support to an extreme form of Islamism closely associated with al-Qaeda.

A fortnight later, on 21 July, while the bomb damage was still being cleared and shocked Londoners tried to get on with their lives, there was a copycat attack: four more bombs were detonated simultaneously on different parts of London's transport network. Thankfully, this time the devices failed to explode and the bombers fled the scene. Suddenly, London was awash with armed police on high alert. Tube passengers eyed each other nervously: anyone with a backpack aroused suspicion.

The next morning came breaking news that one of the bombers had been shot dead by the police as he boarded a Tube train. Some bystanders reported seeing a man in a 'heavily padded jacket' – remarked upon as odd on a warm July morning – or a 'bulky coat with wires sticking out of it' leaping over barriers at Stockwell station and running down the escalators, pursued by armed police. Sir Ian Blair, the Metropolitan Police commissioner, made a public statement that afternoon. 'The information I have available is that this shooting is directly linked to the ongoing and expanding anti-terrorist operation. Any death is deeply regrettable. I understand the man was challenged and refused to obey.'

Initial reactions from many were to breathe a sigh of relief and congratulate the police on a courageous effort to avert another attack. However, news soon began to emerge that the man shot dead was not, in fact, one of the terrorist suspects. The following evening the police named the victim of mistaken identity as Jean Charles de Menezes, a twenty-seven-year-old Brazilian national. Describing his death as 'a tragedy', they admitted that he had not been carrying explosives and was in no way connected with the bombings. He was, it would transpire, an electrician on his way to answer a call-out.

Over the weekend I monitored the news with growing misgivings about the police response. On the Sunday morning, friends of Jean Charles and social justice activists gathered spontaneously at Stock-well station to mourn the dead man and protest about the shooting. That evening, I had a phone call from my colleague and friend Marcia Willis Stewart asking me if I would go with her the next morning to South-West London to help advise members of Jean Charles's bereaved family.

Marcia brought me up to speed. Via Asad Rehman, a stalwart of Newham Monitoring Project (NMP), a community enterprise with a long history of challenging police racism and supporting family justice campaigns around deaths in police custody, Jean Charles's relatives had been in touch with the acclaimed civil rights solicitor Gareth Peirce – our boss.

A founding partner of Birnberg Peirce, Gareth is renowned for her work on miscarriages of justice and has represented many men and women wrongly convicted of IRA bombings, including the Guildford Four and the Birmingham Six. I'd first met her in the 1990s, before I became a solicitor, when she represented Sara Thornton and had been instrumental in securing Sara's release from prison following her second, successful appeal.

Concerns were being raised that the narrative of events surrounding the shooting of Jean Charles de Menezes was being managed by the Metropolitan Police to minimize criticism of the conduct of its officers. Gareth and Marcia had gone immediately to a Kingston hotel where the police had arranged accommodation for Jean Charles's relatives, four young cousins. Two of them, Patricia Armani da Silva and Vivian Menezes Figueiredo, were sharing a flat with him in Tulse Hill in South London, to which they could not return until the police had finished searching the premises as part of their enquiries. The police had also provided the family with two police family liaison officers, purportedly on hand to assist them.

On the Monday morning, I accompanied Marcia to the hotel. By this time, the news had been broken to Jean Charles's parents and brother in rural Brazil and official communication with them was being handled by the police, with the assistance of the Brazilian Consulate. An inquest was opened and adjourned the same day at Southwark Coroner's Court. It heard that Jean Charles had been shot seven times in the head and once in the shoulder.

Gareth, Marcia and I knew from other cases where police officers were responsible for a death that the police invariably sought to control the story by suggesting that some action by the victim had been a contributory factor. Misinformation about the circumstances of the shooting of Jean Charles was already rife. In particular, the fallacy that his behaviour on the day he was killed had been in some way suspicious. The cousins were being advised by the Met family liaison officers not to talk to the media. They were desperate to dispel the rumours and this did not sit well with them – especially with the most vocal cousin, Alex Pereira, who, understandably shell-shocked, tearful and angry, was convinced that Jean Charles's death was solely down to the police and not afraid to say so.

We advised the family to obtain a second post-mortem, a precautionary step when someone dies at the hands of the state to ensure that evidence which might potentially cast doubt on the police version of events is collected and preserved. During the initial post-mortem, an

account of what happened leading up to the death will usually be provided for the pathologist by a police officer. That account may inform
what is examined in an autopsy and has been known to distort findings in some cases. While the cousins were keen to take our advice, the
Brazilian Consulate, urged on by the police, persuaded Jean Charles's
grieving parents, poor farmers who wanted his body sent home to
Brazil to be buried as soon as possible, that there was no need for a
second post-mortem.

The cousins, feeling they were being manipulated, told the
police family liaison officers they no longer wanted their 'support'.
Instead, they relied on a hastily formed family justice campaign
group coordinated by NMP, Justice4Jean, which, with the help of
Birnberg Peirce, convened a big press conference on 27 July at the
Holiday Inn at Camden Lock, where the relatives could set the record
straight, as they saw it, and put forward the questions to which they
needed answers. Jean Charles used a travel card, Vivian told the
assembled press, and 'had no bulky jacket. He was wearing a jeans
jacket. But even if he was wearing a bulky jacket, that wouldn't be an
excuse to kill him.'

'An innocent man has been killed as though he was a terrorist,'
added Patricia. 'An incredibly grave error was committed by the
British police.'

The investigation into the shooting had been handed over to a
new police complaints body, the Independent Police Complaints
Commission. The IPCC, designed to be independent of the police,
can, in the most serious cases, conduct its own investigation into the
circumstances surrounding a police-related death, including consideration of any police misconduct. Any fatality caused by police is
required to be referred to the IPCC immediately but, in this instance,
it was not until 25 July, three days after the shooting, that the IPCC
had announced it would be taking over the investigation and, as we
were soon to learn, 27 July before it was given access to the scene and

actually able to do so. By that time, it was quite possible that incon-venient or incriminating evidence could have been 'lost'.

Once the IPCC were in charge, the former police officer assigned to lead the investigation, John Cummins, reassured me that they were determined to get to the bottom of what had happened and gave me a brief overview of what they had found out so far. He confirmed that Stockwell station CCTV showed Jean Charles was never wearing a padded jacket, but a lightweight denim jacket, which anyone could have seen could not have concealed an explosive belt. He did not vault over the ticket barriers. Neither did he run down the escalators. But when such reports are allowed to circulate unchecked, they never go away. Despite all the evidence to the contrary that would surface; despite two reports, a prosecution and the verdict of a much-delayed inquest, these myths surrounding Jean Charles persist to this day.

On 28 July, Jean Charles's cousins flew back to Brazil for his funeral. We then heard that the Metropolitan Police deputy assistant commissioner, John Yates, was also preparing to travel to Brazil, to offer a personal apology and explanation to the family. The Met had not troubled to inform the family lawyers and we were, of course, immediately concerned about what they might be saying to Jean Charles's parents.

The world's media had descended on their small, remote home town of Gonzaga, in Minas Gerais in the south-east of the country, for the funeral of a son whose death would not have commanded anything like this level of attention in Brazil, a country notorious for police shootings, had he been gunned down by police in the *favelas* of Rio de Janeiro. But Jean Charles had not been shot in Brazil. He had been shot in London by the British police, an institution viewed in Brazil as a beacon of justice and the rule of law. To some in Brazil, then, this looked like the execution by the United Kingdom of an innocent fellow countryman.

Shortly after the funeral, Erionaldo da Silva, a close friend of Alex

Pereira's I'd first met at that Kingston hotel, called me from Gonzaga to tell me they were worried that Jean Charles's besieged parents were being 'bought off' by the police. Erionaldo was a lovely bloke, and a helpful presence in the midst of all the sound and fury. He had not known Jean Charles personally, which perhaps helped him to remain a calmer, clearer-eyed support to relatives overwhelmed by grief, and he had become our main conduit to the family. Erionaldo and Alex felt that someone from the legal team was badly needed over there to provide some guidance.

Gareth agreed. 'Can you go?' she asked me.

I was taken aback. Marcia was in the US and I was essentially holding the fort on this case until her return. Gareth knew I had the legal knowledge to steer the family through the processes available to us to hold the police to account for the shooting of their son. I had come to Birnberg Peirce from Thanki Novy Taube, a firm that had hired me to help set up a new 'actions against the police' department, the brainchild of three ambitious criminal defence lawyers keen to branch out into this relatively innovative and expanding field. There I had found and brought my own cases and had been more or less just left to get on with it.

Through this baptism of fire, I had built up a good deal of expertise in challenging a lack of accountability around bad and often racist policing, advising people on the receiving end of unlawful arrest, excessive use of force or wrongful prosecution on navigating the inadequate police complaints system and bringing civil proceedings against the police using tort law.

I also specialized in inquest law, acting for the bereaved families of those who had died in prison or in police custody or following contact with the police. This included quite a number of self-inflicted deaths in women's prisons referred to me as a result of my work with Emma Humphreys.

All the same, taking the reins of this high-profile and complex case in the midst of a chaotic investigation was pretty daunting. And I had never dealt with a police shooting before. But, as I'd learned, some-times the best way is simply to jump in at the deep end, get as much advice as you can from colleagues and figure it out as you go along.

In between drafting with Gareth an urgent letter to Sir Ian Blair, copying in various key bodies and individuals, to set out our con-cerns, I was on the phone to airlines in search of the flights and connections I would need to get to south-eastern Brazil.

'It is crucial that a thorough and totally independent investigation is conducted without interference from the Metropolitan Police,' our letter concluded. 'Mr de Menezes' death raises significant constitu-tional issues and it must be of paramount importance to all parties concerned that the true circumstances surrounding his death can be seen to emerge without inappropriate interventions from those responsible.'

The letter was dispatched and the next day I was on my way to Heathrow to catch an overnight flight to São Paulo. I had never set foot in Brazil, or indeed anywhere else in South America. I would have only one day to attempt to explain some complicated foreign legal processes to a family poleaxed by grief. Maria, Jean's mother, was being portrayed in the tabloids as either hysterical or zonked out on tranquillizers. Or both. I didn't speak Portuguese and I wasn't likely to get much of a sense of Brazilian customs and manners in such a short space of time. How would I strike the delicate balance between conveying my condolences and empathy and demonstrat-ing the level of professionalism required to help this family take on the British police?

Early in the morning, after twelve hours in the air and not much sleep, I boarded a connecting flight to Belo Horizonte. As I walked into the arrivals hall, I heard Erionaldo's voice shouting urgently, 'Quick! This way!' Apparently, there were reporters milling around the airport. Jean Charles was still headline news and evidently word of the arrival of a British lawyer had spread.

Erionaldo ushered me swiftly into a waiting car, introducing the man at the wheel as his friend Fernando, who drove us to his flat and served us home-made lemonade on his roof terrace overlooking the city while we waited for the mayor of Gonzaga, Júlio Maria de Sousa, to pick us up. The temperature in the southern hemisphere winter was pleasantly warm and it was a relief to be outdoors and away from aircraft cabins and airports.

Júlio appeared, a warm, approachable man in his late forties. Through our short acquaintance, I would be impressed by how well this mayor of an isolated rural town coped with finding himself in the midst of an international incident. Erionaldo brought me up to date as Júlio's driver steered us through the beautiful countryside of Minas Gerais, Brazil's main producer of coffee and milk. 'A bit like Ireland,' I was told. 'Very green and full of poets.' The funeral had been a grand affair. Around 6,000 Brazilians had attended, including a coachload of relatives and friends from São Paulo, some of whom had not been back to the village for years. The mourners were gone now, but Gonzaga was still full of police and news reporters. Between fielding incessant phone calls, deflecting what were presumably media enquiries by claiming that I was still in Belo Horizonte, Júlio warned me I would need to keep a low profile in Gonzaga.

Speculation about how much compensation the family would be paid had been turbo-charged by the arrival of the assistant police commissioner from London, accompanied by an entourage of embassy officials. People were saying the Menezes family could receive a million dollars. The suggestion of substantial compensation brought its own worries in a country like Brazil, where kidnap and blackmail were not uncommon.

The sun was sinking, I had been travelling for twenty-four hours and fatigue was setting in. The drive seemed to go on and on. At last we turned down a track, bumped through a gate across some rough terrain and pulled up outside a farmhouse: the mayor's home, where

I would be spending my two nights in Brazil. Outside, a group of local people were chatting over a beer while Júlio's wife cooked a feast on an open fire. Scenting the wonderful aroma of meat, rice and beans, I realized I was hungry. My business in Gonzaga was men's talk, it seemed – the women all disappeared indoors. Sensing my status as an honorary man, I accepted a beer and joined the men.

By 9 p.m. – midnight back in the UK – I was ready for bed, but I could see the point of the suggestion that I drive over with Erionaldo to introduce myself to the family. They knew I was due to arrive that day and as they did not have a phone, there was no other way of letting them know that I was in Gonzaga. And it would give us a little bit of a head start the next day if we had already met and the ice had been broken.

The mayor's driver took us along a rough road through the valley. At the end of a narrower, rutted dirt track we stopped outside a small house. In the dark I could just make out another small house across the way where, Erionaldo was telling me, Alex Pereira's family lived. The cousins had grown up together. Giovani, Jean Charles's brother, appeared, wearing wellington boots and carrying a fishing rod. He had been fishing, he explained through Erionaldo, because he needed to keep active to distract himself.

I was led into the house, where Giovani's three children were squashed up on a sofa, watching television. I had changed into a suit: I wasn't sure what the family might expect of an English lawyer and I wanted to appear professional and respectful. Given the late hour, and with Giovani in his wellies and everyone else in jeans and T-shirts, I felt a little over-dressed, but hoped the 'uniform' would inspire confidence. None of them spoke English and I was reliant on Erionaldo to translate. He introduced me to Giovani's wife, who seemed to be the one keeping the household running, and Jean's father, Matuzinhos, a skinny, wiry man, with a sad, open face.

Then a small woman entered the room, her long hair tied back, one eye misty, perhaps damaged in an accident. Her sorrow was written across her face, but she bore no resemblance to the zombie depicted in the news. Instinctively, we hugged and I held Maria's hands, as if she were my grandma, an aunt, a dear old friend, willing her to feel the sympathy and reassurance I was attempting to express.

In the morning I headed first with Júlio to his office on the main drag of Gonzaga town to pick up the post-mortem report and other documents arriving by fax from Birnberg Peirce. I allowed myself a wry smile at the unprepossessing Hotel Kennedy a few doors down, picturing the press scrum for its few available rooms a few days earlier when this sleepy, one-horse town had been inundated.

At the de Menezes home, I sat down with the family round a large kitchen table and we embarked on our lengthy meeting, with Alex and Erionaldo translating.

As I wasn't sure if or when I would meet the immediate family again, it was important to cover as much as possible but challenging to do so without over-complicating. I began by recapping where we were, updating them on what had happened since the cousins had left London, explaining the role of the IPCC to Maria and Matuzinhos, going through the overview shared with me by John Cummins and discussing the delay in the handover of the case to the independent investigators.

By now some of the background to this was coming to light. Immediately after the shooting, Met commissioner Sir Ian Blair had notified the IPCC that the investigation would be conducted internally, and not by the IPCC, in view of the 'unique circumstances', on the basis of a paramount need to protect counter-terrorism tactics and intelligence and prevent jeopardizing future operations.

He had written to the Home Office to this effect on the day after Jean Charles was killed. However, the Home Office had refused to allow this exception.

This letter was later released in response to a Freedom of Information request.

If the Met, the media or indeed anyone in the UK imagined that the stereotypical unworldly family depicted in the press would not have searching questions to ask, they had underestimated Jean Charles's relatives. They listened intently and asked the same questions any client would raise: why did this happen? How could it have happened? Who was responsible and how could they be held accountable?

I took the family through the post-mortem report, leaving out some of the more upsetting descriptions of the scene recording how Jean Charles's brain had been splattered across the train carriage. The IPCC, I told them, would investigate whether any criminal offences had taken place and pass on their report to the Crown Prosecution Service, which would consider whether any police officer should be prosecuted.

I explained that an inquest, a public hearing exploring all the relevant circumstances giving rise to the shooting, had been opened, but then adjourned, and that this was standard procedure in the case of any unnatural death, to determine who the deceased was and how, when and where they died. The how – the cause of death – tends to be the question that most concerns those who have lost loved ones at the hands of the police, and the Menezes family were no exception.

When they heard I'd been told there was no CCTV capturing the moment Jean Charles was shot inside the carriage, Alex and Erionaldo were flabbergasted. 'No way!' they shouted in unison. 'That is just not possible!' While it is not unusual for cameras to be broken, of course, it certainly seemed more than a coincidence that neither the camera on the station platform nor the one in the carriage should be working at that precise moment.

I assured Maria and Matuzinhos that if the CPS decided there would be no prosecution, the officers involved in the operation that led to the shooting would be required to give evidence at the inquest. I talked them through the options for pursuing a civil claim.

I spent my last hours in Brazil chatting less formally with Jean Charles's friends and relations. Alex and Erionaldo took me to see Vivian, his twenty-one-year-old cousin and Tulse Hill flatmate, who had arrived in London just three months before he was shot. It was the first time she had left Brazil, and Jean Charles had returned to travel with her. She showed me photographs taken in the places they visited en route – the two of them posing, smiling and carefree, in front of the Eiffel Tower and the Liverpool docks – clearly struggling to grasp how her exciting adventure through European cities deemed far safer than any in Brazil could have ended in this nightmare.

Decompressing that evening at the mayor's house over a glass or two of the national tipple, *cachaça*, before the long drive back to Belo Horizonte airport the next morning, I felt that my flying visit had enabled me to forge a bond with those close to Jean Charles, a basis for an understanding and trust as we moved forward.

Ahead lay three years of legal wrangling that was as much about managing media speculation and political game-playing in the upper echelons of the police and policy-makers as it was about uncovering the truth, achieving accountability and gaining justice for the family.

The shooting of Jean Charles raised issues of constitutional importance. To whom were the police accountable? In what circumstances are they, and should they be, at liberty to devise a shoot-to-kill policy without democratic oversight? Who investigates the police, and to what extent is that investigation transparent?

Details of the Met commissioner's instruction not to hand over the investigation immediately to the IPCC to protect the security of counter-terrorism operations were about to be made public.

These issues were thrown into even sharper relief by the international focus on the case. Elsewhere in the world, as in Brazil, the

British police had always been regarded as the standard-bearers of restraint, the rule of law and the principle of policing by consent.

'Are there any of Jean Charles de Menezes's family members still in London?' asked the ITV journalist on the other end of the line. She was calling not much more than a week after my return from Brazil. I told her that one cousin, Alessandro Pereira, was here.

'Would you both be able to come into ITN to discuss a confidential news story we're preparing?'

I was, of course, intrigued. Alessandro agreed to meet me at ITN, where the journalist elaborated. Some statements and photographs relating to the shooting of Jean Charles had been leaked to them which cast serious doubt on the story, still in wide currency, that Jean Charles had been shot because his behaviour had aroused suspicion. The material, which it was clear came from police files, proved and added detail to what we already knew. Jean Charles had calmly entered the Tube station, used his Oyster card at the ticket barrier and passed through it as normal. He had even paused to pick up a free newspaper. He then descended the escalators showing no sign of being in any particular hurry, breaking into a run only when near the bottom, as many of us do when we hear a train pulling into the platform.

The journalist showed us one photo, taken at the crime scene, of the lower half of Jean Charles's body, lying face down on the floor of the train carriage, grim confirmation that he was wearing jeans and a denim jacket and had nothing strapped round his waist. ITN wanted to use this picture in their report, but as it was so graphic and upsetting, they were requesting the permission of the family.

Alessandro's English was not fluent but when I discussed this with him as best I could, he clearly understood the significance of the photograph. He agreed to its use and gave ITN a short pre-recorded interview.

I agreed to return later to provide my reaction to the finished report before it was broadcast on the six o'clock news. In the event, when I arrived it was still being edited in a race against the clock, and I ended up sitting beside the newsreader as he delivered the headlines and seeing the report for the first time from the studio as it went out live. It was a long piece and contained significantly more new material than had been disclosed to me at the earlier meeting, including fuller details of how Jean Charles had been mistaken for one of the suspects connected with the failed terrorist attack the previous day and had been followed, and the revelation that he had been given no warning before being restrained by a police officer and shot dead.

Being asked to comment immediately on live television with no time to process all this was nerve-jangling but, having spent time with the family very recently, I knew what their reaction would be. I did my best to channel their outrage at the misinformation that had been exposed and how it had been allowed to taint Jean Charles's name.

On my way out of the studio I was intercepted by a producer working for *Channel 4 News*, which occupied the same building. Would I come down to their studio and give a live interview on their programme at 7 p.m.? That done, I left the building and found the BBC home affairs correspondent waiting for me outside with a camera. In the cab home I checked my phone: it was full of missed calls and messages from journalists and broadcasters.

At 11 a.m. the next day, I was still doing the rounds. Alastair Stewart asked me on his morning news show whether I thought Sir Ian Blair should resign. I wasn't sure we wanted to go down that route and gave what I thought in the moment was a measured answer: 'Perhaps, given that the buck stops with the head of the organization.' It's a trap to which every regular interviewee is wise nowadays. Unless the response you give is unambiguously negative, it will appear out of context in the headlines as a call for the person in question to resign. Sure enough, within minutes, the breaking news was that the Menezes family lawyer was demanding the resignation of the commissioner of the Metropolitan Police.

My next call was from Gareth, calmly suggesting that I come back to the office. She had more experience than I did of how commenting on a news story can itself become the news and helped me to put on the brakes before I spun myself completely out of control.

We discussed the significance of the evidence that had been revealed to ITN and drafted a press release declaring that it now appeared the original narrative of events was false and that it was impossible to imagine that this would not have been known by all senior officers and government ministers involved. The family, we said, now asked for only one outcome, and that it be swift: that the entire truth surrounding Jean Charles's death be made public as a matter of urgency. Highlighting concerns about the failure to hand over the investigation immediately to the IPCC, we concluded by praising the person, unknown at that time, who had leaked the information as having performed a public service.

The IPCC was quick to react: John Cummins was soon on the phone asking if he and IPCC commissioner Mehmuda Mian Pritchard could have a meeting with us at the earliest opportunity. We invited them to our rickety office in Inverness Street, where they had to run the gauntlet of a throng of reporters camped outside. They were embarrassed about the security breach and anxious to limit the damage.

August tends to be a quiet month for news and the media stuck with the case, seeking out new angles. As the Justice4Jean campaign attracted new members and started to articulate concerns on behalf of the family, stories appeared in the press focusing on some of its supporters and implying that the family's cause had been hijacked by left-wing extremists.

Alex, Erionaldo, Patricia and Vivian, who had returned from

Brazil, defended the campaigners and began to work closely with them. An interim hearing had been fixed at the Coroner's Court and we discussed with Gareth and Marcia, now back from the States, who we should instruct as counsel to lead on this case. We wanted someone really experienced and hard-hitting and were gratified that Michael Mansfield QC, an obvious contender, agreed to take it on.

Given all the developments, it seemed an appropriate moment for Jean Charles's parents and brother to be brought over, a plan I had explored with them on the basis that the police should be willing to fund their trip. The police agreed and we made the necessary arrangements.

On 25 September, a couple of days before I set off at the crack of dawn to greet the family arriving from Brazil, it was reported that the woman who had leaked the IPCC documents to ITN had been arrested. Lana Vandenberghe, we would later learn, was a secretary at the IPCC who was deeply concerned by the disconnect between what was recorded in the documentary evidence she was seeing in the course of her work and what the public were being told. Although she spent a day in the police cells and lost her job, in the end no charges were ever brought against her, or against her contact at ITN.

With the cooperation of the police and Transport for London, we retraced Jean Charles's last movements with his family. Starting out at his flat in Scotia Road in Tulse Hill, we followed his journey to Stockwell station, where, before descending the escalators to the platform where Jean Charles boarded the train on which he died, they were able to see the poignant memorial created by local people that commemorated their son with photos and other decorations.

At the IPCC offices in High Holborn, all the staff stood up in a show of respect as the family were led through reception to a meeting to update them on the progress of the investigation. By this time, in discussion with colleagues, campaigners and relatives, I had prepared an exhaustive list of questions for the IPCC on issues ranging from the police operation, the shoot-to-kill policy (codenamed Operation Kratos), the command structure and the role of surveillance and the firearms officers; on the contemporaneous evidence from witnesses, forensics and the absence of CCTV footage; on the misinformation after the shooting and whether Sir Ian Blair was under investigation for preventing the IPCC from accessing the scene of the crime and for disseminating, or not correcting, that misinformation.

On the matter of misinformation, the IPCC advised us that since this concerned the commissioner of the Met, the family would need to submit a separate complaint through the mayor's office. This I drafted the following day and it was to lead to the second part of the inquiry, known as Stockwell 2, which dealt with the conduct of Sir Ian Blair.

At the end of a trip that must have been overwhelming for the family, still in the early days of confronting the reality of their loss, we saw them off to Brazil with a small party, hosted by Julie and me at our home, for their friends and relatives, legal team and campaigners. It felt important to reciprocate the warmth of their welcome in Gonzaga and to maintain a personal as well as an advisory connection. We ate, drank, danced and told stories into the early hours.

In January 2006 we were informed that the first part of the investigation into the shooting, Stockwell 1, had been completed and approved by the chair of the IPCC. However, we now learned that the report would not be published. Together with the IPCC's recommendations, it would be sent to the police, the Metropolitan Police Authority, the coroner and the CPS – to consider whether any officer should be charged with a criminal offence arising from the shooting – and, unusually, to the home secretary. But the family would not be entitled to see it, despite previous assurances that they would.

I wrote immediately to Nick Hardwick, the IPCC chair, asking for an immediate explanation for 'how it appears, once again, that the family are the least trusted and the last to know what, after all, concerns them more deeply than anyone else'. I pointed out that we were being bombarded by enquiries from journalists, some of whom claimed to have seen some of the report's findings.

Nick Hardwick's response was that they were willing to share the report, but only with the immediate family in Brazil, despite Jean Charles's closest relatives having made it clear that the cousins in London were representing their interests in any legal processes in the UK. 'The report as a whole is directly relevant to national security and has been classified as "secret"', he said, which meant he was 'simply not at liberty' to publish it.

I wrote to the home secretary, Charles Clarke, who had received the report because of its 'gravity or other exceptional circumstances', asking him if he would publish it, as he had the power to do. Or, at the very least, the findings relating to Operation Kratos, which we maintained had led to the shooting of Jean Charles. There was widespread concern around the country about this policy, formulated to deal with suicide bombers, a set of tactics which included firing a fatal shot to the head. We believed this was unlawful and needed to be publicly scrutinized.

The request was declined and yet leaked stories continued to appear in the press. We read that surveillance officers had altered their logs on the question of whether or not they made a positive identification of Jean Charles as the man they intended to follow. It was said that charges of perverting the course of justice were being considered against certain officers. Other leaks emanating from the police were evidently aimed at discrediting Jean Charles. A tabloid newspaper published a claim that he was a suspect in a rape investigation as a result of an allegation made three years previously but reported only recently. It was an allegation of which his family was aware, and they had already agreed for a DNA sample to be provided which subsequently cleared him.

Eventually, in March, after we had met the director of public prosecutions (DPP) and the Crown prosecutor, who were considering the charges against these police officers, the IPCC offered to provide an overview of their report, under strict undertakings of confidence. Unwilling to be bound by these, the family decided to leave it to the legal team to hear what the two lead IPCC investigators had to say. Marcia accompanied me to the meeting.

Potential criminal charges of police officers included murder, gross negligence manslaughter, misconduct in public office and perverting the course of justice. The senior officer, Commander Cressida Dick, along with her tactical adviser, was being considered for gross negligence manslaughter charges.

Commander Dick was the designated senior officer for the day in case Operation Kratos – the policy developed specifically for circumstances in which the police may need to confront suspected suicide bombers – had to be activated. It allowed for the possibility of a shot to be fired to the head without warning where the designated senior officer had sufficient information to justify the use of lethal force. However, in interview, Cressida Dick had claimed that she never gave the command to shoot.

The surveillance operation had been set up outside the block of flats in Scotia Road where Jean Charles lived after a gym card bearing its address and a photograph of one of the terrorist suspects, Hussain Osman, was found at the location of one of the failed bombing attempts the previous day. At 9.30 a.m. on 22 July, as Jean Charles left his flat, the surveillance officer radioed through that he was 'worth having a look at'. He was followed by two surveillance officers, who recorded that, although they did not believe he was Osman, he was 'a good likeness'.

Jean Charles boarded a bus, got off at Brixton station, made a phone call, then got back on the bus. This was perceived as suspicious behaviour at the time, but in fact the station was closed, which was why he travelled on to the next Tube stop at Stockwell. It was as he re-boarded the bus that Cressida Dick gave the order for him to be stopped and detained. When he stepped off the bus at Stockwell station, with the specialist firearms team still on their way, four surveillance officers followed him down the escalators.

When the firearms team turned up moments later, it was they, not Jean Charles, who some witnesses saw leaping over the ticket barrier and charging down the escalators. They jumped into the train carriage, where a surveillance officer indicated Jean Charles.

There were now nine police officers altogether on the train carriage: four surveillance officers and five firearms officers. They all stated that Jean Charles was challenged and that a warning shout of 'Armed police!' was given. None of the other seventeen passengers in the carriage recalled any warning. Jean Charles, on his feet now, was pushed back into his seat by a surveillance officer, whereupon two firearms officers fired a total of nine shots at him. Seven bullets entered Jean Charles's head, one misfired and one hit him in the shoulder.

Until the death of Jean Charles de Menezes, no one had known that police in our country had secretly introduced, without any democratic debate or approval, a shoot-to-kill policy. Now we believed that ACPO, the Association of Chief Police Officers, was seeking to reinstate this policy publicly before any inquiry into the killing of Jean Charles was completed, confident that the police could hide behind the claim that a criminal investigation was still underway.

As to whether any police officers would actually be charged with a criminal offence, I had my doubts, in spite of the continuing speculation. I was aware that deaths at the hands of the police, whether in custody, following a pursuit or involving firearms officers, almost never result in prosecution.

The CPS did not announce their decision on bringing charges until

July 2006. The outcome of all those months of deliberation was that no individual officer was to be prosecuted for any criminal offence arising from the death of Jean Charles. Mystifyingly, however, we were informed that criminal proceedings were to be commenced against the office of Commissioner of Police of the Metropolis under Section 3 of the Health and Safety at Work Etc. Act 1974.

That the family were shocked and bewildered was hardly surprising. No officer was to be charged with the deliberate shooting of an innocent man, yet there was to be a prosecution related to the endangerment of public health under legislation generally used against restaurants or public facilities that did not comply with health and safety regulations.

Patricia spoke for them all when she accused the CPS of trying to hide behind another law that had nothing to do with their case. 'The authorities here have no shame,' she said. 'I feel sickened by this.'

The effect of this charge was to delay any disclosure about the events that led to the shooting of Jean Charles. As the CPS wrote to the coroner asking him to adjourn the inquest until after the health and safety prosecution, we explored with our counsel team how we might be able to challenge their decision. My request to the IPCC to see their report was refused on advice from the CPS, and the response from the CPS, when I asked for more details of the reasons for not charging any officer with a criminal offence, was less than illuminating.

If the health and safety prosecution did go ahead, could it take place after the inquest rather than before? We made submissions citing the family's rights under Article 2 of the European Convention on Human Rights (ECHR) to an effective and prompt investigation. The coroner determined that the prosecution should proceed first.

On 29 September, I wrote to the DPP and the IPCC threatening a legal challenge to the decision by the CPS not to prosecute any individual officer and taking issue with the IPCC's refusal to disclose its report to the family. When the legal departments of both organizations resisted our arguments, I applied for emergency legal aid in the name of Patricia Armani da Silva to fund the commencement of judicial review proceedings in the High Court.

We then issued an urgent application in the High Court, with grounds drafted by counsel, highlighting the fact that the family had been effectively 'locked out' of the process of investigation and accountability for Jean Charles's death for the foreseeable future.

An application for judicial review requires permission from a judge. The test for the case being allowed to proceed is whether or not it is arguable. His Honour Judge Collins considered our application, noting that 'the family reasonably believed that self-defence can be proved not to be a defence' and that 'there may have been negligence in planning of the operation of a sufficient level of seriousness to justify a conviction for manslaughter'. He further noted that without the IPCC report and the evidence upon which the decision of the CPS was made, the claimant could not make a properly informed assessment as to whether the decision not to prosecute was wrong in law.

With the judge's permission granted, the IPCC report and a report by the CPS reviewing the evidence were disclosed to us under strict undertakings of confidentiality. But the legal to-ing and fro-ing over the challenge of the decision not to prosecute went on for another nine years.

We also lodged a judicial review application challenging the coroner's decision to adjourn the inquest into Jean Charles's death until after the health and safety trial. It was unsuccessful. The health and safety prosecution would proceed in October 2007.

In June 2007 came publication of the IPCC's report of the second part of their investigation, Stockwell 2, into whether Sir Ian Blair, or any other senior officer, had deliberately or negligently misled the public about the events that caused the police to shoot Jean Charles.

Stockwell 2 found that press releases from the Metropolitan Police in the immediate aftermath of the shooting wrongly stated that Jean

Charles had been challenged by police officers and refused to obey before being shot, and that he had been dressed in clothing that added to their suspicions. The investigation revealed that Jean Charles's wallet, picked up at the scene of the shooting, showed that he was a Brazilian national and not their suspect.

Despite rumours circulating within the Metropolitan Police on the day Jean Charles was killed that there had been an 'almighty cock-up' and the police had shot an innocent man, the report concluded that the commissioner had not been made aware of the victim's identity before he put out his misleading press release.

The report went on to consider whether, once he was cognizant of the 'mistake', there was a failure to correct misleading information. It refers to an interview given by Sir Ian Blair to the *News of the World* on 22 August 2005, in which he stated that neither he nor those advising him had known for twenty-four hours that the man shot was not the suspected suicide bomber. However, Deputy Assistant Commissioner Brian Paddick told Stockwell 2 investigators that by 3.30 p.m. on the day of the shooting, the commissioner's staff officer had been aware that the dead man was a Brazilian national. The commissioner insisted that he was not informed till later that evening. DAC Paddick said that when he confronted the commissioner about the misleading information in the *News of the World* article, the commissioner told him it was important that as few people as possible knew for as long as possible. Sir Ian Blair denied this version of events, asserting that DAC Paddick may have had his own reasons for making the allegation. The Stockwell 2 report concluded that there was insufficient evidence to substantiate Paddick's claim.

Brian Paddick, now Lord Paddick, was the first out gay senior police officer. He was also known for the controversy surrounding his policy, while Metropolitan Police commander for the London Borough of Lambeth, of not arresting individuals in possession of small quantities of cannabis. When he found out that I was acting for the de Menezes family, he offered to meet me to see if he could be of any help. The fact that he wanted the meeting to be conducted in the utmost secrecy was telling in itself, and the context he shared with me in confidence gave me further fascinating insight into the internal politicking that had been going on within the Met.

I also got a sense of the discord among the top brass from Assistant Commissioner Andy Hayman, another high-ranking officer who contacted me suggesting a meeting. AC Hayman, who was in overall charge of anti-terrorism at the Met and leading the investigation into the 7/7 bombers, was heavily criticized by Stockwell 2 for failing to inform the commissioner and other senior Met officers and Home Office officials at a management board meeting at 5 p.m. on the afternoon of the shooting that it was believed the man shot dead was not one of the suspects. The report ultimately favoured the commissioner's evidence over that of AC Hayman and he felt he had been left to carry the can.

On 2 November 2007, one month after the health and safety trial began, I hurried to the Old Bailey after being warned that the jury were coming back with a verdict. During the prosecution the Menezes family had to contend with more negative publicity about Jean Charles generated by the police defence team, who sought to suggest that immigration irregularities, and the fact that cocaine had been found in his blood, according to toxicology reports, gave him his own reasons to run from the police. They produced an enhanced composite photograph showing half of Jean Charles's face juxtaposed with half of Hussain Osman's. The intention was clearly to imply that similarities to the suicide bombing suspect were obvious, even though any resemblance was minimal.

As the jury filed in, I took the only available seat in the well of the court: right next to Commander Cressida Dick, by this time promoted to deputy assistant commissioner. On her other side was the commissioner, Sir Ian Blair. Both were in full uniform, an array of bright brass across their shoulders proclaiming their seniority. The verdict was returned. The jury found the Office of the Commissioner of Police guilty of endangering the lives of the public and of Jean Charles. However, they added a specific caveat that they did not consider Commander Dick to be personally culpable in any way. Glancing sideways, I saw Sir Ian Blair nudge Cressida Dick and say, 'You're all right, then.' The judge fined the office £175,000 and ordered it to pay substantial legal costs.

The family issued a statement questioning whether the commissioner should stay in his job in the light of the jury's verdict and the significant failings in the surveillance operation and communications with the command team that had been exposed. However, as the prosecution had been focused on the planning of the operation, it had not examined the role of firearms officers or heard evidence from passengers on the Tube carriage. The big question therefore remained unanswered: how did the firearms strategy effectively become an unstoppable machine intent on extinguishing the life of an unarmed 'suspect'?

With the health and safety prosecution concluded, the IPCC's Stockwell 1 report could finally be published. This lifted a veil on the significant degree of conflict between the statements of the seventeen passengers on the Tube carriage, and others in adjacent carriages, and the firearms officers as to whether 'Armed police!', or indeed any warning at all, had been shouted before Jean Charles was shot dead. It also revealed that the firearms officers conferred with each other before writing up their statements and that the two officers responsible for the shooting did not write up their statements until thirty-six hours after the shooting, when they became aware that they had gunned down an innocent man.

At long last, it was ruled that the inquest could proceed. An inquest is led by the coroner, who decides what evidence is relevant, which witnesses to call and what questions to ask of them. Inquests cannot attribute criminal or civil liability to any single organization. However, if someone dies as a result of an action of the state, there will be what is known as an Article 2 or 'Middleton type' inquest. That means the inquest can explore in more depth any failings by state agencies that may have more than minimally contributed to the death. An Article 2 inquest will be held before a jury, whose verdict will address the key questions the coroner asks. They can also produce a narrative verdict in which they can answer additional questions and comment on specific failings.

While it is for the coroner to decide what evidence to call and what questions to ask witnesses, 'interested persons' can make representations to the coroner as to evidence and put questions to witnesses. The family of the deceased, and any state agencies implicated in the death, may become interested persons.

This inquest included evidence that was subject to public interest immunity. For that reason, a former High Court judge, Sir Michael Wright, was appointed to act as coroner. The venue for an inquest must be in the jurisdiction where the death occurred. Given the number of interested persons to be represented and the high profile of the case, it was going to have to be a big one. The Oval cricket ground was chosen.

In the lead-up to the inquest, we finally began to receive large volumes of disclosure. Henrietta Hill, our frighteningly efficient junior counsel, ploughed through the copious police records, witness statements, reports and other assorted evidence, organized it and pinpointed material we would unquestionably wish to explore further.

In addition to the family of Jean Charles, there would be five other legal teams acting for different interests within the police, including those of the command team, the firearms team, the surveillance team, the Metropolitan Police service and the two firearms officers who discharged the shots, who were to be represented separately from their team as they might be subject to specific criticism. The

IPCC also had their own lawyers. The presence of so many potentially competing interests within the Met dangled the possibility that the agendas of all these legal teams could conflict with each other in a way that would assist the family's goal of exposing serious errors and wrongdoing. We were already aware that there was a significant gap between the statements of the surveillance team, who insisted they never positively identified Jean Charles as Hussain Osman, and the firearms team, who understood him to be the target they were tasked to stop at all costs.

Sir Michael Wright had appointed his own legal team to assist with wading through all the material and preparing questions for witnesses. Live notes would be provided at the hearing, which meant that evidence and legal rulings would be typed up simultaneously by stenographers so that a proper record was kept and counsel would have reliable access to material to enable cross-examination.

Applications were made in advance by the police officers involved for anonymity orders to protect their identities. The normal principle of British justice is that hearings should be held in public and witnesses named, with anonymity granted only in exceptional circumstances, for example, in the case of the police, when a surveillance officer is still working undercover. For this inquest, it seemed that, despite our objections, almost every police officer who applied for anonymity was granted it. A small compromise was that the family and their legal teams would be permitted to observe the officers giving evidence and assess their demeanour. Jean Charles's cousins were planning to be there for most of the proceedings, with his mother and brother Giovani returning to the UK to attend key parts in order to hear the testimony of the firearms officers and of Cressida Dick.

Finally, on 22 September 2008, the inquest hearing began. The key answer we wanted to tease out, since it was clear that the surveillance officers had never positively identified Jean Charles as the suspect, was exactly what command Cressida Dick had given the firearms team. Our second question was whether the officers who fired the fatal shots honestly believed that Jean Charles was a terrorist about to detonate a bomb and that they took action in the belief that they were preventing further deaths.

In the second week of the proceedings, an excited buzz travelled round the press bench and lawyers' desks. News had broken that Sir Ian Blair had announced his resignation as commissioner. Although his role in the shooting of Jean Charles de Menezes did not feature in the reasons he gave for his departure, it played a huge part in undermining confidence in how he had done his job.

Once all the evidence has been heard, the legal teams must make submissions on the matter of what verdicts the coroner can leave to the jury and what questions should be put to them. The possible verdicts that might apply in this case included lawful or unlawful killing or an open verdict.

The family were keen to ensure that unlawful killing remained as an option. We made submissions that there was sufficient evidence to support allegations of murder or gross negligence manslaughter as a result of the acts or omissions of the gold commander, the now promoted DAC Cressida Dick, her tactical adviser and C2 and C12, the two police officers who fired the fatal shots. All the legal teams representing police interests argued that only lawful killing or an open verdict should be available to the jury.

The coroner ruled against us. We had slightly more success framing a series of supplementary questions that the jury would have to answer about disputed facts – for example, whether any officer shouted 'Armed police!' before firing, whether the surveillance officers' view on identification was accurately communicated to the command team and whether there was a failure by the police to ensure that Jean Charles was stopped before boarding a bus or entering an Underground station.

The coroner's decision stripped the family of their remaining faith in the British legal process. As Sir Michael Wright began his summing-up of the evidence, Alessandro, Erionaldo, Patricia and Vivian staged a surprise protest. Walking across to where the jury were seated, they removed their jackets to reveal T-shirts emblazoned with the messages 'Unlawful killing' and 'Your legal right to decide'. They stood there in silence for thirty seconds and then filed out of the hearing.

As that meant their legal team were also obliged to withdraw, we were not in court to hear the conclusion of the proceedings. Apparently, the coroner, not knowing how to react, simply continued with his summing-up as if nothing had happened.

The jury were told that they could only return a verdict of lawful killing if they were satisfied on two matters: that, at the time they fired the shots, officers C2 and C12 honestly believed Jean Charles represented a mortal danger to them, or to others, or both, and that they used no more force than necessary in the circumstances as they honestly believed them to be. Otherwise, they should return an open verdict. And then they were left to come to their decision and answer the thirteen questions they had to consider.

It took them quite a while. It was not until 12 December that we received word they had reached a majority verdict. I alerted the family and campaigners and we all dashed down to the Oval.

The jury returned an open verdict and answered all of the questions submitted in a way that did not let the police off the hook for their gross failures. It was the strongest verdict possible within the permitted parameters. Although the family condemned the inquest as a 'whitewash', we all felt a sense of vindication, not least because the jury's decision reflected, as far as it could, that public sympathy lay with their cause.

The conclusion of the inquest was not the end of my involvement as legal adviser to the Menezes family. We now had the civil claim for damages to prepare, which ultimately resulted in a confidential but substantial financial settlement agreed through a mediation process. We also had the outstanding challenge of the test relied on by the DPP when considering a charging decision. That went all the way to Strasbourg, where it was heard in 2015 by the Grand Chamber of the European Court of Human Rights, which ruled against us.

To this day, not one police officer involved has been held personally accountable for failings that led to the death of Jean Charles de Menezes. Indeed, the two most senior officers in the command team were promoted – and by 2017, Cressida Dick was herself commissioner of the Metropolitan Police. The law as it stands still effectively provides legal immunity for police officers who shoot innocent people in the cause of protecting the public.

3

'Shut Down Yarl's Wood'

THE SPRAWLING MODERN COMPLEX IN the Bedfordshire countryside looks like most out-of-town UK prisons: located in the middle of nowhere, surrounded by high walls and barbed wire, uniformed officers coming and going through a tight, computerized search and security system. At reception, volunteers, lawyers and other visiting professionals are fingerprinted and photographed.

Yarl's Wood is not, however, technically at least, a prison. Those held here are not criminals, but people who have fled the horrors of war, despotic regimes and grotesquely misogynistic societies to seek sanctuary in a safe country, often enduring long and perilous journeys hidden in container lorries or buffeted on the high seas in overcrowded dinghies.

Yarl's Wood Immigration Removal Centre, designed to hold up to 400 detainees, was opened in November 2001 to facilitate the government's commitment to speeding up the asylum process and removing those it had already decided had no right to remain in the UK. The contract to run the centre was awarded by the Home Office to the private company Group 4 Security. While the first detainees were mainly young men, for most of its history a vast majority of them have been women.

Modern asylum law, introduced by the United Nations Refugee

Convention in the wake of the horrors of the Second World War and the Nazi Holocaust, is based on the legal principle of non-refoulement, whereby a refugee should not be returned to a country where they face serious threat to their life or liberty.

Immigration detention has historically been used for people who have entered the country illegally or overstayed their visa. If they weren't willing to leave voluntarily, the state could hold them while arrangements were made for their enforced removal. Many of those sent to Yarl's Wood fell into this category. In addition, there was a new cohort of detainees held under a system introduced in 2000 known as 'Detained Fast Track' (DFT). When someone made a claim for asylum on arrival in the country, or at some later stage, they would be screened by an immigration official to assess whether it was a claim that could be decided quickly. This might depend on the perceived safety of the country they came from and their account of why it was too dangerous for them to return.

Where their claim was considered unlikely to succeed, they would be sent straight to an immigration removal centre (IRC) like Yarl's Wood, which operated a system for rapid determination of asylum claims. They would be interviewed by immigration officers on site and, if a decision was made (as it was in all but a tiny number of cases) to reject their claim, they could appeal at a mini court convened within the centre. If that appeal failed, they would be given 'removal directions'. If they were not willing to comply with those directions, they could be forcibly removed.

While on the face of it, then, the fate of those channelled through DFT was not yet irrevocably sealed, the odds were certainly stacked against them purely on the strength of the method used to process their asylum claims. Indeed, by 2013, according to figures published by campaigners, almost one in five asylum-seekers were having their cases handled by a system with a 99 per cent rejection rate.

The legal grounds for detaining people subject to immigration control who have committed no crime is based on the Immigration Act 1971. It is an administrative process, not a criminal one, with migrants held on the decision of an immigration official, not a court or a judge. Depriving someone of their liberty without the use of a proper judicial process is a serious sanction, however much time and money it may save, and it had been subject to much Parliamentary debate.

The rules governing decision-making and the operation of immigration detention provide clear guidelines on the circumstances in which a person can be detained. In particular, it is Home Office policy that detention must be used sparingly and for the shortest possible period, and that it must not be used at all for torture survivors, unaccompanied minors or those suffering from significant mental illness. The Home Office thus rightly acknowledges that detention can cause further harm to the most vulnerable and that it is therefore inhumane to keep them under lock and key.

In my first job with Winstanley Burgess, I had helped advise people from all parts of the world who had escaped some unspeakable situations to seek sanctuary in the UK. Their stories resonated for me with my own history: I come from a family of refugees myself, and if it hadn't been for the sanctuary found by previous generations in the UK, I wouldn't be here today.

My father arrived in England as a teenager just before the start of the Second World War, eluding the Nazi invasion of Poland by the skin of his teeth. His mother, my Granny Ewa, and his sister Renee, only eight years old when he left, managed to survive the whole war in Poland, hiding their Jewish identity as they watched the creation and then the destruction of Jewish ghettos and heard news of other family members being taken to the woods and shot or transported to the concentration camps.

My mother's immigrant background was only one generation

further back. She was born into London's Jewish community to parents who settled in the East End at the turn of the century.

As a child I had for a while lived alongside refugees from Africa, after Idi Amin, the president of Uganda, expelled the country's Asian population in 1972. Many of these displaced people, forced to leave everything they owned behind them, were UK and Commonwealth citizens and headed for Britain. Horrified by the parallels with the Jewish experience in the Second World War, my parents invited Mr and Mrs Patel and their son Akesh, who was my age, to live with us until they found their feet, and Akesh went to school with me.

It was after joining Birnberg Peirce in 2002 that I first started taking on immigration detention cases at Yarl's Wood. It would soon become clear that many asylum-seekers, refugees just like my father or the Patel family, were being unlawfully held here for long periods of time and in breach of the regulations, and that there was a huge demand for lawyers to assist them.

Yarl's Wood was controversial from the start and has seen, during its relatively short history, numerous internal protests and frequent calls for its closure from campaigners on the outside. It faced its first hunger strike almost as soon as it opened, and in February 2002, just a couple of months later, a protest by detainees upset about one of their number being harshly physically restrained was badly handled by the guards. It escalated into a riot and a fire was started. According to one of the custody officers, staff complied with orders to 'lock detainees in the burning building'. The centre was gutted. Five people were injured; it was fortunate no one was killed.

Those identified as possible troublemakers were segregated, held in freezing cold conditions, then transported to prisons and detained incommunicado. A number of them were charged and prosecuted for arson, riot or violent disorder, in some cases on the flimsiest of evidence. Nigel Leskin, a partner at Birnberg Peirce who represented several of the accused, all of whom were acquitted at trial, asked me if I could advise his clients on possible civil claims for damages.

A friend and former colleague from Winstanley Burgess, Mark Scott, was also acting for several clients in the same situation. At that time, Mark was just about the only lawyer in the country bringing civil claims on behalf of immigration detainees. We decided to join our cases together to bring a group claim against Group 4, the private contractors to which the management of Yarl's Wood had been outsourced. Mark and I were able to obtain substantial damages for our clients at a joint settlement meeting.

The legal landscape in this area was, Mark told me, a bit like the 'wild west'. The widespread failure to adhere to the immigration rules often had a dramatic impact on the most vulnerable people you could imagine, including children, torture survivors and those suffering from serious mental and physical illnesses who should not have been there in the first place.

I knew from Mark about a related case he had taken to court on behalf of a Czech Roma family, a mother, father and two children, who had arrived at Yarl's Wood on the day of the fire. They had been locked in a room for several hours to await processing when the protest erupted. They escaped the blaze only as a result of the intervention of other detainees. Mark was pursuing damages in the County Court, claiming, among other things, that the family had been unlawfully detained and subject to violations of a number of their rights under the European Convention. The Home Office, as the defendant in the case, successfully applied to strike out their claim, arguing that any challenges to a decision of an immigration officer had to be brought in the administrative court, where judicial reviews are decided. The family were given permission to appeal the case.

The judgment, if upheld in the Court of Appeal, would have significant implications. It would massively restrict the legal remedies available to anyone subject to potentially arbitrary decisions taken

by an immigration officer and to the critical and far-reaching consequences those decisions could have. It would also limit the impact of
such legal interventions as could be made to hold the immigration
authorities to account.

I was approached to act for members of the Children's Refugee
Legal Consortium in a third-party intervention in the case and eventually instructed by two member organizations, immigration
detention specialist voluntary bodies, to produce evidence for the
Court of Appeal.

A third party can be granted permission to intervene when it can
add something new in terms of evidence or legal argument which
might assist the judge in considering the wider implications of any
judgment he or she may reach.

Lord Justice Henry Brooke, in delivering judgment for the appellant family in *ID and Others v. The Home Office* in January 2005,
quoted from our evidence in his conclusion:

> The evidence of the interveners showed, however, that when the
> Home Office determined to embark on the policy of using powers
> of administrative detention on a far larger scale than hitherto, the
> practical implementation of that policy threw up very understand-
> able concerns in individual cases. The transition from a world
> where decisions affecting personal liberty are made by officials of
> the executive who operate according to unpublished criteria, and
> where there is no way of compensating those who lose their liberty
> through administrative muddles and misfiling, to a world where
> the relevant criteria have to be published and where those officials
> are obliged to ensure that their decisions are proportionate and to
> justify them accordingly, is bound to be an uneasy one in the early
> years, and mistakes are bound to be made. But so long as deten-
> tion, which may cause significant suffering, can be directed by
> executive decision and an order of a court (or court-like body) is

not required, the language and the philosophy of human rights law, and the common law's emphatic reassertion in recent years of the importance of constitutional rights, drive inexorably, in my judgment, to the conclusion I have reached.

The ruling of the Court of Appeal recognized that there was a legal remedy available in the civil courts for bad decisions made by immigration officials – decisions which had the potential to wreck already damaged lives. Over the following years I would test out this judgment in many cases where I was seeing the appalling human consequences of the simplistic political mantra of 'being tough' on asylum-seekers.

The operation of immigration detention is governed by the Detention Centre Rules 2001, which form a crucial part of the legal framework to which lawyers refer when assisting those who claim they should not be in detention or have been maltreated there. Key provisions include Rule 34, which requires that all detainees should be seen by a medical practitioner within twenty-four hours of their arrival, and Rule 35, which states that a 'medical practitioner shall report to the manager on the case of any detained person whose health is likely to be injuriously affected by continued detention or any conditions of detention'.

The purpose of those Rule 35 reports is to flag up those at risk who may have slipped through the net. An initial medical examination will usually pick up any physical scars that point to torture and should also include an assessment of an individual's mental state. If evidence consistent with torture is found, an immigration officer should be notified and authorize the detainee's release. But at Yarl's Wood, this system was patently not functioning.

Through my work on the Yarl's Wood fire, I got to know various local people concerned about the welfare of those being held at the centre. Campaigner Emma Ginn, the founder of SADY (Stop Arbitrary Detention at Yarl's Wood), had been visiting detainees since the IRC opened. A lot of them had no friends or family in the country, and on several occasions Emma offered her home to bail applicants with nowhere to go. Gill Butler, a member of the Yarl's Wood Befrienders group and active in her local church, volunteered as a visitor, expecting to be there to offer straightforward friendship and practical support. It had not been long before it became obvious to both Emma and Gill how many alarmingly vulnerable people were languishing at the centre, some of them bearing the additional mental torture, sometimes for months, of anticipated repatriation to countries from which they had fled for their lives.

Emma and Gill began to bring cases to my attention, and gradually I became known as a solicitor who could challenge unlawful decisions and fight for compensation for victims of unlawful detention and excessive use of force.

One woman whose experience typified the abject failure to apply Home Office policy at Yarl's Wood was Patience. She was from northern Uganda, where she had been relatively well-to-do. She and her husband owned land and ran a successful motor spares company. Patience did the accounts and bookkeeping for the business. Theirs was a philanthropic family, providing food and clothing for the destitute and paying the school fees of a number of children from poor homes in their village.

One day soldiers came to their house and arrested both Patience and her husband. He had been financially assisting the People's Redemption Army, a rebel group associated with the opposition party, FDC, and had hidden arms at their home. Patience was separated from her husband and never saw him again. She later learned that he had been shot and killed while trying to escape. She, too, had sustained a gunshot wound and, during about five months of being held captive in atrocious conditions, was also violated and tortured.

A week after her arrival in the UK in May 2005, she claimed asylum. Her claim was channelled through the DFT scheme and she was taken to Yarl's Wood, where she was examined by healthcare staff. She told them that she had been tortured in Uganda and complained of pain in her back, legs, waist and bottom as a result. The medical staff duly noted this in their report, which was forwarded to the Home Office in accordance with Rule 35.

A few days later Patience was interviewed by an immigration official. She recounted how, in Uganda, she had at first been held in a small, dark, damp room. What little food she had been given was contaminated with insects and she had been severely beaten and raped by her guards. She had then been taken to an interrogation centre, where her captors had tied her to a bench and poured water over her, thrown her into a pit with snakes and other reptiles, bound her and suspended her above a pit of crocodiles. She was told that she was to be executed by firing squad. With the help of a brother-in-law, she had eventually managed to escape by bribing one of the guards and had fled the country.

Her solicitors wrote to the Home Office stating that, as a victim of torture, Patience was not suitable for the fast-track system. Before any steps were taken to address the legitimacy of her detention, her asylum claim was rejected. Patience exercised her right to appeal. With no access to legal aid (it is available for initial advice in fast-track cases, but not for appeals), she represented herself in the small courtroom at Yarl's Wood. The judge dismissed her entire asylum claim as 'an elaborate charade'.

Three weeks later, Patience was served with removal directions and escorted by guards to board a flight to be returned to Uganda, the country she had fled. She refused to get on to the plane and was taken back to Yarl's Wood, where she remained in limbo.

Gill Butler met Patience soon after the aborted removal attempt that summer, about two months into her detention, and her first impressions were of a 'highly intelligent and vivacious person with a good command of English'. It was not until the following winter, when Gill talked to me about bringing a case against the Home Office on Patience's behalf, that I entered the picture, by which time this strong and capable woman had no more capability than a small child.

On Gill's second visit, Patience told her about her arrest and subsequent torture. 'She was obviously extremely distressed,' Gill said. 'At that time, I had never heard anything like it. I found it hard to believe that in this day and age there could be such cruelty. Subsequently I spoke to others who knew more about the situation in Uganda and discovered that her account of the sort of torture she was subjected to was not uncommon.'

By the time Gill next saw her, Patience had joined other detainees on a hunger strike and had been refusing food and drink for four or five days. She told Gill she would not be able to bear being sent back to Uganda. 'She gave me a letter she had written but told me not to read it until after my visit. The letter requested my help to end her life.'

Unsure of what to do, Gill spoke to the Yarl's Wood chaplain, the Reverend Larry Wright, a former police officer who had become an Anglican priest and taken up the role of head of religious affairs at the centre in 2004. Larry had already heard Patience's story. 'I found her utterly credible. Her demeanour was of someone recounting something awful. Her eyes were lowered – she couldn't look at me directly. It felt as though her memories were literally weighing down upon her.'

After Patience lost her appeal, he observed that, like many detainees, she found it extremely hard to understand why she was being punished, as she saw it, for telling the authorities what had happened to her and seeking sanctuary. That lack of comprehension was massively compounded by being disbelieved.

Following the failed removal attempt, Patience told Larry that the officers who had tried to get her on the plane had been abusive and racist towards her and that she had been handcuffed. She was, he recalled, bewildered. It was from this point on that he dated the rapid deterioration in her physical and mental health.

The hunger strike was growing and a number of those joining the protest, according to Larry, were from Uganda and Zimbabwe. Patience seemed very committed to it. 'She had by this time given up hope of getting justice from the British government and, like many other detainees, she expressed a desire to die in this country rather than being returned home to further torture and certain death.'

In August 2005, Alistair Burt, the local MP, visited ten of the hunger strikers, including Patience, who had already written to him. I met Alistair later, in Parliament. A thoughtful man from the decent wing of the Conservative Party, he told me he visited Yarl's Wood regularly, taking an interest in issues involving both staff and detainees, had tabled numerous Parliamentary questions in connection with the centre and had spoken in debates in the House on related matters. He had asked the hunger strikers to consider giving up their protest. 'I did not believe it was in their best interests. This was obviously because of the danger to their health and also because I felt it would be made more difficult for the authorities to deal with them fairly.'

Alistair stressed to me that he was not somebody who opposed the use of immigration control. 'I believe that in limited and clearly defined circumstances, detention is necessary in order to enforce policy. I understand that enforcement is a difficult job, but it is essential that it is undertaken as justly and fairly as possible and at all times with reference to basic human rights.'

Through August, Gill saw a marked deterioration in Patience's condition. Her concentration was decreasing and she was becoming forgetful. 'She was always cold and had developed pitting oedema of her ankles. She complained of increasing tiredness and dizziness. Although she loved to participate in singing in chapel services, she complained that she could not get enough breath to sing properly.'

Gill contacted Dr Frank Arnold, who had previously examined some Zimbabwean hunger strikers, to ask if he would assess Patience. Frank, an American settled in the UK, was a member of the Royal College of Surgeons and an expert in wound healing. He had volunteered with the Medical Foundation for the Care of Victims of Torture and was visiting detainees regularly to document their scarring as evidence to corroborate accounts of torture. He made arrangements to examine Patience as a matter of urgency over the bank holiday weekend.

On his advice, she was transferred to Bedford hospital to begin a controlled re-feeding programme. He visited her there to examine her for a torture report, noting a number of lesions and other marks on her body which he considered consistent with her account of having been tortured in Uganda.

On requesting and receiving her medical records, he saw that the healthcare centre at Yarl's Wood had already twice sent Rule 35 torture reports to the immigration authorities, who appeared to have done nothing in response. Having made several phone calls to try to speak to somebody at immigration, he contacted an official at the Home Office to ask what steps were being taken to verify Patience's account. He was informed that since her asylum claim had been refused and her credibility had been doubted, no further steps needed to be taken.

Patience was discharged from hospital a week later. Gill was staggered that she was deemed fit to be returned to Yarl's Wood. 'I think even the medical staff were quite surprised,' she said. Although she had been rehydrated, she was still very weak and had barely been able to walk out of the hospital. The staff had had to put her in a wheelchair to get her into the security guards' van.

Back at Yarl's Wood, she was having problems with her vision and appeared to be hallucinating frequently, insisting that there were Ugandan soldiers in her room.

On 21 September, there was another crisis. A fellow Ugandan hunger striker, Margaret, who had become good friends with Patience, described how the DCOs (detention custody officers) came to Patience's room, handed over her suitcase and told her to pack her things because she was going to be removed. Realizing that Patience was not in a fit enough state to manage this, a couple of the DCOs started packing her belongings themselves. When Margaret asked where the removal directions were, they said Patience had them among her papers. 'They told me I had to leave the room. I said that I was going to stay as I was becoming very concerned for Patience. They tried to push me out.' Eventually, there were about ten to fifteen DCOs in the room, plus a manager, who was adamant that Patience was going to have to be ready to leave in two minutes. Patience, frantic with fear, was overcome by a panic attack.

In the chaplain's office, Larry Wright took an emergency call from a staff member to say that Patience had collapsed in her room. Could he could come quickly? When he got there, the duty manager told him about Patience being given notice of imminent removal. 'The scene in her room was chaotic. Patience was lying on the floor, propped up against a suitcase. She was having difficulty breathing and being attended to by officers and other detainees.' It was obvious to Larry that she was hyperventilating and he noticed that her eyes kept rolling backwards. Outside the room, distressed and angry detainees were gathering. Apparently, while some officers were trying to calm the situation and provide medical help, others were still demanding that she get up and pack.

Margaret left to call Gill and Patience's solicitor, Paul Nettleship. When she returned, 'Patience couldn't take in what I was telling her. She was sweating madly and could no longer recognize me. I got her to the phone to speak to Gill but she was hysterical and incoherent.' The guards seemed, at last, to become concerned about her condition and left. A manager told Margaret: 'Good news – the flight is cancelled.'

But Patience was becoming more and more unwell. Paul Nettle-ship, a quietly spoken immigration lawyer from one of the few really good firms of immigration solicitors, Sutovic and Hartigan, had recently taken on her case and instructed Dr Felicity de Zulueta, a consultant psychiatrist and lead clinician at the Traumatic Stress Service in the Maudsley hospital in London. On 4 October, Felicity spent about an hour and a half assessing Patience in the IRC health-care centre. There was, she said, absolutely no doubt in her mind that Patience was reliving traumatic events from the past.

> My extensive experience of working with patients suffering from trauma enables me to distinguish between genuine sufferers and those who are inventing symptoms. Patience displayed all the char-acteristics of somebody who was in a state of autonomic arousal. When patients experience PTSD flashbacks it is almost like there is a camera playing back their unprocessed memories. Patience liter-ally showed me, with her hand movements and from the terror on her face, a very vivid picture of the torture she had experienced in Uganda. There were very evident signs of increased arousal and I was convinced that she could not be inventing her account.

Felicity was concerned that, as a result of her hunger strike, Patience might be suffering from Wernicke's encephalopathy, or 'wet brain', a serious neurological condition that can be brought about by the exhaustion of vitamin B1 reserves. She made an emergency med-ical referral to move Patience once again to Bedford hospital.

But within a few days Patience had been returned to Yarl's Wood where, apparently, she lay on her bed in a catatonic state, unable to speak or recognize anyone, before being taken back to the hospital, this time to the psychiatric unit.

In Dr Felicity de Zulueta's professional opinion, the episode pre-cipitated by the second failed removal attempt on 21 September had been a significant catalyst in Patience's dramatic deterioration, and it followed that if she was returned to the environment that had triggered her decline, the chances were this would be repeated. And yet, three weeks later, Patience was back at Yarl's Wood. On learning this, Felicity swiftly arranged to reassess Patience and concluded that it was 'the last straw'. If she had remained out of detention and begun treatment, there would have been opportunities to help Patience recover from her severe symptoms. As it was, Felicity believed, detaining her at Yarl's Wood once again at this juncture had caused 'permanent and irreversible damage'.

It was around this time that Gill filled me in on Patience's story and asked me about the prospects of bringing a case against the Home Office. After reviewing the documents she sent me, I took the view that, in addition to contravening the Human Rights Act, the ongoing detention gave Patience a strong claim of false imprisonment.

Incredibly, given the state she was in, there was then a third attempt to put Patience on a plane to Uganda. Gill made contact with Paul Nettleship and local MP Alistair Burt and the removal directions issued for 6 December were cancelled. But Patience seemed past the point now of grasping what was happening to her and it was, according to Margaret, largely left to other detainees to take care of her – changing her sheets when she became incontinent, bringing her back to her bed when she wandered in the middle of the night and generally coping with her erratic behaviour.

One evening in early January 2006, Gill had calls from several panicked detainees saying they thought Patience was dying. She phoned the duty manager. She heard the next morning that he had come to see Patience but had refused to believe there was anything wrong with her. Later that day, Gill discovered that she had been rushed to Bedford hospital on oxygen. Visiting in the evening, she found an apparently comatose Patience lying in a bed with the side rails raised to prevent her from falling out, even now, to comply with the regulations, being guarded by two Yarl's Wood DCOs, as if, despite all the evidence to the contrary, she might suddenly leap out and escape.

A few days later, Patience was transferred to the Maudsley hospital under the care of Dr de Zulueta. I went with Gill to see her. Patience was literally mute. Unable to speak, she had to communicate in scribbled messages. I did my best to explain that I was going to explore a claim for damages against the Home Office because of the way she had been treated. As it was questionable whether Patience was fit to instruct a lawyer, we agreed that Gill would apply to be her litigation friend, a person who can be appointed by the court to act in the best interests of children or adults who lack the necessary mental capacity.

I called upon Richard Hermer, a barrister with whom I had worked on the Yarl's Wood fire cases and the intervention in the appeal of the Czech Roma family. Together we mapped out the basis of a substantial claim for damages, identifying the multiple failures to act in accordance with Home Office policy or guidelines in the detention and treatment of Patience throughout the asylum process.

Normally, a claimant's own statement is a critical document in a civil claim for damages, but in this case all Patience could state was: 'My claim has been explained to me by my solicitor and by Gill Butler, who I refer to as "my mum". It has been explained to me that the claim relates to a period of time that I spent at Yarl's Wood Immigration Removal Centre. However, I have no recollection whatsoever of being at Yarl's Wood and find it hard to believe that I was there for (I am told) seven months.'

The particulars of claim, a formal legal statement of case, set out how Patience was subjected to violations of her human rights and unlawfully detained for an extended period of time, giving rise to a claim in false imprisonment. The case was contested by the Home Office and it trundled along for some months as I prepared and reviewed disclosure schedules, witness statements, expert reports to deal with damage, loss and care needs and a trial bundle. In the meantime, on her discharge from the Maudsley, Patience went to live with Gill and her husband David, who looked after her as she slowly began to recover and regain the power of speech.

Patience was finally awarded refugee status in 2008 after a successful appeal allowed her to submit a fresh claim for asylum, backed by the evidence of an array of medical experts. The following year, after a mediation, we settled her civil claim for damages for a substantial sum, which was paid into a special investment account managed by the Court of Protection. While her condition has improved considerably in the years since, she still struggles with her health and the legacy of the damage she suffered at Yarl's Wood.

As Patience's story demonstrates, failed asylum-seekers sometimes have very good reasons to resist attempted removals. And resistance has sometimes been met with a level of force amounting to assault.

Along with Gill Butler, Frank Arnold and several former detainees, Emma Ginn set up the charity Medical Justice, a coalition of campaigners and doctors committed to safeguarding the physical and mental wellbeing of people in immigration detention. Its independent doctors, usually volunteers, have recorded evidence of both recent and historic injuries consistent with the excessive use of force by guards.

Journalist Robert Verkaik reported some of these cases in the *Independent*, referring in one article to a 'dossier' of around 200 allegations of assault. After a senior civil servant working in immigration enforcement wrote to the newspaper declaring that if there was evidence of mistreatment 'we would expect it to be provided to the police and Border and Immigration Authority for investigation', various government ministers cast doubt on the veracity of the complaints by accusing the *Independent* of refusing to supply proof of this 'dossier' and campaigners of making unsupported assertions about the treatment of detainees.

If the government wanted more proof, Emma, Frank and I decided, we would give it to them. In July 2008 we published *Outsourcing abuse: the use and misuse of state-sanctioned force during the detention and removal of asylum-seekers*. Our report contained forty-eight detailed case studies, selected from the 300 allegations we now had on record from several IRCs and presented with the consent of their subjects. There were accounts of women being handcuffed from behind and put in leg restraints as they struggled to resist being shoved on to a plane; of protests by passengers; of screaming detainees being gagged; of racist abuse from some guards; of the deployment of batons and other 'distraction' techniques. The use of such force had resulted in both physical injuries and, in a significant number of instances, exacerbation of PTSD in survivors of torture.

Lord Ramsbottom, a former British army officer and chief inspector of prisons, wrote in the foreword he contributed to our report of a 'culture of disbelief' among officials dealing with immigration and asylum. 'If even one of the cases is substantiated,' he said, 'that amounts to something of a preventable national disgrace.'

Some of the case studies featured in our report were families with children. The provision for the detention of children was one of the most controversial aspects of the policy introduced by the Labour government in 2001. Like torture victims and those suffering from mental illness, unaccompanied minors were not supposed to be sent to IRCs. But families seeking asylum with their children were not excepted from immigration detention. And when the stipulation that this measure must be 'used sparingly, and for the shortest period necessary' was so routinely flouted, the consequences for those children could be devastating. As one mother put it: 'Yarl's Wood isn't a proper place for children to be. It felt like they were in prison. The children themselves were very frustrated and it was really disturbing their minds.'

By 2009, reports from the inspectorate, the children's commissioner and others were repeatedly raising concerns about the detention of minors. That June, a group of mainly African families at Yarl's Wood staged a peaceful protest in a bid to draw the attention of the United Kingdom Border Agency (UKBA) to their worries for the long-term physical and psychological health of their children.

The UKBA was the Home Office department responsible for the enforcement of immigration rules and the contract to run Yarl's Wood. By this time, the contract had been awarded to a different private company, Serco, which had taken over in 2007.

After a couple of days, with the protest showing no sign of petering out, the response from the Yarl's Wood management was to send in a posse of guards to break it up, resulting in violence, pandemonium and the separation of some families.

In the aftermath, my assistant, Sheila, and I took accounts from members of ten families as we prepared a case against the Home Office on behalf of those parents and children who were harmed by the unlawful use of detention and by the aggressive handling of the protest. As well as recording what had happened that day, we dug into why and how they had been brought into detention in the first place and the issues that had prompted their demonstration.

Together their stories painted a picture of inadequate paediatric healthcare, nutrition and education, of fear, boredom, bad dreams and behavioural problems, for the children of Yarl's Wood.

Baby Abbo, for example, had been listless and refusing to feed for several days, developing diarrhoea and a raging temperature, when, according to his mother, she was told by healthcare staff that if she wanted him to cool down, she should open a window. It wasn't until, in desperation, she phoned 999 and the IRC was notified of the call to emergency services that some custody officers took her to a doctor, who put him on antibiotics.

Five-year-old Moussa, from Senegal, had already been detained twice before with his mum. Now he was having nightmares and wetting the bed. He was asthmatic, and not only was the eczema that flared up when he was under stress getting worse, he was having coughing and vomiting fits as well.

Ensuring their children ate reasonably healthy food, if they could get them to eat at all, was an uphill struggle for parents. In the canteen, 'every day it's chips and rice', said one woman who had previously tried to bring up her son on a varied diet. Many parents relied on the milk and yogurt on offer but too often found it past its sell-by date and sour.

The Crane Unit, the facility assigned to families with children, had a schoolroom and children's paintings added splashes of colour to the institutional walls. Otherwise, there was not much to distinguish it from the other three units at Yarl's Wood. Although internal doors were not locked, people were not able to leave unless accompanied by a guard with keys to other areas.

The school was not, said the detainees, equipped to provide much more than recreation. 'Children of all different age groups are put together in one classroom with no planned programme of study,' explained Grace, from Malawi, who was being held with her fourteen-year-old daughter and her son, seventeen by the time we talked to her. 'There is nothing for them to do apart from play games all the time. There are very few books and children are not encouraged to work at their education.'

Grace's son Chimwemwe recalled being brought to Yarl's Wood in handcuffs when he was sixteen. 'It felt really strange to be placed in prison when we had done nothing wrong . . . Because I was one of the older children in the family unit there was nothing for me to do. I spent a lot of time sitting in my room waiting for the day to go by. I was planning on going to college in September . . . The school in the family unit had nothing to offer me.'

It was after their requests to be given the chance to raise their concerns directly with the UKBA led nowhere that the families collectively decided to mount their peaceful protest. On the third afternoon, they were ambushed by around thirty or forty Serco officers forcing entry into the corridor where they were sitting quietly on mattresses, some of them reading, some of them asleep, while the smaller children played near by.

Witnesses spoke of how the few adult men in the unit were apparently targeted, aggressively manhandled and restrained. It seemed that the authorities had opted to hold them responsible for the protest. 'I remember when my daddy was thrown to the floor and hit the radiator,' a nine-year-old boy told us. 'There were lots of officers and they were pulling his hair and kicking him. They also kept blocking his nose and it looked like he couldn't breathe. They were shouting bad things at him and I was scared.'

Along with three fathers, Chimwemwe was forcibly removed and segregated. 'I was woken by about six men grabbing, pulling and pushing me down on the floor,' he said. 'They twisted my hands behind my back and were pushing me down. Then one of them grabbed hold of my hand and twisted it and then together they dragged me down the corridor . . . My boxers were falling off me.'

Amid the chaos, frightened people were crying and shouting and fire doors were locked, separating some of the sobbing children from their mothers. There were reports of infants being roughly handled and even trodden on. Several detainees described how, after removing one of the husbands, the officers came back for his wife. In the struggle to keep hold of her baby daughter, the traditional African wrap she was wearing came off and they dragged her away, naked and screaming, treating her 'like an animal', in the words of one of her friends. 'When I saw her crying, I fell down to the floor,' said another. 'It was for things like this that I left my country.' It would be two or three days before all the families were reunited.

The violent suppression of the protest, on top of the trauma of detention itself, was to have a profound psychological impact on some of the children.

I instructed Sheila Melzak, a child and adolescent psychotherapist and one of the founders of the recently established Baobab Centre for Young Survivors in Exile, to assess some of the affected children who were still in the UK and used the extremely detailed reports she prepared on four of them as evidence in successfully suing the Home Office in a series of linked civil claims settled with damages being awarded to each family.

In all the reports, Sheila found that the impact of the detention conditions and of what the children witnessed during the break-up of the protest, on top of pre-existing stressors arising from the histories that led to them being detained in Yarl's Wood in the first place, had caused significant damage. In one case, she attributed unevenness in the child's behaviour, problems with thinking and capacity for reflection, mood swings, loss of hope and depression to a profound deterioration in developmental functioning. In two sisters, symptoms of complex PTSD were, in Sheila's clinical opinion, likely to become entrenched and to have a similar effect on their moods and thinking, as well as on their learning and relationships. She was concerned about a four-year-old boy who felt he was sometimes treated as a criminal and sometimes abused, noting that he was particularly preoccupied by events where he had observed uniformed officers being verbally and physically aggressive.

The ordeals of these children, and so many others, led to renewed political pressure to end the detention of all minors for immigration purposes. In December 2009 a joint report prepared by a coalition of the Royal Colleges of General Practitioners, Paediatrics and Child Health and Psychiatrists, along with the UK Faculty of Public Health, set out how detained children were at risk of mental health problems, self-harm and even suicide. 'It is time for this inhumane practice to end,' said Sir Al Aynsley-Green, the children's commissioner for England.

Following the general election in May 2010, the Conservatives formed a new coalition government with the Liberal Democrats, who were committed to ending the detention of children. In July, Nick Clegg, the new deputy prime minister, declared: 'This coalition government will once again restore a sense of decency and liberty to the way in which we conduct ourselves. That is why I can confirm that the government will make an announcement shortly about how we will deliver on our pledge to end child detention and to close the Yarl's Wood detention centre for good.'

Some fourteen years later, Yarl's Wood remains open for business.

The 'culture of disbelief' described by Lord Ramsbottom is endemic in the immigration detention context. A general public scepticism in the UK towards asylum-seekers and a strong narrative that they make up stories to stay in the country is inevitably amplified when an asylum claim is rejected and the refugee ends up in an IRC. if they are being detained, the logic goes, it stands to reason that they must have done something wrong.

And when that other societal context where we find a huge culture of disbelief – so huge that the CPS has had to publish detailed guidance to try to dispel rape myths and stereotypes – also comes into play, what happens then? What happens when an immigration detainee makes an allegation of sexual assault against a detention custody officer or other member of staff?

A setting like Yarl's Wood, where half the staff were male, and in a position of power over an overwhelmingly female population, was ripe for exploitation. The so-called 'relaxed environment' led some male officers to take advantage of young and often extremely vulnerable detainees. To what extent is hard to know because abuse was so under-reported. Many women were too afraid of repercussions to complain of sexual assault; some may not even have perceived it as abuse, because of favours they may have received in return. Others may have sincerely believed themselves to be in a loving relationship with the man.

Those who did complain did not find it easy. Towards the end of January 2011, the coordinator of Yarl's Wood befrienders, Heather Jones, asked me whether I might be able to advise a young detainee who alleged that she had been sexually assaulted by a male nurse. After speaking briefly on the phone to Sana, who was originally from Pakistan, I arranged to visit her with an interpreter. Although she had been in the UK for a few years, her English was not fluent and it was essential that my understanding of her account was accurate. Escorted from reception through a series of locked doors and corridors up to 'Legal Visits', I was shown into a room to wait with the interpreter.

Sana entered tentatively: a woman in her late twenties, eyes downcast. She was, she told me, a regular at the healthcare department, to have her blood pressure checked and her medication dispensed, having suffered throughout her time at Yarl's Wood from a range of medical problems, mainly associated with anxiety exacerbated by her circumstances. More than once she had been flagged as a suicide risk and put on a RASP (raised awareness support plan). She had been seen a few times by the nurse about whom she had complained and initially she had thought him very kind and caring. Until the day when, alone with her in a consulting room, he had made sexually suggestive comments before exposing his erect penis and inviting her to give him oral sex or to touch it. She returned to the wing in tears. One of the other women, Mira, asked her what was wrong, but for two days Sana couldn't bring herself to tell her.

When she finally did, Mira encouraged her to report the incident to an officer. Sana took no action. She was too worried that she wouldn't be believed.

About three weeks later she found herself once again alone in the healthcare centre with the same nurse. He told her how much he liked her and pulled her hand towards his penis, which was hard, telling her that he needed to have sex with her. She snatched her hand away and fled back to the wing, where she told Mira what had happened. Again Mira urged her to report the assault, but by this time things were not going well with Sana's immigration case and she was scared to do anything she felt might jeopardize it.

One evening, they were among a group of women who were discussing the big news of the day: apparently, one of the detainees was pregnant by a DCO. While it seemed the woman in question believed herself to be in a romantic relationship with the guard, others could see that it was exploitative and were shocked. One of the DCOs, Maureen, came over and asked what all the fuss was about. When Mira explained, Maureen said she was not allowed to talk about it. The forming of a sexual relationship with a detainee by a member of staff, whether or not it was apparently consensual, would of course constitute serious misconduct, and potentially amount to the criminal offence of misconduct in public office.

Mira made it known to Maureen in no uncertain terms how unsafe some of the women were feeling and told her about the sexual advances made to Sana by another member of staff. Now the officer was listening. It took some coaxing from Maureen and Mira to get Sana to speak, but eventually she disclosed a few details. 'One girl pregnant and another assaulted?' said Maureen, appalled. 'I wonder what else is going on here?'

Sana was now crying and shaking and Maureen was concerned enough to send her to healthcare. She called on two guards to accompany her and assured her she would be safe with them. But at the healthcare centre, Sana was left in a consulting room on her own to be seen by the very nurse who had assaulted her.

While taking her blood pressure he fondled her breasts and rubbed her groin. He told her he could 'satisfy her'. Sana stood up and got out of there as quickly as she could. On the wing she went straight to Maureen. This time Maureen called the manager and submitted a formal complaint on Sana's behalf.

The following morning Sana was asked to provide the manager with a statement. There would, in the end, be three so-called investigations into her allegations. At this first meeting, the manager, employed by Serco, took down her account without the assistance of an interpreter.

The statement was passed to the UKBA. On 12 January, before Sana heard any more about her complaint, she was called to Legal Visits and informed by an immigration officer that removal directions to Pakistan had been fixed for two weeks' time.

This was deeply troubling. Sana had found a new immigration lawyer who was in the process of obtaining fresh evidence in support of her asylum claim. She told him about the sexual assaults and he advised her to report them to the police, but Sana was extremely reluctant to do this. It already seemed to her that the UKBA were trying to get her out of the country so that they wouldn't have to investigate her complaint and that the removal directions were punishment for making the allegations.

On 18 January, Sana was summoned again to Legal Visits, where she met two UKBA officials, equipped with a tape recorder, who announced that they were there to obtain a fuller account of her allegations before her removal. She asked for an interpreter, but they said her English was good enough. She now stated that she wanted to report the assault to the police.

Three days later, an officer from Bedfordshire Police arrived to speak to her – a male officer, again with no interpreter. He spent no more than half an hour with Sana and didn't write down anything she said, merely telling her that the authorities believed she was lying in an attempt to avoid being deported. As soon as she returned to her wing from Legal Visits, she was handed her removal directions for a flight to Pakistan on 26 January.

Sana's solicitor issued judicial review proceedings and obtained an injunction to stop her removal. At a bail hearing at Yarl's Wood on 4 February, the judge concluded that she should stay in detention on the basis that the judicial review would be decided quickly and Sana would soon be deported – arranging for her release was not worth the trouble, in other words.

In the meantime, Sana was exposed to the hostility of some of the guards who believed she had fabricated allegations against one of their colleagues and put his job at risk. She was too scared to go anywhere near the healthcare centre. When I saw her just after the bail hearing I was worried by the state she was in and promised her I would set up an urgent mental health assessment.

In the Legal Visits area, Sana pointed out Maureen, the officer to whom she had reported the sexual assaults. Given the uneasy atmosphere, I wasn't at all confident that Maureen would feel she could speak to me, but, perhaps a little warily, she agreed. 'Did you believe what Sana told you?' I asked her. She was in no doubt that the disclosure had been 'entirely spontaneous' and she had no objection to me seeing the account she had given to Serco and the UKBA.

I was grateful that Dr Georgina Smith, a clinical psychologist specializing in trauma with experience of treating victims of sexual violence, was available to see Sana at short notice, because a couple of days after the bail hearing Sana received the outcome of the UKBA's investigation. The claimant's 'desire to remain in the UK,' they said, 'coupled with her knowledge of the other Yarl's Wood IRC case, encouraged her to formulate allegations which are unsubstantiated'. Now her anxiety was off the charts.

An interim report from Georgina enabled me to raise concerns with immigration about the serious impact on Sana of her ongoing detention and, thankfully, she was released to bail accommodation in Manchester. In the meantime, I rolled up my sleeves and went into battle on her behalf over the handling of her complaint and the lawfulness of her continued detention after the assault and in view of her deteriorating mental health.

The duty of the state to safeguard the wellbeing of those it holds in custody is implicit in the protections of the Human Rights Act, and with that comes the duty to conduct an effective investigation of any allegation of assault made by somebody in custody where there is evidence that the complainant has come to harm. If such harm is shown to have been caused by unlawful acts, the state may be liable.

If the decision-making of the UKBA in relation to Sana's detention, or any stage of it, contravened the published Home Office policy, she would have a claim on that score, too, for civil damages.

I wrote to the prison and probation ombudsman, listing the defects in the UKBA investigation and inviting them to consider the complaint afresh. The investigators had failed to take statements from the two key people who could have corroborated Sana's account: Mira and Maureen. The UKBA investigator had implied that Sana had made up the sexual assault allegation as a way of avoiding deportation, even though, at the time she reported the assault, she had not been notified of, or received, any removal directions. The police officer who had spoken to her, ostensibly to establish whether a crime had taken place, hadn't even bothered to take notes.

I looked carefully into whether part or all of Sana's detention was unlawful, starting at the beginning – what had led Sana to be detained in the first place? – and examining her immigration history and experience of detention.

Sana had come to the UK from Pakistan on a spousal visa in 2000, at the age of seventeen, forced into a marriage to a distant cousin arranged by her authoritarian father. Her husband was very controlling and when she failed to get pregnant, he became violent. After throwing her out, he ultimately divorced her on the basis that she could not conceive. She couldn't return to her family in Pakistan: being divorced by her husband was perceived as shameful in their community and her father had disowned her. Lost and alone in the UK, she was taken in by distant relatives in return for looking after their children.

A few years later, encouraged by friends, she married another Pakistani national, only for him to turn out to be even more violent. She tried to leave him but, trapped by the impact of her abandonment by her first husband on her visa conditions, she could not live independently: she was not allowed to work and had no access to benefits or other resources. In the end she was compelled to leave by her second husband's escalating abuse. She stayed temporarily with a friend and sought help from a refugee charity. They referred her to an immigration solicitor, who advised her to claim asylum.

In October 2010 Sana was assessed by the asylum screening unit, deemed eligible for the DFT system and sent to Yarl's Wood. This was unexpected and traumatic. 'I had never been to prison,' she told me. 'I had no idea what a prison looked like. I thought I was going to die.'

Sana was interviewed about her claim within a week and her application was swiftly rejected. She had no legal representation when her appeal was heard at Yarl's Wood and the judge was not persuaded. With her options exhausted, she no longer had any right to remain in the UK and would be sent back to Pakistan. She was terrified. How on earth was she going to survive there?

I obtained Sana's Home Office file under the Data Protection Act and instructed Alison Pickup, an immigration specialist barrister with whom I had worked on previous immigration detention civil claims. Alison was not only very thorough but passionate about the issues central to Sana's case. In her view, it could be argued that, in the light of the reported sexual assaults, both the length of Sana's detention and the conditions in which she was held constituted the basis of a claim for damages. In addition to making a claim against the Home Office, we decided to bring proceedings against Serco, who were vicariously liable for the sexual assaults, and against Bedfordshire Police for their failure to investigate them.

Georgina Smith assessed Sana for a second time to explore what, if any, psychological damage she had suffered. She diagnosed depression and PTSD, the latter caused by the sexual assaults and the former exacerbated by the experience of detention.

The upshot of the ombudsman's investigation into the sexual assaults was that there was insufficient evidence for the UKBA investigator to have concluded that Sana's allegations were untrue. However, neither could it be concluded that the allegations were true. Ultimately, in short, it was one person's word against another's.

I escalated the complaint about the police failure to investigate by taking it to the IPCC. They upheld my appeal and required a reinvestigation, which eventually found that the officer's investigation was inadequate due to the failure to interview a critical witness, Mira.

All three defendants – the Home Office, Serco and Bedfordshire Police – initially resisted the claim for damages. After the 'close of pleadings' stage, the parties were required to list the documents in their possession that were relevant to the issues to be tried in the claim. Serco included their internal investigation report into Sana's allegations against the nurse. Sana had never been told about the outcome of this report. I requested a copy. I was gobsmacked to read what it said and the conclusions it drew.

'The allegations made are very detailed and have been consistent each time Sana has relayed them in interview,' the report stated. Usually, those who provide accounts of sexual assault are criticized when they are inconsistent, but here Serco were saying that her consistency cast doubt on her credibility. This was a new one on me.

As for the nurse: 'It would appear to be very out of character' for him 'to make inappropriate sexual advances to another person'. He was seemingly 'a family man with strong religious beliefs and would have a lot to lose through this type of alleged behaviour'. This beggared belief. Had they never heard of anyone being abused by clergy or priests? And what had being 'a family man' to do with anything?

'Sana shares the same solicitor as another resident who has recently made an allegation against a member of staff. It has also transpired that Sana receives social visits from the same befriender . . . It is possible that there could be an element of coercion in order to thwart her removal directions.' The befriender 'could also be involved in the coercion' and it was conceivable that Sana was 'being advised by her solicitor and befriender of actions to take'. I assumed that the author of the report meant to use the word 'collusion' rather than 'coercion'. Even so, to imply that those seeking to support a detainee would encourage her to lie, let alone collude with her or coerce her into it, was utterly scandalous.

The only staff member to be criticized was, ironically, the DCO who had helped Sana to make her initial complaint. It was recommended that Maureen should be 'given advice and guidance to assist her in being more objective in the future. Maureen must understand that she should not be making judgments without knowing all the facts.'

As the Serco report pointed out, and seemed for some reason to find suspicious, I was acting for another Yarl's Wood detainee in a sexual assault case at the time. I also had several clients there who were victims of sex trafficking. Many of these women had suffered abuse and violence in the countries they had escaped, like Patience, or in the UK, like Sana. Or both. On top of this, they were having to bear the loss of liberty and stresses of detention. The initial investigations into Sana's allegations were an indisputable illustration of the multiple barriers victims of assault and abuse had to overcome to have their voices so much as heard, let alone believed. It was crystal clear that, as well as the same scepticism faced by so many women reporting sexual violence in any sphere, they had to overcome imputed motives of fabricating allegations to avoid being deported.

I was able to settle the civil claim for damages against the police and Serco. The case against the Home Office went to trial, following which a judge ruled that the final two weeks of Sana's detention were unlawful and made a small award of damages. Sana's new immigration lawyer later succeeded in establishing her right to asylum and she was able to start rebuilding her life in the country where she had lived all her adult life. For a number of years, she battled depression. She became involved in a support group for women refugees in her local area and has spoken publicly about what happened to her to help raise awareness of the treatment of detained asylum-seekers in the UK.

I sought permission from Serco to pass on their internal report on Sana's case to the Parliamentary Home Affairs Select Committee, to other relevant statutory bodies and to Marc Townsend, who covered some of the Yarl's Wood cases for the *Observer*. It was refused.

The *Observer* had to wage a six-month legal battle in the High Court before they were allowed access to the report. They then published a major exposé featuring allegations of sexual assault and sex for favours at Yarl's Wood. Serco were summoned to appear before the Home Affairs Select Committee. In June 2014 their chief executive issued an apology after it was revealed that ten of their employees had been dismissed following allegations of improper sexual contact with detainees at Yarl's Wood.

The Detained Fast Track procedure faced various legal challenges and appeals. The Court of Appeal ruling in 2015 that it was unlawful was ultimately upheld by the Supreme Court, obliging the Home Office to discontinue it. In August 2020, it was announced that Yarl's Wood was being 'repurposed' and would no longer be used to detain women. But it remains one of ten IRCs in the UK, which now include a women-only detention centre recently opened by the Home Office in County Durham.

In the meantime, successive Conservative governments apparently more focused on keeping asylum-seekers out than dealing with a backlog of asylum claims promised to 'speed up the process' and set up more detention facilities, with some of their more radical proposed solutions liable to face legal challenges in the courts. The highly inflammatory rhetoric used by some in government to discuss the issue has played into media coverage of the number of asylum-seekers crossing the Channel in small boats that has bordered on the hysterical. The number of desperate people reaching the UK by this dangerous route has certainly rocketed, but it is still relatively tiny compared with the overall increase in the net migration figure.

The indefinite detention of asylum-seekers, including children, looks set to increase with the Illegal Migration Act, which became law in July 2023, giving the home secretary extensive powers to detain without time limit those arriving in the UK irregularly.

It is concerning that the climate of hostility being created in some quarters will lead to more inhumane treatment of adults and children alike; of women like Patience and Sana – just two victims among many of a system geared to enforcing removal without regard to the human stories involved. Seeing cases like these while hearing so many asylum-seekers speak of their belief in the UK as a land of fairness, compassion and justice has filled me with shame and sadness.

4

Challenging the Failure to Investigate

'LOTTO LIE CABBIE DRUGS AND RAPES 5 – HUNT FOR SPIKED BUBBLY BRUTE' screamed the headline in the *Sun* newspaper on 15 February 2008. A Metropolitan Police cold case review team running a routine computer check on recent unsolved rape and sexual assault complaints had spotted four allegations against a driver of a black taxi which looked very similar. The information had been passed on to the specialist crime directorate, which conducted further computer searches and found more offences with strikingly common characteristics, including one dating back to 2002.

The police made a public appeal for potential victims to come forward. The details they shared of the rapist's modus operandi rang alarm bells with a number of people. Two of them had been on a night out five years earlier with a close friend, Fiona, which had ended for her in an assault that had blown her life apart. They both got in touch with her straight away.

For Fiona, this news stirred up painful memories, and she was reluctant to re-engage with the police after the way they had treated her at the time. It had destroyed her relationship with her partner, left her battling depression and she was only now beginning to put her life back together.

It had all started in May 2003, after her first evening out since the birth of her child eight months before. Leaving the baby with her partner, Mike, Fiona had met up with a group of friends she hadn't seen in a while to celebrate the birthday of a former flatmate. They had dinner in Soho and then decided to go on to a club. Fiona had a few drinks and was a bit tipsy when her friends hailed a black cab to take her back to Mike's North London flat. The couple lived separately and, unable to remember the exact address, she just gave the cabbie the address of her previous flat, which was practically next door.

The cab driver was very chatty. When he offered her a nightcap and handed a cup of something through the open window behind him, she declined. But he was very insistent and, not wanting to offend him, she relented and took a few sips of the drink, which had a strong orange liqueur flavour and tasted 'slightly sickly'. She asked if she could smoke and he said to go ahead. Then he stopped the cab, got out, climbed into the back with her and put his arm round her. To this day, Fiona remembers nothing else until she woke up the next morning and found herself in hospital.

She leaped out of bed, confused and completely disorientated. What on earth was she doing in hospital? Needing the loo, she managed to find the toilet. When she sat down, the tampon she was using fell out and she was horrified to discover a lot of lubricant inside her. Her vagina seemed very open and stretched. She felt so spaced out and weird she was convinced she must have been drugged and it dawned on her, to her distress, that she had been raped. She immediately retrieved the tampon from the toilet, thinking it might be needed as evidence, and wrapped it in tissue. Unable to locate a nurse who might be able to tell her what was going on, she ran out of the hospital in tears.

She needed to call Mike but remembered that she had left her phone at home the night before. She had no idea where her handbag was, with her purse and glasses in it. She went back into the hospital and asked a member of staff if she could use their phone. It took her about five or six attempts to get the number right. Mike, not surprisingly, was beside himself with worry. She told him she thought she had been raped and he rushed over to the hospital with their baby.

Urged by Mike to phone the police, Fiona made the call and two officers arrived from Islington police station. They took an account of what she could remember, collected the tampon and a urine sample and accompanied her to Ilford rape suite, where she was examined by a doctor. The examination was extremely upsetting and it was only now that she broke down.

Two days later, Fiona was invited back to the police station for an ABE – Achieving Best Evidence – interview. These are used to produce video-recorded verbal statements from vulnerable witnesses, or those at risk of intimidation, and are seen as a more effective way of capturing their evidence than the traditional written statement. First introduced for children, and designed to take a victim-centred and trauma-informed approach, ABEs were extended in 2002 to adult victims of sexual offences.

Fiona was briefed by the detective assigned to her case, DC Stephens, to be as factual as possible and to try not to become too emotional. She knew this was going to be a tall order. To get through the interview as calmly as possible, she dissociated, describing what she could remember as though it had happened to someone else. Towards the end of the interview, the male officer who had been sitting with her commented: 'To be honest, no one will believe you. You aren't crying or showing any emotion.'

After the ABE interview, Fiona felt that the police lost interest. She mentioned that she had noticed some bruising coming up on her arms and thighs and asked if it should be photographed. She was never contacted about this. She did, however, discuss the bruises with her GP, who made a detailed note of them.

Fiona was desperate to make sense of what had happened that

night. She had never blacked out before and still had no idea how she came to end up in hospital. She got in touch with the SOIT (sexual offences investigative-trained) officer who had come to the hospital. He explained how she had been sent there by ambulance, in a barely conscious state, from Hornsey police station, where she had been driven in a black cab with another passenger, called Kevin, who lived at her previous address.

Fiona arranged to meet Kevin, an Australian student sharing the flat with several others, to thank him for helping her and he filled in some of the gaps. He told her how he had been woken in the middle of the night by a noise that sounded like someone trying to break in. Going downstairs to investigate, he found a cab driver attempting to open the front door with a set of keys that did not fit, which he must have taken from Fiona's bag. The cabbie said he was dropping someone off. Kevin went out to the taxi and saw Fiona unconscious in the back, covered in vomit. He told the driver he didn't know her and suggested he took her to the local police station.

But there was something about the cab driver that made Kevin uneasy. He claimed that the woman was roaring drunk when he picked her up but, to Kevin, she seemed drugged. And he had always been under the impression that taxi drivers refuse to carry passengers in this bad a way. Kevin decided to get into the cab and go to the police station with her, just to make sure she was OK.

At Hornsey police station, they got Fiona out of the taxi and spoke to someone at the desk. The driver told the police she was drunk, that he had picked her up in that state and then he quickly cleared off. As the police called the ambulance, Kevin tried to raise his concerns but the officer didn't seem very interested.

After meeting Fiona and hearing her story, Kevin made several unsuccessful attempts to provide the police with a statement. They also failed to take accounts from any of the friends Fiona had been with in Soho that evening, including one who, having put her in the cab and spent a few minutes chatting with the driver, could have provided a description of him and possibly even have identified him. He went to the police station several times to try to give a statement and was promised that someone would be in touch to follow this up. It never happened.

In fact, the only statement the police did take was from Mike, who hadn't been there and knew nothing of the events of that night until Fiona called him from the hospital in the morning. He told her that the questions they asked him were mainly about her behaviour. All this achieved was to raise Fiona's anxiety levels and doubts in Mike's mind about whether she was telling the truth.

Fiona was losing confidence in how rigorously the police were pursuing their inquiries. She had a call a few weeks after the assault from the SOIT officer with the news that they had received the results of the forensic tests and no semen had been found – though this could, he explained, be because a condom had been used. And that, it seemed, was that. The investigation appeared to have stalled. She phoned a few times for updates and to ask if the police were gathering any additional witness statements but, despite assurances that they would be, neither Kevin nor any of the friends she had been with that night were contacted and critical witness identification evidence was never obtained.

A few months later, Fiona and Mike were in the park with their child when she had a phone call from DC Stephens. They could find no evidence to support her allegations, he said, and were closing the case. 'I believe something happened to you,' he told her, 'but you weren't raped.' DC Stephens reasoned that a licensed London cab driver would never jeopardize his entire livelihood by raping a customer, nor would he drive her straight to a police station afterwards. Besides, the officer mansplained, she could not have been raped because intercourse was impossible with a tampon in place.

He asked her if she would like to come and collect her clothes.

Fiona was really upset and angry. She felt she was being accused of being a liar. 'You will need to hang on to them,' she replied, 'because one day you may need the evidence. I believe this man will do it again.'

Now, in 2008, it seemed she had been proved right.

The public appeal had been sparked by a chain of events that began with a phone call to the police from one of the staff at the Havens, a London specialist sexual assault and rape centre, who saw the report in the *Sun* and remembered examining a rape victim the previous year with a remarkably similar story.

In July 2007, nineteen-year-old Meena went out to a nightclub in the West End with two friends from university. At 2 a.m., having become separated from her friends, she decided to make her own way back to her halls of residence in Greenwich. She'd had a couple of drinks but was by no means drunk. She didn't feel confident, on her own, about catching a night bus home as planned and, noticing a taxi rank outside the club, thought the safest option was to take a black cab. The driver was talkative. Showing her a bag containing a large sum of money, he told her he had just won £3,000 and invited her to have a drink to help him celebrate. He handed her a glass of something bubbly through the window, which she declined. But he kept pressing her and, in the end, she drank a little bit just to shut him up.

The driver hit the brakes hard, jolting the glass from her hand. It fell to the floor and broke. He handed her a plastic cup with a clear liquid in it, again urging her to have a drink. Uneasy now, she took just a small sip or two. Then he pulled over, got into the back of the cab, sat down next to her and offered her some pills. When she refused to take them, he became aggressive and forced her to swallow one by holding his hand over her mouth. That was the last thing she remembered.

Meena woke with a start the following afternoon at about 2 p.m., in her own bed, dizzy and confused. Suddenly, she had a flashback of the cab driver forcing her to take the pill. She registered that she was still fully dressed, then that there was a lot of blood on her mattress. Recalling that she was on her period, she realized that the tampon she had been using was no longer there. She noticed there was a button missing from her shorts and grazes on her knee and elbow.

She spoke to the security manager on campus, who checked his CCTV and advised her to call 999 and report a suspected sexual assault by the cab driver.

Two male police officers arrived and noted down her story. One of them went to look at the CCTV. It showed a black cab pulling up outside at 4.25 a.m. The driver got out and opened the passenger door. Meena nearly fell out. The driver could be seen holding her up, possibly embracing her, before leaving her to stagger towards her halls of residence.

Meena found the attitude of the police officers very insensitive. One of them joked about her falling over. They asked what she saw as stupid questions, such as whether she was sure it was a black cab and how much she'd had to drink. They then called in a SOIT officer, who wrote down her account. A mouth swab and urine sample were taken, and some of her clothing collected, but, inexplicably, not her bra or bedsheets. The SOIT officer drove her to the Havens, where she was subjected to a full medical examination.

The police were able to identify the registration number of the cab from the CCTV. A check with the Public Carriage Office revealed that it was registered to one John Worboys. They went to his home to arrest him and search the premises but he was not in. They asked the Public Carriage Office to give Worboys a message inviting him to report to Plumstead police station.

The following afternoon, John Worboys duly showed up at Plumstead, where he was arrested on suspicion of sexual assault. Samples were taken from him but a decision was made not to bother with a search of his home or his taxi. He was then interviewed, with a solicitor present, despite evidence not yet having been gathered on which to question him.

Worboys said he had picked up Meena at 3.50 a.m. and that she had fallen asleep in the back of the cab. He denied giving her any drugs or alcohol. When they arrived at her address, she told him she had no money to pay him and he decided to let her off the fare. He claimed that she kissed him and said he was a 'lovely man'. The CID police officers conducting the interview allowed him to explain his version of events and made suggestions as to what might have happened as if they wanted to help him out. Could her tampon have dropped out in the cab? Did she look like somebody who might have been taking drugs? And, in one of the most jaw-dropping lines of questioning I've ever seen in a police interview: 'Forgive me for asking, because obviously we've got to investigate this matter. Is it a case that she engaged in sexual activity to pay for her fare?'

'No.'

'Did she offer to pay you in any sexual way? Am I right that her response in cuddling and kissing you was because she knew that you wasn't expecting any money?'

'Yeah. I suppose.'

They concluded that his account was credible and consistent with the CCTV. And yet there had been no search, nor had they taken a full statement from Meena, opting to wait for the forensic test results to come back first.

The taped interview with Worboys was reviewed a week later, and the inconsistencies between his account and Meena's considered further. He said he had picked her up at 3.50 a.m.; she said it was 2 a.m. Worboys had not dropped her off until 4.25 a.m., after a journey that should have taken no longer than forty minutes. The obvious way to verify the pick-up time was to check the CCTV from outside the nightclub. The police now collected the recording but by the time they got round to viewing it, they realized it was from the wrong evening. By then it was too late: the relevant CCTV had been wiped. Worboys was never re-interviewed about this discrepancy, or indeed about a number of others that later came to light.

When Meena's blood test results were received, there was no indication of the presence of any date-rape drugs, although this was unsurprising as such drugs remain in the system only for about six hours and the sample had not been taken until much later the next day. However, the toxicology results that would subsequently be examined did record various types of antihistamines and anti-inflammatory medication. This report was never shared with her and she was never asked about whether she had taken any over-the-counter medicines. There was no evidence of alcohol intoxication. So why could she be seen on camera staggering from the taxi, barely able to stand?

No trace of semen or blood was found in the fingernail scrapings taken from Worboys when he was arrested and, with nothing conclusive to go on, the police closed the investigation on 28 October 2007. And like Fiona, Meena felt she had been disbelieved. And, just like Fiona, she had been told by the police that no driver of a black cab would put his licence at risk by sexually assaulting a fare.

Meena's was the only case reported to the police that had resulted in Worboys' identification and arrest. As would soon become apparent, their failure to investigate more meticulously had left him at liberty to attack again on a prolific scale. Had the sharp-eyed member of staff at the Havens not seen the *Sun* story, joining the dots might have taken even longer than it did.

When the Plumstead team closed their investigation, they had, in their wisdom, relegated the case to a 'crime-related incident' in order to improve statistical data about their clear-up rates. It was therefore not classified as an unsolved sexual assault. But the link with Meena's allegation was made at last and Worboys was arrested at his home address. This time, the police conducted a thorough search of his home and his cab. They found a 'rape kit' consisting of alcohol, an array of sedative drugs, a vibrator and notebooks containing some of the victims' names and addresses. They also found notes appearing to anticipate questions that could potentially be put to him in connection with the assault on Meena.

It was at this point that they made their appeal for other victims to come forward. The details they released, of the rapist's tactics, his garrulousness and the offers of a drink to toast a gambling win, played over and over in Fiona's mind. She sensed that he had perfected his technique since attacking her. She was right: it would be established that after 2006 Worboys followed an identical routine with all his victims, and yet still the police failed to see a pattern, throughout the six years before he was finally arrested and charged, in the reports made by a number of women who had been assaulted or had had a troubling experience as a passenger in a black cab. After a fitful night's sleep, Fiona told me later, 'my conscience got the better of me'. Despite her misgivings, the next morning, she phoned the hotline.

The call handler told Fiona that the new investigation team had already identified her as someone they wanted to speak to and she soon had a visit from DI Steve Warrilow, who couldn't have been more different from the officers she had dealt with before. However, he didn't seem to have much to work with. He told her that her video-taped ABE interview couldn't be located. Nor could the full file of evidence, or the clothes she had left with Islington police. She could not escape the conclusion that the original team had buried the evidence to cover up for their past failings.

Fiona was invited to attend an ID parade to see if she could pick out the taxi driver. Shown into a waiting room full of women there for the same purpose, she was seized by a terrible guilt. If only the police had believed her back in 2003, she wondered, how many of these women would have been spared what had happened to them?

According to a CPS closing report, by the time Worboys' trial began on 20 January 2009, the police had identified eighty-nine linked offences. Five years on, Fiona wasn't a hundred per cent confident she could identify him. For this reason, and because so much of the evidence from her attack had been lost by the police, a decision was made not to prosecute him in relation to her allegation. There were plenty of evidentially stronger cases, and Fiona was assured that the CPS did not need to prosecute every offence for Worboys to be sent away for a very long time.

The prosecutor was 'crafting the indictment': taking care not to overload it, especially with cases that had a lesser chance of succeeding, to avoid complicating matters for the jury – and indeed a very lengthy and unwieldy trial – while at the same time bringing enough solid charges to ensure that, if convicted, Worboys would be sentenced to a period of imprisonment that would protect the public.

While Fiona was not one of the women on the indictment, Meena was, which meant she had to give evidence at Croydon Crown Court. Worboys was pleading not guilty to all charges. The court heard that he incapacitated his victims using alcohol laced with sedatives, and it was only then that Meena learned of the mostly over-the-counter drugs that forensic testing had revealed in her bloodstream after the rape. In combination, it must have been these that had caused her to lose consciousness. She had not taken any of these medications and was outraged to discover that the police had not checked this with her as soon as the toxicology results were back.

John Worboys, by this time fifty-one years old, was found guilty of nineteen offences in relation to attacks on twelve women, the earliest in 2006, and jailed indefinitely, with a minimum term of eight years. The judge said he would not be released until the Parole Board decided he was no longer a threat to women.

By the time the trial ended, 105 women had come forward to say they believed they had been among his victims.

It was in March 2010 that I first spoke to Fiona. She had been given my phone number by another solicitor, Alison Ludwell, who was advising her and several other Worboys victims about making a compensation claim against Worboys himself, and/or the company that licensed his taxi, for the harm caused to them by his attacks. While Fiona certainly thought Worboys should be made to pay for the suffering for which he was responsible, she was just as angry about, and felt she had been just as badly damaged by, the way the police had let her down, and let down all the other women Worboys assaulted after her.

Alison, who had no experience in suing the police, had seen a news report about a case I had advised on, a claim against the Cambridgeshire police force for the inadequate investigation of another rape. We had secured both compensation and a public apology for the victim. Although the case had been settled without admission of liability, it was a legal milestone: one of the first reported cases in which a rape victim had successfully sued the police for such a failure.

It has been a long-established legal principle that the police cannot be sued in negligence for a hopeless investigation. In 1989, this principle was upheld and set in stone by the House of Lords, who were at that time the final court of appeal in our jurisdiction. *Hill v. The Chief Constable of West Yorkshire Police* concerned a claim brought by the mother of Jacqueline Hill, the last known victim of Peter Sutcliffe, dubbed the Yorkshire Ripper, who was convicted of the murders of thirteen women and seven attempted murders between 1975 and 1980.

The West Yorkshire Police investigation into his crimes was disastrous. Blinded by a prejudicial view of his victim type and an obsession with a hoax caller who goaded them, they missed many key opportunities that might have stopped Sutcliffe in his tracks much sooner. Jacqueline Hill's mother, Violet, firmly believed that her daughter would still have been alive had it not been for the police failures.

As a matter of law, the House of Lords struck out Violet Hill's case on the basis that there was no 'cause of action', ruling that the police do not owe a duty of care to the general public in respect of the investigation of a crime and there is a public policy reason why they should not be under such a duty, namely that it could lead to the police conducting themselves in 'a detrimentally defensive way'.

However, when the Human Rights Act (HRA) was passed into law in 1998, lawyers like me, who specialized in actions against the police, could see that it opened up the possibility of new ways of holding them accountable for investigative failures. The HRA, which came into force in 2000, incorporated the European Convention on Human Rights (ECHR) into UK law. In effect this meant that the UK government and all state agencies had to act compatibly with the rights set out in the articles of the ECHR. Those rights include, among others, Article 2, the right to life, Article 3, the right not to be subjected to torture or inhuman and degrading treatment, and Article 4, the right not to be subjected to slavery or forced labour. Any violation of a convention right can lead to a declaration of incompatibility by the court and a payment of compensation.

The police might therefore be held accountable not just for wrongful acts, such as the shooting of Jean Charles de Menezes, but for failures to enforce positive obligations, such as the duty to protect a person from a death threat or to prevent someone from being raped or trafficked. How far this duty might extend was to become the subject of an eight-year battle in the courts when I took on Fiona and Meena as clients and we decided to sue the Metropolitan Police.

After the conviction of John Worboys, as a result of formal complaints made by Fiona and Meena, the IPCC had been asked to conduct an independent investigation into failures by the police that may have contributed to leaving Worboys free to continue preying on victims. Their report, published in January 2010, made a series of criticisms and identified eight officers whose conduct was investigated. Despite complaints against five of these eight officers being upheld, not one of them was subject to any sanction more serious than a written warning. Fiona was upset by the report's findings and aggrieved that nobody was carrying the can. As far as she was concerned, DC Stephens, the officer handling her case, should have lost his job.

When she got in touch with me in 2010, I explained that it would not be possible to appeal the IPCC decision. However, it might be possible to sue the police, relying on the Human Rights Act. She was keen to go ahead, but she did not qualify for legal aid, which was available only to those on the lowest level of income. Neither did she have enough money to pay the legal costs herself. This left me with just one viable option: to represent her on a 'no win, no fee' basis, otherwise known as a conditional fee agreement (CFA).

Taking this route is a gamble for both lawyer and client. You have to carefully assess your prospects of ultimately winning the case and the costs therefore being met by the losing party. If you lose, the lawyer will earn nothing and the client might be left having to pay the other side's costs. Although we were walking a relatively untrodden path, I reckoned that, after the police had been so roundly criticized, there was a good chance they might wish to settle early on, as they had done in the Cambridgeshire case. I asked Phillippa Kaufmann, an extremely able barrister with a feminist instinct with whom I had worked previously, whether she would be interested in advising on a CFA basis. She considered the papers and confirmed that she would, although she warned me that we might face 'limitation' issues.

A claim under the HRA should be started within a year of the events giving rise to the claim, otherwise it will be 'out of time'. In Fiona's case the failures dated back to 2003. There were arguments we could make to persuade a judge to exercise his or her discretion to extend the limitation date, but this was a significant stumbling block. I took steps to issue 'protective' proceedings in court as soon as possible to stop the limitation clock ticking. I also wrote a 'letter before claim' to the Metropolitan Police solicitors. Their response was robust. They countered that Fiona's case was well out of time and that, in any event, there was no legal basis for such a claim under the HRA.

I arranged for a psychiatric report on my client to serve on the defendant. This could address any psychological reasons for delay, as well as potentially increase the amount of compensation that could be awarded if it showed that Fiona had suffered damage as a consequence of the police failures.

I chose Dr Charlotte Harrison, a psychiatrist I had used in a number of other cases, who had a good understanding of sexual violence and trauma. I provided her with papers relating to the case, Fiona's medical records and a set of questions I wanted her to answer.

In the course of the assessment, as well as describing her background, Fiona had to give her account of the attack by Worboys and the police investigation and detail the ways in which they had affected her mental health. Dr Harrison needed to base her report on both Fiona's account – and any contemporaneous medical or other evidence that supported her narrative of how she had been impacted – and on her own clinical observations of Fiona's demeanour. If she found psychological damage, she would have to separate the potential causes, which might include pre-existing trauma, the rape itself and the repercussions of Fiona's treatment at the hands of the police.

Dr Harrison concluded that Fiona had not sustained any specific psychiatric injury as a consequence of the rape. She had, however, suffered a depressive episode as a consequence of how she had been dealt with by the police during the investigation. In particular, great distress and anxiety had been caused by her sense that people did not believe she had been raped. An adjustment disorder experienced in 2008 was triggered to a large extent by the guilt that overwhelmed her when she learned how many other women had been attacked by Worboys after she had reported him to the police.

We requested disclosure from the police and were supplied with the limited material that had not disappeared from the original investigation. One item of evidence was the toxicology report, which showed the presence of a range of sedative drugs (including traces of morphine/codeine and citalopram) in the blood sample provided by Fiona after she was assaulted. Like Meena, although Fiona had been told that no date-rape drugs were found in her system, she was never informed of her full test results and she was shocked that no one had bothered to ask her if she had been taking any of this medication (she hadn't). Not only should this, of course, have been a significant point of enquiry, but had Fiona been given the complete picture by the police, she would also have been spared years of anxiety about how she could have ended up so ill on the night of the attack.

That November, I was contacted by Meena, who had also been referred to me by Alison Ludwell. She, too, was unhappy with the toothless IPCC response to her complaint and wanted to see the police take more responsibility. She, like Fiona, was ineligible for legal aid and would face limitation issues. In her case, I was less sure of our ground. Although the first police investigation had without question been woefully inadequate, Worboys had in the end been prosecuted and convicted for his crime against Meena. It could therefore be argued that, ultimately, the police failures had been put right. But I was willing to give it a go.

I issued a claim in court on Meena's behalf and sent a letter before claim to the Met solicitors, who once again responded that my client's claim was years out of time, legally flawed and had no prospect of success. The disclosure of evidence they were obliged to provide in both cases included statements and other evidence obtained for the original investigation and used at trial, complaint documents and a copy of relevant parts of the Met's own internal critical incident review of the Worboys investigation, codenamed Operation Danzey. Extracts from the internal review proved to be very useful in their own right as they revealed that another eight women, in addition to Fiona and Meena, had reported Worboys to the police before he was eventually charged with any offence.

With the police taking a bullish stance and showing no signs of softening it, Phillippa and I were nervous about proceeding full steam ahead on a CFA basis with a lengthy, complex and expensive litigation in an area with little precedent, if it could be avoided. I decided to approach Andy Fairbrother, the Met Police solicitor, to sound him out on whether they might be willing to have a 'without prejudice' meeting to discuss a possible out-of-court settlement that would involve no admission of liability on their part.

Andy said he would take his client's instructions. They were prepared to meet our clients but with the proviso that no financial offers would be on the table. At the very least we would be able to explore non-financial remedies such as a public apology.

Up to that point, Fiona and Meena had never met. I had expected Meena's approach to me to be welcomed by Fiona: usually, people with shared experiences fighting the same or related legal battles are glad of the opportunity to support each other, and appreciate that the more claims there are, the stronger their prospects of success. So I was surprised at Fiona's muted response to this proposed meeting. She said that while she had every sympathy for Meena, she didn't really want to meet her. She explained that this reluctance was rooted in her abiding sense of guilt. She felt that, somehow, her own inability to make the police believe her had led to the assault on Meena. Here was living proof of the lasting psychological damage wreaked by the way the police had dealt with her.

But Fiona was nothing if not committed to their common cause and agreed to come with Meena to the structured settlement discussion we arranged at Doughty Street Chambers. The women spoke powerfully of what had happened to them and Phillippa spelled out the strength of the legal case. The police representatives, though sympathetic, were not willing to budge an inch on settlement. The only 'offer' on the table was to invite Fiona and Meena to present their experiences as part of a police training programme.

Effectively, we came away with nothing more than the certainty that if we took the claim forward, we would face strong resistance. We had tried the conciliatory approach. Now it was all or nothing.

I had one safety net in place. I had managed to agree a deal with an 'after-the-event' insurer whereby, if the clients wanted to go ahead and the lawyers' view was that the prospects of success were good, they would cover any risk that the clients would be out of pocket. Phillippa and I would still be running the risk of undertaking a huge amount of work for no pay – as would Birnberg Peirce, as my employers – but if we lost, at least Fiona and Meena would not have to pay the police's legal costs.

We decided to go for it.

The first hurdle was the limitation issue. If we fell at this one, that would be the end of the claims. In anticipation of the police argument, we set out reasons in the particulars of claim as to why it would be equitable for the court to apply its discretion to extend the limitation deadline. Neither woman could have reasonably brought a claim before Worboys' arrest in 2008 as they would have had little evidence to show the extent of the police failing. Furthermore, it was reasonable for the claimants to wait until after the trial and the outcome of the complaint investigation before exploring the civil claim.

I also served on the defendant a Part 36 offer, a device available to either side to encourage early settlement by pitching a claim for, or offer of, compensation at a slightly lower level than the claimant might expect to receive if the case went all the way to trial and a judge awarded damages. If you 'beat the offer' at trial there are very significant costs consequences. My offer therefore deliberately cited a more modest sum than I estimated my claimants might win in court.

The claims had been issued in the Queen's Bench division of the High Court in the Royal Courts of Justice in the Strand, where I'd first protested with Justice for Women twenty years before to raise awareness of our campaigns. Nowadays it was more familiar to me as the home of the masters' chambers in the East Wing, reached by way of the Bear Garden, so named, apparently, because the clamour of argumentative litigants here in Victorian times was reminiscent of bear-baiting.

A master is a procedural judge who will deal with the management of cases before they reach trial. Hearings take place in their spacious, old-fashioned chambers furnished with desks and leather armchairs. Most masters are men; those who are not are also, slightly confusingly, known as masters. Phillippa argued our case on limitation before Master Leslie, one of the male majority, an affable judge who was, in my experience, often empathetic towards claimants. He ruled it would be equitable to extend limitation. Our case would proceed to trial, unless the defendant decided to accept our Part 36 offer. They didn't.

We set to work preparing the case. While Fiona and Meena were subjected to more psychiatric assessments with the defendant's experts, the legal team carefully reviewed all relevant disclosure from the two investigations, the prosecution and the complaint investigation and compiled detailed statements from the claimants and any witnesses we might wish to call. In Fiona's case, in addition to calling one or two of the friends she had been with that night, I was very keen to get a statement from Kevin, the student who had answered his door to Worboys in the early hours and insisted he take the unconscious Fiona to the police station.

This was a challenge: Fiona had heard that Kevin had since returned to Australia. We managed to track him down and he was happy to provide a statement, but there was still the practical problem of exactly how he could give oral evidence in court. It would have been far too expensive to fly him back to the UK and the technology used by the creaking old Courts of Justice had not really caught up with the modern age. I was surprised and pleased to discover that they did actually have a video-link facility, although they hardly ever used it. We just had to hope they could operate it, that it worked on the day and that Kevin was up for potentially having to testify in the middle of an Australian night.

As the trial date approached, Phillippa was furiously researching ECHR case law that might assist the tricky legal arguments we were going to have to make and I was digging into evidence on what might have been known about Worboys' offending and into what we knew about policing and rape more generally.

The *Guardian* crime journalist Sandra Laville, who had reported extensively on Worboys, was able to give me a figure for the number of women believed to have been attacked after Meena's case was dropped and before he was arrested and charged: twenty-nine. That is twenty-nine women assaulted by the same serial rapist taxi driver in a four-month period who would never have suffered potentially life-changing psychological damage if the police had not failed to follow basic investigative leads. And that is just the number we know of. There will almost certainly be others who did not come forward. The charity Rape Crisis estimates that only about 15 per cent of rapes are ever reported to the police.

In the seven-volume trial bundle I put together with the painstaking help of Cassie, my paralegal, I included the IPCC report on the Kirk Reid case, an equally disastrous Metropolitan Police investigation into another serial rapist who targeted lone travellers on South London public transport. Reid is believed to have attacked around a hundred women. He was active at the same time as Worboys and therefore subject to the same Met Police standard operating procedures and guidance for the investigation of rape.

The soundings from Phillippa's barrister colleagues indicated that the judge we were assigned, Mr Justice Green, was both sharp of mind and fair, which boded well. Counsel for the defendant was Jeremy Joseph QC, a barrister who seemed to be instructed on the other side for virtually every case I brought. Although he was, in my opinion, fighting to defend the indefensible, he did make one wise, as well as merciful, decision, to the huge relief of Fiona and Meena: to accept their written statements as true. This meant they were not required to give evidence in court and would be spared having to recount the extremely traumatic background to this action, which, for Fiona, stretched back ten years, and being cross-examined about their behaviour.

The trial began on 25 November 2013 (rather aptly, International Day to End Violence Against Women). In setting out our stall, Phillippa included a survey of the European case law which, taken together, provided a compelling argument as to why an investigative duty arises under Article 3 of the ECHR. The witnesses were called. With neither of the claimants giving evidence, our case was concluded fairly swiftly and we had reached the point Fiona and Meena had been waiting for: the chance to cross-examine the police officers who had so badly failed them.

Among the disclosure with which we had been provided were documents that set out policy, guidance and standard operating procedures for investigative techniques in rape and sexual assault cases. One we were to refer to again and again with the police witnesses was the guidance on the investigation of drug-facilitated sexual assault. It was carefully crafted and laid down detailed steps and considerations from a starting point of treating the victim's account as truthful, at least until a full and thorough investigation had taken place.

There has been much debate in recent years about the risks of this approach. But, as feminist campaigners and advocates for rape victims have argued, we operate in a victim-blaming culture where a majority of women and girls who are raped or sexually assaulted feel shame or guilt that they are somehow responsible for 'getting themselves raped'. This reaction is not seen in the same way in victims of crimes like theft, assault or criminal damage. If the police and others show they are sceptical of a rape victim's account, most victims will either not report or withdraw from the process at some stage. The upshot is that rapists will get away with, and be emboldened to repeat, their offending. The Worboys case, in which victims were disbelieved, their behaviour and actions queried and the prejudices of officers concerned infected their whole attitude to investigations, perfectly exemplifies the consequences not only for the victim but for the public at large.

As each investigating police officer gave evidence in court, they admitted they had not been trained in the guidance or that they hadn't read much or any of it. These were officers in Sapphire teams, the Met's specialist rape and sexual assault investigation units, which the force had boasted of nationally as 'gold standard'. Whatever the standard was in theory, the practice, as this case so dismally demonstrated, was at best poor and at worst contemptible.

The pièce de résistance came in the cross-examination of Inspector Underwood from Plumstead police. When Phillippa asked him whether he had read the relevant policy, he dismissed it as something he didn't consider necessary to apply. Pushed to explain why, then, he thought such policies had been created, he said that, in his view, the only reason was to protect the police from legal challenges. I couldn't believe what I was hearing. This was one of the officers against whom the IPCC report had upheld complaints – an officer who was fully aware that his own professional shortcomings may have contributed to many more women being raped. And yet, even now, he did not have the grace to show a hint of contrition.

Fiona and Meena were sitting in court and their jaws dropped open. In the break, Fiona said to us, at last, 'Now I get it! It wasn't my fault I wasn't believed. It was the police. It was their fault.'

As the trial drew to a close, Mr Justice Green announced that, after taking some time to consider his conclusion, he would produce a written judgment on liability only. If he found in the claimants' favour, he would go on to consider quantum, in other words, the amount of damages to be awarded. There was nothing to be done now but wait, so I went back to the office to catch up on other case-work I'd had to leave on the back burner.

On 28 February 2014, Mr Justice Green handed down judgment in the case of *DSD and NBV v. Commissioner of Police of the Metropolis*. It was a whacking 118 pages long, but its conclusion was a victory for Fiona and Meena and the countless other women whose lives have been blighted by being disbelieved.

Even though a conviction had been secured for the attack on Meena, the judgment emphasized that the Article 3 ECHR violation was a failure of means, not result. Setting out why and how the investigative duty arises, it provided guidance as to the circumstances in which such a violation might occur. Mr Justice Green concluded that, on the facts, 'there were both multiple systemic and operational failures which individually and collectively meet the test of liability under Article 3'. He identified systemic failures in five different areas: providing training; supervision and management; using available intelligence sources; having in place proper systems to ensure victim confidence; allocating adequate resources.

Having found in the claimants' favour, the judge now invited submissions on quantum. The amount of compensation awarded in any case tends to be determined by precedent. As this was the first finding in the High Court under the Human Rights Act of an Article 3 investigative violation, we had to look to European case law for guidance. The sums awarded in that court were generally lower than average damages in the UK. But, in addition to the figure for the human rights violation, we could also argue for compensation for psychological damage. The psychiatric evidence we had served for both claimants identified damage suffered specifically as a result of police failures as distinct from other causes. Fortunately, as the defence expert largely agreed with our expert, there was no contested evidence on this point.

However, the police argued that the claimants were not entitled to any damages on the grounds that they had both received small payments of compensation from the Criminal Injuries Compensation Authority and from Worboys himself. But these were for the damage caused by the assaults themselves, which Mr Justice Green recognized in his quantum judgment. He found there was clear evidence that Fiona had suffered significant harm over a long period of time as a consequence of the way she was treated by the police. He awarded her £22,500 in total. Significantly, in Meena's case, he found that, but for the earlier failures by the police, she would not have been raped at all. He awarded her a total of £19,000 damages.

This judgment was a valuable yardstick for future awards in such cases. I was able not only to breathe again, but to smile: we had beaten by some margin the Part 36 offer made much earlier in the proceedings and the police were now going to have to fork out substantial indemnity legal costs.

Police action lawyers, human rights specialists and women's groups were delighted with the outcome and I found myself nominated and shortlisted for Liberty's Human Rights Lawyer of the Year 2014. I was so happy to be accompanied to the awards ceremony by my elderly parents, who had joined Liberty's predecessor, the National Council for Civil Liberties, in the early 1950s after witnessing the impact of McCarthyism in the USA when my mother took a one-year post at a university in Massachusetts. I was thrilled to hear my name called out as the winner, but the look of pride and joy on my parents' faces was something else: a memory I will always treasure, and one that is especially precious as it was only a few months later that my father died, just days before his ninety-second birthday. I know how blessed I am to have had hugely supportive parents whose politics, intellect and open-mindedness enabled me to make the choices I have and ultimately to pursue my vocation.

A case is never over until all avenues have been exhausted, and the news that the Metropolitan Police were going to appeal the judge's decision on liability took some of the wind out of our sails. It was possible that this massive victory could be reversed.

A date was fixed in May 2015 for the appeal to be heard. It would be decided by three Court of Appeal judges purely on legal argument. As the solicitor, the preparation for me was mainly confined to reviewing counsel's draft response and her skeleton argument and discussing any strategy. It was just as well: I was in the midst of a murder retrial and by now my father was very ill in hospital. He died just before the appeal hearing and I was only able to attend part of it.

I had full confidence that Phillippa would be able to hold her own, and so it proved. To my great satisfaction, the police appeal was dismissed in June. This affirmation in a higher court of Mr Justice Green's judgment only strengthened the precedent we had set. But the police now decided to challenge the decision before the Supreme Court, the highest in the land. And then, to my horror, I received a request from the government's legal department asking for our consent for the secretary of state for the Home Department to intervene in the case as a third party. Going by the outline of their proposed intervention, the Home Office were taking the side of the police.

The Supreme Court had to decide whether to grant permission for the appeal. Having reviewed the papers, three judges concluded that, while the police grounds of appeal were not arguable, the secretary of state's submissions were potentially of 'general public importance'. They invited the police to amend their grounds dealing with two issues: whether Article 3 is engaged where the state is neither a party nor complicit, and whether the investigative duty under Article 3 should be confined to having a system of laws in place rather than an operational duty to investigate an individual crime.

The Met now instructed Lord Pannick QC, one of the country's most highly regarded advocates, to lead on the case. The Home Office drafted their intervention and were represented by 'Treasury Devil' James Eadie QC, a quietly fierce and effective opponent.

Given the heavyweight line-up, civil society groups were keen to intervene to ensure that the interests of those subject to state violations were heard. A counterpart of mine at another firm, Sarah Ricca, who also specialized in actions against the police, applied to intervene on behalf of the End Violence Against Women (EVAW) coalition, Rape Crisis England, Southall Black Sisters and the Nia Project, as did my former Birnberg Peirce colleague Debaleena Dasgupta, now employed by, and intervening on behalf of, Liberty.

On 13 and 14 March 2017, all the parties pitched up at the Supreme Court for a hearing before five judges. There was an amazing polarity in the large room. To the left sat all the claimants' and civil society solicitors and their instructed counsel, all women. On the right were the police and government legal teams, virtually all men.

After a somewhat rushed two-day hearing, we left the Supreme Court to wait for what turned out to be almost a year for their judgment. At long last, on 21 February 2018, we heard that our victory was complete. Eight years after setting out to open up a new route for victims of serious sexual violence to challenge terrible policing, we had succeeded in clearing the path and embedding this important principle in English law.

5

A Perversion of the Course of Public Justice

'I WILL REGRET REPORTING THIS for the rest of my life. I did that as my duty to this country and to women. I have given up caring if he does reoffend ... What happens if I lose? Will I go to prison?' These were the words of twenty-three-year-old Eleanor de Freitas on learning that she was to face trial for perverting the course of justice after going to the police with a rape allegation. On 4 April 2014, four days before the trial was due to begin, Eleanor killed herself.

The number of prosecutions for perverting the course of justice (PCJ) which involve allegedly false accusations of rape is small, and they tend to involve defendants with mental health problems. Statistics on false reporting are limited and unreliable. Some research commissioned by the Home Office back in 2005 indicated that 3 per cent of reported rapes were false. But it all depends on what we mean by 'false reports': a deliberate lie or an allegation that seems unfounded? In my experience, women hardly ever lie about rape – I have only ever come across one who admitted to it. Why would anyone groundlessly put themselves through such a gruelling reporting and investigation process?

However, the disproportionate coverage such cases are given in the media can create a very different impression and I had been concerned for some time about the narrative this was helping to create that women lie about rape and should be prosecuted for going to the police with an allegation that is subsequently deemed unfounded. By bolstering the victim-blaming culture, this narrative exacerbates reluctance to report and the tendency for victims to reproach themselves for getting into a situation where they could be raped. I have advised and spoken to other vulnerable women prosecuted for PCJ where they may have suffered a history of previous sexual abuse and/or had mental health issues and were themselves convinced of the truth of their allegations, even if the surrounding circumstances seemed inconsistent with the account they had given.

Six months after Eleanor de Freitas died, I was contacted by Shona Crallan, a caseworker at Inquest, the charity that provides support and expertise for bereaved relatives dealing with the investigation of state-related deaths, asking whether I might be able to assist Eleanor's family with the forthcoming inquest into her death. They were in no doubt that her suicide had been triggered by her impending trial for PCJ and they wanted the inquest to examine the handling of the case by the CPS. The coroner was resisting their request, arguing that this matter was outside the scope of his inquest, which should focus only on issues related to the management of her mental illness.

I met Eleanor's father, David, a kind, smartly dressed, City gent type, determined in the calmest, most reasonable way to get justice for his only child. He told me his daughter's story and provided me with the background to her heartbreaking suicide.

Eleanor – Ellie – had been a bright, bubbly child, brought up in a comfortable, middle-class home in Fulham, West London. She did very well at the private all-girls Putney High School and went on to Durham University to study geography. But there she had a mental health breakdown and had to drop out at the end of her first year. She was referred to a psychiatrist who eventually diagnosed bipolar disorder, which is characterized by dramatic mood swings from severe depression to hypermania. It can cause feelings of utter

despair, with an increased risk of suicide, at one extreme, and gran-
diose delusions and disinhibited social behaviour at the other,
resulting in impulsive and high-risk actions.

In her early twenties, a reckless phase which included wild spending sprees had her parents really worried for Eleanor's welfare and
safety. She was referred to a local mental health trust, where it was
decided that she should be sectioned under the Mental Health Act.
Her experience under section was awful, unfortunately, and led to
her doing everything she could to ensure she would never have to
repeat it.

By the end of 2012, however, Ellie was on an even keel and her
moods were relatively stable. She was taking her medication and
avoiding drinking too much alcohol. With the support of her parents, who were very protective and kept a close eye on her, she had a
job at the Body Shop and was studying for financial services exams.

At a party in November, she ran into Alexander Economou, whom
she had known slightly for three or four years through her cousin
Lizzie and other mutual friends. The son of a wealthy Greek ship-
ping tycoon, with his own flat on the King's Road, Alex was seen in
his social set as a 'good catch'. They flirted with one another at the
party and subsequent Facebook messages exchanged between them
revealed sexualized banter involving fantasies of bondage and drug
rape. They arranged to go out on a date, meeting up for Sunday
brunch on 23 December. Afterwards they went to Harrods, where
Ellie said she needed to pick up some Christmas decorations for her
grandma and a few last-minute presents, and then back to Alex's flat.

What happened next became the subject of disputed accounts and
perhaps demonstrates how each participant in a sexual encounter
can come away from it with different recollections or interpretations
of the experience.

Ellie's story was recorded in an ABE interview she gave to police.
She recounted how, having arrived at Alex's flat and been offered a

glass of cider, she realized she didn't have her phone. Alex told her it was in the car. When she asked for the keys to fetch it, he said no. Ellie explained that she needed to let her parents know she was OK. 'Use my phone,' he said. She called her dad, telling him that she was on a different phone because hers was out of battery. As she and Alex drank their cider, she was coughing a bit and mentioned that she was getting over a chest infection. He offered her two vitamin C tablets, which he told her were really good.

After a while she began to feel very woozy. A bit anxious about being without her phone, she asked Alex again if she could go and get it. He said he would get it for her, but he didn't trust her alone in his flat – 'You will go through my drawers and find out all my dirty secrets. I am going to have to tie you up . . . I bet you love this kinky shit.'

Bound up and unable to move, Ellie recalled feeling panicked and scared by the loss of control. Her memory of what happened after Alex eventually untied her was hazy. She asked if she could have a shower. She remembered washing her hair. At some point she gave Alex a massage and he was angry with her for spilling massage oil on the floor. They had unprotected sex at least twice, once on the sofa and on the bed. At another stage she registered that it was 3 a.m. and she still hadn't been back in touch with her dad, who worried about her. Alex had switched his phone off.

Ellie described waking up on Christmas Eve feeling really confused and groggy. Her body felt weird and she was aware that she had had sex. There were at least three messages on Alex's phone from her dad, sounding increasingly alarmed and asking her to please let him know she was OK. She sent him a text message to say she was fine.

Alex went to get some coffee from Starbucks and she asked him to collect her gym bag from the car, so that she had her phone and something to change into. They drank their coffee and then she went to the bathroom and vomited. She changed into her gym clothes, tracksuit trousers and a hoodie, and told Alex she had to work that afternoon. He said he needed to pick up some things from a shop in Kensington High Street. They drove down there in his flashy car and went into an Ann Summers sex shop. Struck by a sudden urge for some retail therapy, Ellie began to put items into the shopping basket at random. Alex offered his card to pay for them but she insisted they split the cost and gave him £180 cash (Ellie didn't carry credit cards because of her weakness for impulsive shopping). They returned to his flat, where she collected her stuff and her own car.

Ellie was due at work in a couple of hours but she was reluctant to go home first. She didn't want her parents to see her in this state and ask uncomfortable questions. So she went directly to work. She was conscious that she was behaving quite oddly there. After her shift, having arranged to drive up to her grandmother's in Northamptonshire that evening, she called her dad and asked if he could bring her medication and some other bits and pieces down to her car so that she could set off straight away. She was keen to avoid him getting too good a look at the shape she was in.

She then texted Alex saying that she was feeling very weird and confused. She was about to drive up the motorway and she was scared. Alex called her cousin Lizzie and told her that Ellie was suicidal. En route Ellie spoke to Alex on the hands-free. He said he thought she was being really manipulative and that he didn't want to see her again. She took a wrong turn, got lost, then ran out of petrol and ended up having to be rescued by her mum at 4 a.m. and taken to her grandma's.

By now, Eleanor's parents were, naturally, very worried about her. On 27 December, she told her mother, Miranda, that she believed she'd had unprotected sex and that she was in pain. Miranda took her to the GP for emergency contraception. Ellie was also prescribed antibiotics for what appeared to be a urinary tract infection. David, her father, called her psychiatrist and arranged an urgent appointment.

Ellie spoke to her psychiatrist, and, a couple of days later, to her GP

and claimed to them both that she had been sexually assaulted by
Alex. In the meantime, she was receiving furious messages from
Alex, who, it would become apparent, was hearing from people they
both knew that Ellie had been making some serious allegations about
his behaviour towards her.

'Stop telling nasty lies!' he texted Ellie.

'Continued lying by you will result in both criminal and civil proceedings against you. Now fuck off!'

Ellie spoke to a police community support officer she knew
through her job at the Body Shop, who encouraged her to talk to the
police, and, on 4 January, she decided to go to Chelsea police station,
where she made her allegation that Economou had raped her and
gave an account of her version of events. Miranda had alerted David,
who went to meet her there. While waiting for Ellie to arrive, he had
received a message from Alex. 'I'm on my way to Chelsea police station to file an official report ... I'll have no mercy and I will do
everything to prosecute Ellie for her allegations.'

Alexander Economou's account of the events of 23 and 24 December
differed in some key details and recorded his firm belief that everything that had taken place between Eleanor and himself was
consensual. His version was set out in the prosecution case summary given to me by David de Freitas, which had been compiled by
Edmonds Marshall McMahon, the firm of solicitors Alex had gone
on to instruct to prepare a private prosecution of Ellie.

Economou said that, after realizing she had left her phone in the car,
Ellie asked if she could borrow his to let her dad know where she was.
Then she asked if she could have a shower and reappeared wearing a
shirt of his and nothing else. They drank some cider. Alex took a vitamin C tablet and offered one to Ellie. She asked Alex if he could fetch
her phone from her car. He replied that he wouldn't leave her alone in
his flat as he had heard she had gone through the drawers of a man she

had dated in the past. She said, 'You can tie me up if you want,' and he did so. Once he untied her, they had unprotected sex on the sofa. After this she gave him an intimate massage and they had sex again.

At 1.55 a.m. Ellie asked if she could text her dad to let him know she was safe. This led to a conversation in which she explained that she had previously received psychiatric treatment in a hospital. They had sex a third time and fell asleep. The following morning, he requested sex again. She said she was sore, so he masturbated instead.

Ellie texted their mutual friend Freddie and thanked him for matchmaking them. She told Freddie they'd had 'huge fun' and were still together.

Later that morning, Alex had to run an errand in Kensington High Street and Ellie accompanied him. She insisted on going into the Ann Summers sex shop, where between them they spent nearly £400 on sex toys and paraphernalia. They parted company and Ellie went off to work at the Body Shop.

After Ellie left, Alex started reflecting on some of their conversation. In their sexual banter, Ellie had said she was a qualified masseuse, and during their night together she told him she used the pseudonym 'Portia'. Alex did some Google searches and discovered advertisements posted online by Ellie representing herself as 'Portia', illustrated with soft-porn photos, offering 'tantric massage'.

He then received a number of text messages from Ellie that suggested she was suicidal. He messaged her cousin Lizzie to raise concerns. That evening he and Ellie spoke on the phone and she acted as if nothing was wrong. Alex was angry with her emotionally manipulative behaviour and told her he didn't want to have any further contact with her.

The case summary also contained evidence in the form of text messages exchanged within their social circle in the days following the encounter between Ellie and Alex. On Christmas Day, Ellie texted a mutual friend, Henriette, to say she was on 'suicide watch' and that Alex had 'fucked me and chucked me'. A later message to Henriette read: 'I don't know what I have done wrong'.

On Boxing Day, Ellie's cousin Lizzie texted Alex to tell him she had received 'some very disturbing and unsettling news' about his treatment of Ellie and that he should stay away from her family.

On 31 December, in a message to Henriette, Ellie commented that she was going to 'make herself look hot' to show Alex what he was missing. She attended a New Year's Eve party, where her behaviour was described by others present as very hyper and sexualized. She emailed Alex asking: 'Can we be grown-ups and forget everything that happened last week?'

On 1 January, she said in a message to Freddie that she didn't want to fall out with Alex and hoped they could remain friends. But two days later, she was telling another mutual friend, Tanya, that Alex had assaulted her, drugged her and wouldn't let her out of his flat. She also emailed Alex on 3 January: 'I am sorry for the trouble I have caused you . . . I hope we can bump into each other and talk again one day.'

Alex's anger and indignation were evident in the messages Ellie received from him before she went to the police. The next afternoon, 4 January, he emailed to inform her that he had consulted a lawyer, and that unless she contacted everyone immediately to retract 'her lies', he would be reporting her to the police that evening. At 6.30 p.m. he went to Chelsea police station with the intention of making a complaint against Ellie for harassment. Instead the police arrested him on suspicion of rape and he was held in a cell overnight before being interviewed with his lawyer present.

I subsequently learned that he read out a pre-prepared statement in which he vehemently denied the 'baseless and false' accusations and strongly maintained that all sexual activity was consensual. Thereafter he answered 'no comment' to police questions, laughing at some of the allegations put to him. He was then released on bail. He would later say that he found his arrest 'very scary'.

Following a police investigation, the evidence was reviewed by DI Julian King, who decided that no further action – 'NFA' – would be taken. The rationale for his decision was (i) that Ellie had communicated with Alex in a manner inconsistent with a rape having taken place; (ii) that the two had gone together to the Ann Summers sex shop the day after the alleged rape; and (iii) Ellie's 'fucked me and chucked me' text to Henriette, which made no mention of any non-consensual sex having occurred.

I could see from the case summary why the police had decided not to charge Alex. Ellie's behaviour after the alleged offence was bizarre and inconsistent. Some of her actions and communications would have been a gift to any defence lawyer in a rape trial and a jury might well have been sceptical – indeed, may have taken the view that she was motivated by revenge after Alex rejected her.

But however difficult a rape prosecution is made by evidential weaknesses, and however damaging to her credibility a victim's behaviour may have been, that does not mean she fabricated her account and I was not convinced that Ellie had deliberately lied. It seemed to me that if, reflecting in the cold light of day on what had happened, she felt she had not truly consented to sex, her belief that she had been raped would have been honestly held.

Many victims behave, both before and after a rape, in ways that may seem contradictory. Indeed, inconsistent behaviour and reactions are so prevalent in rape and sexual offence cases that the CPS now provide detailed guidance on their website, giving examples of common myths and stereotypes. It warns that 'there is no typical response to rape – the traumatic nature of the offence means that the victim can behave in a huge range of ways, some of which might seem counterintuitive' and that 'consent cannot be implied from what might be interpreted as flirtatious behaviour or from the way a person is dressed'.

If the case summary showed me why the NFA decision had been

taken, it also revealed Alex to be a pretty unpleasant man. It seemed to me that he had been happy to indulge in sexualized chat with Ellie online about his bondage and 'masseuse' fantasies until he discovered that she might actually be an escort. And after he learned from Ellie that she had a mental illness, it had not, apparently, taken him long to distance himself from her. His immediate response to her allegation of rape was to threaten her with legal action to 'restore his reputation' rather than to take into account that she may not have been well. He had to make her suffer for the insult she had caused him. This vindictive streak was a side of his character of which I was to see a good deal more over the following months and years.

The police informed Ellie of their decision not to charge Alexander Economou on 21 February 2013, explaining that they didn't want her to be put through the trauma of a trial when they weren't confident that it would result in a conviction.

As soon as he was notified, Alex sent Ellie several texts telling her that he was going to take court action. His family, he said, had 'pooled together their resources and instructed the best lawyers that money could buy to ensure you will be sent to prison for your crimes'. He also emailed David at his work address making the same threat. David reported these communications to DC Dial of the Sapphire unit, who issued Alex with a harassment warning.

In the ensuing months, Alex asked the police to investigate Ellie for perverting the course of justice. He would later say that, having been 'widely and repeatedly accused of a crime he simply did not commit', he had been 'in despair' and 'naturally' wanted to see Eleanor 'behind bars'. When the police declined to investigate, on the basis that there was no evidence Eleanor had lied, he instructed Edmonds Marshall McMahon, who had expertise in bringing private prosecutions. He also made a complaint against the police for their refusal to investigate her. Ellie was very upset to discover that many of her friends, her cousin and her employers had been approached for statements.

On 14 August, she received an email from Edmonds Marshall McMahon, attaching a private prosecution summons, together with the prosecution case summary – the document I was now going through – which was based on Alex's version of events and contradictory accounts given by Ellie to several mutual friends. This concluded that the text messages, CCTV of the visit to the Ann Summers sex shop and the positive tone of Ellie's communications with Alex before reporting him for rape constituted 'prima facie evidence' of the falsity of her allegation.

Distressed and frightened, Ellie suffered a panic attack. To support her through the effects of the alleged rape, she was having counselling with the Women and Girls Network, part of West London Rape Crisis, which she had found helpful. She asked for an emergency counselling appointment. But now that she had been served this summons, her counsellor explained, they could no longer discuss the issues that would be the subject of a criminal trial as it could be argued that her testimony might become compromised by the counselling process.

The pressure of this prosecution seriously destabilized Ellie. Feeling bullied and persecuted, she complained to the police that Economou was harassing her. She was growing increasingly paranoid and began to exhibit the grandiosity associated with the manic phase of her condition. She became convinced she was being followed. Having instructed solicitors, and discovering that she would have no right to anonymity, she took to wearing a burka to court for the necessary pre-trial hearings and when out and about, fearful of being recognized. She was picked up by the police from a local supermarket where she was seen throwing items from the shelves. Her father phoned her psychiatrist, who wrote to the court stating that she was too unwell to attend.

Ellie's defence solicitors were of the view that the private prosecution was an abuse of process and that the best way to stop it in its tracks would be to invite the director of public prosecutions to take it over. That would bring the Code for Crown Prosecutors into play, which involves considering whether the evidence is sufficient for there to be a realistic prospect of conviction and, where that test is satisfied, whether the prosecution is in the public interest. If the CPS decide that the case meets the test, they can take over the prosecution and the court may be ordered to pay the costs incurred by the private prosecutor. If they do not, the prosecution will be stopped.

Eleanor's solicitors believed it was highly likely that, after reviewing the case, the CPS would decide not to proceed, not least because she had never been arrested or asked to answer questions concerning the allegations against her. Sarah Maclaren, head of RASSO (Rape and Serious Sexual Offences unit) at the CPS, had a meeting with the police and was provided with all the evidence they had on the rape allegation. The police stood by their decision that no further action should be taken against Eleanor.

Meanwhile, Ellie was served with the evidence obtained by the private prosecutor and further upset to see statements there from people she had assumed were her friends. A report by the psychiatrist instructed by her solicitors, noting the specific risk of suicide for those suffering from her condition, was sent to the CPS. 'Clearly, such a trial would be an extremely stressful event,' the psychiatrist emphasized, 'and there is no doubt that this could be a destabilizer for her, precipitating an episode of affective illness.'

On 5 December, after considerable delay and pressure from the judge, the CPS announced, contrary to expectations, that they would be taking the prosecution forward. Ellie, her family and their solicitors were dismayed. Ellie wrote in her diary: 'I reported a crime in good faith . . . I'm treated like a criminal.'

The CPS said that they were proceeding on the same basis as the private prosecution case. They told Ellie's solicitors they would be making a bad character application and seeking to adduce evidence of a previous rape complaint by Ellie. This was an allegation she had made against a former landlord at a time when she was very unwell. No one had been arrested and nothing had come of it. They also notified the defence they would allege that she was an 'escort'. This approach was in conflict with their own guidance, which cites as falsehoods the misconceptions that 'prostitutes/sex workers cannot be raped' and 'other complaints of rape which have not resulted in successful prosecution outcomes always mean the victim lacks all credibility as a witness'.

On 1 April 2014, Ellie learned that her trial would begin in less than a week. At that point the CPS had not yet disclosed the recorded ABE interview she had given after reporting that she had been raped, which was potentially a critical part of her defence evidence. On Thursday 4 April, Ellie was due to meet her solicitor, Martin Lee. While at home on her own for a few hours that morning, she made the decision to take her own life. When Miranda came in at lunchtime, she found her daughter hanging.

'I am so sorry to do this to you,' Ellie had noted in her diary for her parents, 'but I feel trapped and there is no way out . . . I feel I have battled with bipolar and the reckless decisions that I have sometimes made and their consequences for too long . . . If I were to lose the case I know that I would have brought acute shame to the family.'

As it happened, the CPS had finally disclosed the ABE interview to Ellie's solicitor the day before her death. He had viewed it and noted that she provided a coherent account. It seemed from the interview that, in retrospect, she felt uncertain about whether she had communicated with sufficient clarity that she did not want sex. When asked if there was any way that Alex could have realized that she didn't want to have sex with him, she replied:

I certainly didn't say yes . . . I didn't say anything, actually – I was literally frozen with fear after the whole tying-up thing . . . I guess what I want to make clear is I don't feel that I would have consented to sex, and I certainly would have insisted on using a condom. I'm the daughter of a sexual health nurse. Why would I put myself through trying to get emergency contraception on Christmas Eve?

In the context of the PCJ charge against Ellie, her solicitor considered that this cautious articulation of non-consent would make it hard for the prosecution to prove that she intended to pervert the course of justice. It also meant that Ellie would not have been required to give evidence: the ABE video could have been played to the jury instead. Had Ellie been informed of this it would have been a huge weight off her tormented mind.

On the day the trial was due to begin, the prosecution were notified of Ellie's death. Judge Taylor made the extraordinary observation in open court that her death was 'a tragedy from both the prosecution and defence point of view'. She ordered that the costs incurred by Economou in preparing the private prosecution would be repaid to him from central funds. These amounted to in excess of £200,000.

When David de Freitas came to see me some six months after these terrible events, and as I got on top of the facts, I was both mystified and horrified by the apparent complicity of the CPS in the actions that resulted in this young woman taking her own life. I told David that the inquest could give us an opportunity to explore the role of the CPS in the circumstances leading to Ellie's death and to gain some understanding of their decision-making and accountability.

David had been referred to Inquest by the mental health charity Mind. He had already received some advice from Victim Support, who were concerned by the use of a private prosecution in a case of this nature. David had written to the coroner asking him to adjourn the inquest, which had been fixed for mid-October, to give him time to seek advice and more detailed disclosure. The coroner did agree to an adjournment, but only until 7 November, and, as Shona Crallan had told me, he was clearly resistant to holding a fuller inquest which would explore the role of the CPS.

I made more detailed representations to the coroner, inviting him to broaden the scope of the inquest and asserting that the involvement of the CPS engaged Article 2 of the European Convention on Human Rights – the right to life.

The ECHR requires the state to take steps to refrain from conduct that may threaten an individual's right under Article 2. That will encompass putting in place necessary safeguards to protect the right to life and ensuring there is a proper investigation where there is a loss of life, including in circumstances where the state may be implicated. Given the part the CPS played in continuing the prosecution of Ellie, I argued that a fuller inquest was required in which this decision should be examined. I also argued that the case raised significant wider public concern – another reason why an inquest with a broader scope, and potentially a jury, should be held.

The coroner replied two days later refusing my request and stating that the inquest would proceed on a limited basis the following Friday. David and I discussed our options. In theory it was possible to challenge this refusal by threatening judicial review proceedings against the coroner, but I wasn't convinced that would be effective. It would also involve a massive amount of work in a very short space of time. And David was not eligible for legal aid, nor could he afford to run the risk of having to pay the coroner's costs if the challenge failed.

In the circumstances, I felt our only chance of delaying the inquest was publicity. David was at first a little reluctant to go down this road. He had absolutely no experience of dealing with the media and

he was, understandably, worried about serving up Eleanor's vulner-
abilities for public scrutiny or provoking further ire from Economou.
Miranda, he knew, was even more anxious about this. But an inquiry
of sorts into the wider circumstances surrounding Eleanor's death
was important to them both, and David could see that opportunity
slipping away. He discussed it with Miranda and they agreed he
would go for it.

I suggested approaching Sandra Laville of the *Guardian* and June
Kelly of the BBC, both of whom I believed would be able to understand the underlying issues and deal with the case sensitively. David
was happy with this and provided quotes for them. It was arranged
that he would be interviewed live on the *Today* programme on the
Friday the inquest was due to open. Sandra's *Guardian* article went
up on their website the night before. That morning I awoke at around
7 a.m., as usual, and switched on Radio 4 ready to catch David's
interview. Checking my phone, I saw that he had sent me an email at
5.43 a.m. 'We had a ring on our doorbell last night at about 12.30 a.m.
which we ignored. On leaving the house this morning I discovered
this note on the doormat in an envelope. This will distress Miranda
enormously. She feared he would do something. What can we do?
Concerned. David.'

Attached was a photograph of a printout of an email from Alexander Economou, sent to David at his work address. At the end of this
communication, Economou indicated that if David made 'any further comments twisting the facts' he would issue a public statement
in which he would make it clear that Eleanor de Freitas was 'a prostitute'. In my view this letter constituted a threat, particularly since it
had been left at the de Freitas home in the middle of the night. It was
harassment, and it needed to be reported to the police.

David duly gave a very dignified and powerful interview to John
Humphrys in which he criticized the CPS for taking over the PCJ
prosecution. Asked whether he believed his daughter, David replied

simply, 'Yes.' BBC TV News then requested an interview, which David did. In the meantime, ITN, Sky News and Channel 5 were emailing asking to talk to David.

I put any further press on hold, however. At that stage, my priority was the inquest hearing we had to prepare for that afternoon with the relatively newly qualified barrister I had recently instructed, Catherine Oborne. I hadn't worked with Catherine before: I had been hoping for a more experienced barrister to challenge the coroner but no one had been available at such short notice. As it turned out, Catherine was a great choice: passionate, smart and up for a fight when she needed to be.

The publicity we had already attracted did the trick. That morning, Alison Saunders, the DPP, made a public statement in which she said she was 'saddened' by Eleanor's death, had 'asked the legal team involved for a full explanation' and 'would welcome a meeting with the family to discuss the case and the law surrounding it'.

Later that day I would have a call from Martin Lee, Ellie's solicitor, who told me that the DPP's office was desperate to get hold of a copy of her ABE interview. He thought this was significant as he did not believe that Alison Levitt, the most senior CPS lawyer to sign off on the decision to prosecute Ellie, had actually viewed the recording.

By the time I arrived at the small coroner's court in Fulham, it was packed. Catherine, David and I had decided that the note posted through his letterbox in the early hours should be brought to the coroner's attention prior to the public hearing on the basis that it represented a veiled threat with regard to any evidence Mr de Freitas chose to give in the court. The coroner announced that he was going to adjourn the inquest until after the DPP's inquiry.

In view of the threatening letter, we decided it was better that David did not do any further interviews. Instead we put together a statement which he read out to the media outside the court.

Early the following week, Alex Economou called my office

wanting to speak to me. I was somewhat less keen to speak to him, not least because of the unpleasant email he had delivered to David. I was in any case tied up with other matters so I left a message requesting that he send me an email.

An email duly appeared in my inbox. Economou said he wanted to give me some information 'to help the media situation for us both'. I replied a couple of days later, after discussing with David the best tack to take, asking him what he meant by this. I thought it was interesting that he seemed to think this case was somehow about media relations rather than two parents trying to explore all the circumstances surrounding their daughter's death at an inquest. This prompted, within hours, a series of emails from Economou. The first made a number of criticisms of the police conduct and suggested that Eleanor's lawyers had told her to plead guilty on the morning she killed herself (Martin Lee would confirm that this was completely untrue). He also threatened to release CCTV of himself and Eleanor at Ann Summers and sent me a lot of individual pictures of sex toys they had bought. This felt like a type of sexual harassment. I did not respond.

The next day came a photograph of a letter containing a death threat allegedly sent to Economou's mother the previous day, as a direct result, Economou claimed, of David speaking to the press. I replied suggesting that his mother should report this to the police. There followed a series of screenshots from a website called Tantric Temple, which included pictures of Eleanor de Freitas posing as 'Portia'. It was, wrote Economou, 'some more of the CPS evidence you can look forward to viewing with Alison Saunders and at the inquest'.

This continual bombardment of emails and screenshots made me really angry. I could feel my blood pressure rising and had to resist the temptation to reply in some very unlawyerly language. But I confined myself to warning that any communications from him would have to be shared with my clients, and that this could amount to a form of harassment of these bereaved parents.

I also received an email from Sebastian Gosden-Hood, who knew Economou personally and wanted to share some information. He told me Alex had made clear to him that his aim was to bankrupt Eleanor's family.

On 20 November 2014, David and I attended the meeting offered by the DPP, Alison Saunders, who was accompanied by her principal legal adviser, Neil Moore. We brought with us David's niece Lizzie and my colleague Debaleena Dasgupta as back-up. The DPP began by offering her condolences and moved on to set out how the case had developed from the CPS perspective. What we were hoping for was an apology and explanation of how things had gone so badly wrong and we were deeply disappointed not to get it. Instead the DPP was justifying the CPS decision.

She did acknowledge that the case raised issues about the propriety of private prosecutions for PCJ in rape cases. She told us that once the CPS were invited to review the case, they applied the usual two-stage Code for Crown Prosecutors test: was there the evidence to ensure a reasonable prospect of conviction and, if so, was it in the public interest to prosecute? Their analysis led them to conclude that the rape allegation was false. We asked if we could see the evidence underlying their decision but this request was refused.

It was, however, significant that Alison Saunders fully accepted that any suggestion Eleanor de Freitas may have been working as an escort would have been entirely irrelevant to the question of consent and would not have formed part of the prosecution's case. She also said the CPS would not have relied on the fact that Eleanor had made a previous allegation of sexual assault at a time when she was very unwell.

Neil Moore told us that the psychiatric report submitted by Ellie's solicitors, which we had not yet seen, read more like a document prepared for the prosecution than for the defence. He made it clear that the DPP could not have discontinued the prosecution on the basis of this report, or any other submissions they may have received from Eleanor's criminal defence team, because they did not address the public interest test.

The one concession Alison Saunders made was to accept that there was a considerable delay in the disclosure of Ellie's ABE interview. However, the CPS blamed the police for this. Because the police had been so strongly opposed to prosecuting Eleanor, we now learned, in order to get approval to proceed with the investigation, the DPP had to go above the heads of both DI Julian King, who was in charge of the case, and a superintendent who backed his position, right up to Assistant Commissioner Martin Hewitt.

I raised the wider issue of how bringing cases like this against women who reported rape would deter them from going to the police. Alison Saunders was quite defensive about this, arguing that the impact on the 'falsely accused' also had to be taken into account. The meeting was brought to a close with an indication from the DPP that she would be issuing a public statement and writing to the coroner about the outcome of her review.

The conflict between the police and the CPS over pursuing the prosecution was, in my experience, highly unusual – and for the police to be the ones opposing it, rather than the CPS, was rarer still. Curious about how this clash had come about, I emailed DI King to ask him if he was able to shed any light on it, sharing my own hunch that perhaps the reason for the difference of opinion was that the police, unlike the CPS, had had the opportunity to assess the characters of both Eleanor de Freitas and Alexander Economou in their direct dealings with them.

DI King confirmed that, in his view, Eleanor should not have been prosecuted for PCJ and that there were no clear facts either way as to whether she had falsified the rape allegation. Equally, the allegation could not have been proven, hence his decision to take no further action against Economou. But 'we never doubted as to whether Eleanor's complaint of rape was genuine or not', he wrote, from which I inferred that, in his view, Ellie honestly believed she had not given consent and had not deliberately fabricated her account.

David and I remained convinced that the CPS decision had been wrong, when you looked at all the evidence in the round. When I wrote to the DPP thanking her for meeting us and raising some further questions I hoped she could address, I alerted her to Economou's recent behaviour. Worried that publication of the outcome of her review would embolden him further, I asked her to make clear in any statement that the analysis was based only on the evidence that she had seen, and also that a decision to prosecute did not mean Ellie was guilty, as this had never been tested in court.

Another flurry of emails from Economou began popping up in my inbox late in the evening of 27 November and into the next day, the first headed 'A serious warning about any future misconduct'. This made assorted threats of legal proceedings and concluded by urging me to 're-read the above ten times so that it is etched in you and your client's memories'. Another gave me some examples of cases where people had been prosecuted for intimidating witnesses. It wasn't entirely clear to me what exactly he was threatening, or indeed what he was suggesting might warrant a legal threat.

Economou then suggested that I might be approached by journalists looking into his side of the story, and that I ought to be available to advise my client in case he was tempted to comment – followed by the bullet I felt he had been waiting to fire: 'I am the owner of EleanordeFreitas.com. The truth is coming out in 48 hours just get ready . . . I can give you a complimentary viewing of the new edited six minute version of the Ann Summers video before publication.'

I was shocked and appalled that he could feel it was appropriate to buy a website in the name of a vulnerable young woman who had taken her own life partly as a consequence of his actions. After pointing out that David was speaking to the press only because he wished to raise issues regarding the CPS and the inquest – he was focused on these and had never mentioned Economou by name – I informed Alex that his behaviour was causing distress, and possibly psychological harm, to a grieving family; once again, that it may amount to harassment; and that I would be forwarding his emails to the police. I advised him to show my message to his lawyer.

That Saturday night, I was alerted to an interview already up online that would hit the newsstands the next morning in the *Mail on Sunday*. 'THE DOUBLE LIFE OF TRAGIC SUICIDE GIRL WHO ACCUSED ME OF RAPE' ran the headline. 'Tycoon's son says don't judge me before you know the whole story'. It was illustrated with photographs for which Alexander Economou had evidently posed.

I was livid. This piece contained a number of significant inaccuracies. I complained to the editor, who agreed to make several corrections. It did little to ease my fury at the way this newspaper had seen fit to so casually rub salt into the wounds of Ellie's parents.

More correspondence from Alex arrived, this time via the coroner, Mr Chinyere Inyama, to whom it had been addressed. It contained various fallacies we had seen before: that on the day of Eleanor's death, lawyers had tried to get her to plead guilty; that she had a history of making false rape complaints. Alex was demanding that the coroner put a stop to the inquest on the basis that the family had a hidden agenda. Mr Inyama, I was relieved to learn, had been robust in his response. It was 'wholly inappropriate', he had informed Economou, for him 'to write in the terms that he had chosen to use'.

To me, Alex claimed that the police had not looked at the Ann Summers CCTV. He placed great emphasis on this visit to the sex shop the day after the purported rape as conclusive evidence that the rape did not occur. This incident was also, of course, taken into account by the DPP as probative of the false rape allegation. But, however many times I studied the CCTV, I couldn't see that it provided proof of a lie. Yes, it showed Ellie behaving bizarrely but, as David pointed out, she also looked dishevelled, not her normal self. She appeared to be going round the shop just throwing items haphazardly into a shopping basket, as if on autopilot. In my view, if it was evidence of anything, it indicated that she was not well, and quite possibly in the throes of a hypermanic episode.

On 9 December, the CPS published a statement in which they justified their role in the prosecution of Eleanor de Freitas. We had been expecting this and had decided to prepare our own press release in response. The *Daily Telegraph* ran the story and David wrote a comment piece for the *Guardian*, with some additional input from me, which called attention to the reasons why we remained critical of the CPS analysis and of their actions in taking the prosecution forward.

Three days later I received a letter from Field Fisher solicitors, sent on behalf of Alexander Economou, threatening legal proceedings against David for libel and harassment. By this stage, I was getting past the point of being shocked by anything this case threw up, but I was somewhat taken aback that a respectable firm of solicitors would be willing to represent such a vengeful claimant, not to say puzzled by how they could think there was an arguable case for anything David had said to be regarded as defamatory in law. This was followed by an email from Alex stating that he had warned me repeatedly not to libel him. The *Guardian* article had been the 'last straw', he said. 'Tell your client to shut the fuck up!'

I showed the solicitor's letter to a barrister with libel expertise and he suggested I reply making it clear that at this point David would not be commenting further on the issues in the case. I enclosed their client's aggressive letter and asked the solicitor to tell him to desist from contacting me personally again. Then I sent this correspondence, together with the other recently received material, to the police, to add to the harassment complaints from David they were already dealing with.

Just before Christmas, Field Fisher dispatched a formal 'pre-action protocol' letter setting out the basis of a claim by Economou against David. Interestingly, he did not seek to sue me, or any of the media outlets that had published anything David had written. This was personal.

It was time now for David to instruct a libel solicitor. This was not something he could afford, but I hoped, given the facts of the case, that someone would be willing to take it on a conditional fee agreement. It was 22 December – hardly the best moment to be looking for a lawyer in a hurry. Debaleena suggested Roísín Gad el Rab, a young trainee solicitor, trained up in media law, who had recently joined media law specialists Manleys. We talked to Roísín and her boss, Eddie Parladorio, and they said they would take a look at it. Meanwhile I was also liaising with Catherine Oborne about the submissions we needed to send to the coroner, who was now proposing to fix a date for the inquest.

I was exhausted. The pain and anger generated by this case was taking its toll, on top of an already full caseload. It was demanding a lot of my time as well as draining my emotional energy and the firm weren't being paid for the work. But I certainly couldn't abandon David now. I took a break over Christmas and went away over New Year to recharge the batteries, but there was to be little respite from Economou's crusade.

On New Year's Eve he posted on a number of websites a secret recording of a telephone conversation he'd had with a police community service officer who had called him after Ellie had gone to the police station to report him for harassment. This was at the stage when her mental health was collapsing in the wake of the private prosecution summons. In the recording PCSO Tulsi and Economou are heard joking together about her 'mental' behaviour. 'I could have smacked her,' Tulsi remarks. Economou laughs.

It flummoxed me why or how Economou felt that this recording helped his case in any way. I immediately brought it to the attention of DI King, who was horrified by the behaviour of the PCSO and initiated a complaints investigation. As a result, a gross misconduct hearing was convened, but PCSO Tulsi resigned from the police a couple of days before this was due to take place.

To meet the coroner's deadline for filing legal submissions on the scope of the inquest, Catherine worked over the Christmas break drafting our arguments that Article 2 of ECHR was engaged and that the case should be heard before a jury.

In a separate document, she marshalled our concerns about the DPP's internal review, which had been communicated to the coroner on 3 December, the week before the DPP's public statement. We quoted from the CPS's own guidance on the circumstances in which PCJ should be pursued against rape complainants: 'If there is any question as to whether the original allegation might in fact have been true, then there is not a realistic prospect of conviction, and no charge of perverting the course of justice should be brought.'

We criticized the failure of the CPS to gather evidence that might have supported Eleanor's belief that she had been raped – from her GP and her mental health and counselling records, which would have noted her disclosure and discussion of the impact of the alleged rape, among other sources. We highlighted that because Eleanor had never been interviewed under caution about the alleged false allegation, the CPS could not take into account her response to that allegation, and that their decision-making in adopting the private prosecution case summary was at risk of relying on rape myths and stereotypes which they themselves recognized.

We questioned the applicability of the second stage of the Code for Crown Prosecutors, namely the public interest test. We drew the coroner's attention to the report of the defence psychiatrist, Dr Rogers, who affirmed the diagnosis of bipolar disorder, and its particular risk of suicide, and recorded Eleanor's history of hospitalization under the Mental Health Act. We also pointed out that although Economou had been arrested, he was never charged with an offence of rape and his name was never made public in connection with the allegations until he himself went to the media.

I delivered our submissions to the coroner. He promptly rejected them.

He now scheduled the inquest for 17 March 2015. Until David was granted probate, Eleanor's defence solicitors were not permitted to give us the criminal file. Once we had sight of this, in mid-February 2015, we drafted some additional submissions to the coroner, to the effect that even if we hadn't met the Article 2 threshold, the scope of the inquest should be broadened to ensure, in accordance with a pre-Human Rights Act test, that it would be 'full, fair and fearless'.

The coroner rejected these submissions as well. He told us there would be an opportunity to make further representations on the morning of the inquest. But 'there needs to be a recognition that any further representations need to address points that have not already been the subject of extensive and detailed oral and written representations'. Catherine and I decided we might be able to strengthen our position if we had a 'silk' to argue the points. Leslie Thomas QC, a leading inquest lawyer at Catherine's chambers, was happy to assist.

Just one week later we attended the inquest hearing into Eleanor's death. At the opening, Leslie made further submissions for an Article 2 inquest relying on a recent inquest into the death of Frances Andrade, a violinist who had been sexually abused as a pupil at

Chetham's School of Music in Manchester in the 1970s and 1980s and subjected decades later to fierce cross-examination as a witness at the trial of her music teacher. She found the process so distressing that, after giving evidence, she took her own life.

The coroner yet again rejected our submissions, ruling that a decision to prosecute is not conduct and could be distinguished from the case of Frances Andrade. He then proceeded to call his witnesses, who included David, Ellie's GP and her treating psychiatrist. After hearing the evidence, he reached his verdict. In concluding that Eleanor took her own life, he acknowledged that the impending trial was clearly a significant stressor.

While we had been preparing for the inquest, Economou had stepped up his campaign, which was purportedly to prove his innocence but effectively did more to cause David and Miranda intolerable pain. When he posted more documents and links about Ellie on the website he had acquired in her name, yet again his sense of righteous entitlement and the relentlessness of his cruel disregard for the grief of the de Freitas family left me gobsmacked. I helped David to compile details of these posts to append to the formal complaint of harassment the police were still considering.

In late January 2015, I had been invited to participate in an edition of the Radio 4 programme *Unreliable Evidence*, hosted by Clive Anderson, on rape and the law. Also participating were Alison Saunders, the DPP, and Assistant Commissioner Martin Hewitt, the senior police officer who had overruled DI King and his senior superintendent in the matter of pursuing Eleanor's prosecution. The DPP and AC had been working together on a national action plan to improve the investigation and prosecution of rape. While we were waiting to go into the recording studio, I took the opportunity to speak to Alison about the awful posts Economou was putting on 'his' website. To give her credit, she was quite shocked and agreed that if evidence of harassment could be sent to her, she would look into ensuring that it would be considered by a senior prosecutor.

In the meantime, Field Fisher solicitors served particulars of claim setting out Economou's libel action against David. While Manleys – who had found counsel also willing to advise on a no win, no fee basis – handled that case on David's behalf, we decided to launch a judicial review of the coroner's decision not to extend the scope of the inquest. At the same time, I was looking at an additional route of challenge: calling for a public inquiry arising from the circumstances of the prosecution of Eleanor. There were so many ripples flowing from this case with important implications for the investigation and prosecution of rape as a whole.

I wrote to the attorney general, the government minister who oversees the office of the DPP and also had the power to order a fresh inquest, setting out the wider issues and requesting one of three remedies: an attorney general's fiat, an order that would quash the original inquest and initiate a fresh one; an independent investigation into the conduct and decision-making of the CPS; or a public inquiry into the wider questions arising. In support of our call for a proper, independent public inquiry, I submitted over twenty letters from national women's organizations, including Rape Crisis and the End Violence Against Women coalition, as well as from concerned individuals, among them Vera Baird, who wrote in her role as police and crime commissioner for Northumbria.

The response of the attorney general's office was that we should pursue the judicial review in the High Court but could come back to them subsequently if needed.

On 26 March 2016, following an oral hearing before two judges of the Divisional Court, our application for a judicial review of the coroner's decision not to examine the role of the CPS in relation to Eleanor's death was rejected.

The next day I was in Westminster magistrates' court, where I was due to give evidence alongside David in the prosecution of Alexander Economou for harassment. At the start of the trial, as I was waiting to be called into the witness box, I learned that Economou had sacked his counsel and asked his solicitor in the libel action to defend him. The case was heard by District Judge Ikram, who came to the verdict that Economou was not guilty. 'I do not find,' he said, 'that, taken as a whole, the defendant's communications by email, or indeed the first delivered by courier, reach the threshold of oppressive and unreasonable.' I could not believe my ears. What next, I wondered, from the criminal justice system?

Two weeks later, David's trial for defamation commenced in the High Court before Mr Justice Warby. It was the first case to be fully tried under the relatively recent Defamation Act 2013, which had introduced a new statutory defence of public interest. This gave David a defence to libel if it could be shown, first, that he had spoken out in the public interest and, second, that he had done so because he reasonably believed his statement to be in the public interest.

I felt a terrible weight of responsibility for encouraging David down a route that had allowed him to be dragged into these defamation proceedings. After one meeting with his libel solicitors, David and I had gone for a drink and I'd asked him if he regretted speaking out. He said that although defending the libel claim was taking its toll, he felt he had to pursue any angle he could to get accountability. This was something of a relief, but I still felt bad about it.

In court, Economou appeared in the witness box and a number of statements from family and friends were read with the aim of illustrating the ways in which his reputation had allegedly been harmed by the publication of statements made by David. For the defence, as well as David and myself, witnesses included Shona Crallan of Inquest, Jon Clements from Victim Support, Sebastian Gosden-Hood, whom Economou had told of his intention to bankrupt David, and Gideon Wagner, who worked with Eleanor's defence solicitors.

Julian King, the police inspector who investigated the rape allegation, was unable to give evidence in person because he was subject to a misconduct investigation precipitated by the complaint Economou had made against him for refusing to investigate Eleanor for PCJ.

After everything I had been through with David, I would have liked to have been able to be more present in the courtroom and it would have been fascinating to hear all this evidence. I just couldn't afford the time off. The day I was due to give my own evidence kept slipping until it was in real danger of clashing with a holiday I had booked with Julie, our niece and my elderly mum, by this time afflicted with Alzheimer's.

As it was, I was finally called on the day we were due to leave and gave my evidence with one eye constantly on the clock while Economou stared at me from the well of the court with what appeared to me to be a glare of pure hatred. When I was eventually released, I had to sprint from the court into a taxi and made the flight only by the skin of my teeth.

I was, though, back in London when Mr Justice Warby published his judgment a month after the conclusion of the libel trial. He found in favour of David and awarded him costs. The judge said:

> Mr Economou has pursued this case with sincerity but, as I find, in anger and with elements of vengefulness . . . Mr Economou has made the error of seeing this case from his own perspective as a victim, paying too much attention to the impact on him and his feelings, and giving insufficient consideration to the other perspectives, indeed the other rights and interests, that demand and deserve consideration.

It was a huge relief. I hoped it would free David to speak out once more about the issues raised by this case. But his libel lawyers warned against doing so: it was always possible Economou would appeal. As indeed he did. It would be another two years before the Court of Appeal decided that Mr Justice Warby's judgment was correct. Further costs were awarded against Economou, who was now facing a bankruptcy petition from David's libel legal team. He had spent hundreds of thousands of pounds hounding David and there was little left in his personal coffers to pay David's lawyers' fees. Yet still he pressed on, seeking to appeal to the Supreme Court. This time permission was refused.

I was determined to fight on for an independent investigation or public inquiry to shine a light on the flaws in the justice system that had so badly let down the de Freitas family. I had gone back to the attorney general with a fresh request, updating him on developments concerning the two officers involved in the Economou case. They had been subject to a lengthy police misconduct investigation which included having to account for their refusal to pursue Eleanor de Freitas for PCJ. When initiating his police complaint, Economou had written to both officers in his own inimitable way, threatening that if the IPCC did not go after them, he would bring a private prosecution for misconduct.

It was unacceptable that police officers could be at risk of misconduct proceedings every time a man arrested for rape demanded that his accuser be arrested and charged for lying and it fundamentally undermined the extremely fragile system we have for the investigation of rape.

The attorney general sought the view of the DPP to our renewed request. The DPP said that the decision had 'already been the subject of substantial scrutiny'. But the scrutiny given had been neither independent nor external. Effectively they were marking their own homework. I asked for disclosure of the Neil Moore advice, which had been the basis of Alison Saunders' internal review into the original CPS decision, and which the office of the DPP had sent to the AG as evidence of their review. The DPP refused to provide it, claiming it was 'legally privileged'. Eventually, the AG decided to deny us any form of independent scrutiny.

But we weren't about to let this go. Why wouldn't the CPS allow independent examination of their decision-making? Why wouldn't they disclose the material on which their decision and retrospective review was based?

I asked Kate Ellis, a solicitor with whom I was working, if she could take forward a legal challenge to the AG's decision. We got advice from a public law barrister, Jenny MacLeod, who considered it to be at least procedurally wrong. Given that we would be challenging a government minister, she felt we should have a senior barrister on board and recommended Martin Chamberlain QC. After we issued proceedings, the AG agreed to provide us with Neil Moore's advice. However, it was shared with David and the legal team only on the very strict undertaking that we could not disclose or discuss its contents with anyone, on pain of being in contempt of court. I am bound by that undertaking to this day, as is David, despite a number of requests from him to be released from it.

After eight years of seeking accountability for a CPS decision that, in my view, was a significant trigger in the death of Eleanor de Freitas, her parents still do not have justice. However, neither David nor I have given up yet. We have applied for a review of the case under the Optional Protocol of the UN committee CEDAW (Convention on the Elimination of All Forms of Discrimination Against Women). CEDAW stands alone in recognizing how sex stereotyping can amount to discrimination against women, and we are setting out the ways in which prosecuting a woman who reports rape for perverting the course of justice may do just that.

The safeguards that have evolved to support victims of this uniquely complex crime immediately disappear the moment a woman becomes a defendant in a PCJ case. She loses her lifelong right to anonymity; she loses the protections in place to prevent cross-examination on her past sexual history; she loses the right not to be directly cross-examined by her alleged rapist. The jury, moreover, will not be given guidance on rape myths and stereotypes.

The issues at the core of this case extend far beyond the terrible tragedy of Eleanor's death. They go to the heart of the criminal justice system's approach to rape allegations, to questions about the accountability of our prosecution service and to the use of wealth to silence and crush those who speak out.

6

Undercover Police: The Personal Is Political

THE RIGHT TO PROTEST IS a cornerstone of democracy. Since my teens I have been active in the political causes in which I believe passionately, demonstrating against racism and violence towards women and defending entitlement to abortion and lesbian and gay rights. In my youth I dabbled in forms of civil disobedience like sitting down in the road or spraying graffiti on sexist advertising.

Activists, and especially those belonging to groups involved in direct action, have always recognized arrest as an occupational hazard and are, naturally, aware that the police will try to gather intelligence on their organizations and plans. But the idea that the British police would embed officers in such groups, deep undercover for years at a stretch, in circumstances conducive to forming long-term intimate relationships, was, until relatively recently, beyond most people's imaginations. As a police action lawyer, I have represented numerous protesters who have fallen foul of excessive use of force, unlawful arrest or malicious prosecution, and I had heard about such infiltration methods being used in Apartheid South Africa, or by the East German Stasi. But I would simply not have believed it of a country like the UK, widely regarded as a world leader in policing by consent, justice and the rule of law.

That all changed in 2011 after the collapse of a major criminal trial of political activists charged with conspiracy to commit aggravated trespass. The police had pre-emptively arrested 114 protesters preparing to break into and occupy Ratcliffe-on-Soar power station in Nottinghamshire to call attention to its damaging levels of carbon emissions. A long-haired, tattooed eco-warrior known as Mark Stone, who, according to the climate activists, had played a central part in planning the occupation, was exposed as an undercover police officer.

Stone, real name Mark Kennedy, was widely believed to have been the source of the intelligence that led to the arrests. It would emerge that he had been working deep undercover for seven years within the environmental activist movement as a member of the clandestine National Public Order Intelligence Unit (NPOIU). Unbeknownst to the general public, and even to most of the Metropolitan Police, two covert units – initially the Special Demonstration Squad (SDS), and, later, the NPOIU, whose operations for a time overlapped – had been secretly infiltrating groups designated as a 'threat to the state' and feeding back intelligence to Special Branch for over half a century.

As the *Guardian* and the BBC's *Newsnight* dug into this shady business, a particularly insidious element surfaced: that Kennedy, in the guise of his alter ego, had been involved in a number of sexual relationships with female members of the protest groups he had infiltrated. He told his story in the *Daily Mail* – ' "I'm the victim of smears": undercover police officer denies bedding a string of women during his eight years with eco-warriors', nevertheless admitting to two relationships, one of them serious. 'He was unmasked as a spy,' reported the *Mail*, 'after his beautiful redhead girlfriend of five years found his real passport.'

According to the *Guardian*, Jon Murphy, the Association of Chief

Police Officers lead on undercover policing, said that undercover officers (UCOs) were prohibited from sleeping with their targets in all circumstances. 'It is absolutely not authorized. It is never acceptable for an undercover officer to behave in that way.'

But as more women began to come forward to the press with stories about the activities and relationships of UCOs, the 'one rogue officer' argument the police sought to present began to look decidedly thin.

When Gareth Peirce asked if I would be interested in advising a former Birnberg Peirce client, Helen Steel, along with 'Lisa' – the longstanding girlfriend Mark Kennedy had talked about to the *Daily Mail* – I immediately said yes.

I had not met Helen Steel before but I knew of her by reputation. She was famously one of two defendants in the longest-running libel case in English legal history. She and Dave Morris, a fellow member of a very small environmentalist group, London Greenpeace, had defended themselves in a libel claim brought by the global fast-food giant McDonald's over a leaflet criticizing the corporation that had been handed out at protests outside its restaurants. Some of those criticisms Helen and Dave were able to prove as facts during the long trial, but they lost in relation to other claims and damages were awarded against them. They both refused to pay. Ultimately, McDonald's scored a massive own goal by pursuing the two determined and impecunious activists in this David and Goliath battle and wisely, given the damaging PR around the case, they decided not to hound them for the damages or legal costs.

When Lisa came with Helen to see Gareth, she was, not surprisingly, extremely traumatized by some of the prurient media coverage on top of the shock of discovering that her 'soulmate' of six years was in fact a police officer who had betrayed her, her friends and her family in the most fundamental way. What Gareth had not been expecting to hear was that Helen Steel had been similarly betrayed, eighteen years previously, by another police officer with whom she had formed a long-term intimate relationship and who had then disappeared without explanation.

When I first met Helen, she seemed quite shell-shocked and zonked out and, I felt, rather guarded and initially reluctant to trust me. I would come to know her as an impressively courageous person, utterly political in her outlook and driven by a thirst for justice. She wanted to take legal action against the police to expose these abusive relationships and to prevent more women being abused by undercover officers. Helen told me that she had met the man who called himself John Barker, also known as New Zealand John, in about 1987 at a London Greenpeace meeting. She was twenty-two. He had a van – a useful commodity to young idealists with few material possessions – and was always happy to drive campaigners to protests.

John had made the running in their relationship, Helen said. At first she had rejected his advances, but they became closer after his mother died (or so he said) and 'fell in love'. They moved in together. He said he wanted it to be for ever and to have children with her. But about a year into the relationship, Helen came home to find a letter from John saying that he couldn't cope any more. He had left and was not coming back. This was 'a bolt from the blue. I was extremely upset and couldn't stop crying. But I had no means of contacting him. Within a few days he rang and apologized.' He returned soon afterwards, but increasingly 'appeared to be going through some sort of mental breakdown'.

In April 1992, he wrote to her from Heathrow airport to tell her he was on his way to South Africa. There were two more letters from South Africa, the first contrite, attempting to explain how messed up he was and declaring that he would never contact her again. In the second, he said he really missed her, still loved her deeply and that, 'once he had sorted out his head', he would get back in touch. 'This gave me hope again,' Helen told me. 'But it was the last I ever heard from him.'

Desperately worried about John's mental health, she had gone to great lengths to try to find him. Her painstaking detective work over many years led her to the discovery that the details used in his records related to a John Barker who had died at the age of eight, and, eventually, to New Zealand, where she learned that his real name was John Dines and that he was married. Examining the marriage certificate she traced 'was like being ripped to pieces. I recognized John's signature, even though the surname was different from the one I had known him by. He was ten years older than me, not five. But the worst part was reading his occupation: "police constable". My blood ran cold and I felt really sick and violated.'

Helen's worst suspicions, that John had remained a serving police officer and had been working undercover the whole time she had known him, were conclusively confirmed in 2010, when Rosa, a political activist she had known a while back through Reclaim the Streets, made contact with her via a rather cryptic letter passed on by a friend. It turned out that Rosa had also been deceived and manipulated by an undercover cop. She had two children with Jim Boyling, one of the officers I'd read about in the wake of the Mark Kennedy scandal.

Helen asked if I would visit Rosa. It was difficult for Rosa to travel as she lived in a remote rural area and both of the children she'd had with Boyling suffered from a serious genetic degenerative condition and required round-the-clock care. We arranged to meet in her nearest big city while she had a week's respite support. Rosa greeted me at the railway station, a newborn baby strapped to her front in a sling. We went for a walk by the harbour and chatted.

Rosa, warm, funny and quick-witted, had a history of activism that embraced environmental, animal rights and social justice campaigns and causes. She talked about her traumatic experience, about Jim's attempts to use their children to continue to manipulate her and about her determination to care for them at home to make two lives that were not expected to be long as comfortable and full of love as she could. Her new baby had been conceived through artificial insemination: her trust in men, and indeed in everybody, had been shattered.

Rosa knew the man she had fallen in love with as Jim Sutton. Arriving in London in early 1999, having just finished her master's degree in political theory, she had met him at the first Reclaim the Streets meeting she'd attended, where he was already an established and trusted member of the group. Little did Rosa know that Jim already had access to information about her – through another SDS colleague posing as an activist.

Her relationship with Jim had been very intense. In many ways, she said, he seemed to be the partner she hadn't known she was looking for. He moved her into his flat and broached the topic of having children with her. Then one day he announced out of the blue that he had to go travelling – alone – in a few months' time 'to sort his head out'. He seemed to be having some sort of breakdown. At times verbally cruel, he would disappear for days on end, then, on his return, he'd be hugging her, sobbing and saying he never wanted to lose her. He confided that he had been adopted, and had never known what it was to have someone there for him.

Setting off on his travels, Jim told Rosa he was going to Turkey and planned to hitchhike across Africa. He phoned once from Istanbul. Then he just completely vanished.

Beside herself with worry, she embarked on a search for him that would end up taking her halfway round the world. In the process she discovered that everything he had told her about himself, his family and his past was a lie.

She phoned the Foreign Office to report Jim as missing and then, fearing that he may be running from the state, later rang back to say that he was now safe. She got hold of his phone billing records and called all the numbers. One was answered by someone who asked her how she'd got hold of the number and hurriedly hung up; another by a man who took a message for Jim despite claiming never to have heard of him. Shortly after that, in the post, she received an email address and a long love letter from Jim. In subsequent communications, he intimated that he was being controlled or trapped in some way. These were full of riddles that would draw her into a labyrinth of false leads.

Although Rosa cut contact with Jim for the sake of her own well-being, she was determined to get to the truth. After spending some months in South Africa, following a false trail in the hope of a face-to-face conversation, she found someone able to track where Jim was picking up his emails. She was shocked to learn that the man she had thought was on the run had been in England the entire time. She flew back to the UK, increasingly scared for her own safety and of whatever it was Jim had got himself involved with.

Back in London, Rosa unearthed evidence that Jim's real name was not Sutton, but Boyling, and that he had been to school in Kingston in South-West London. Returning to the phone billing, she was able to establish through a contact that the numbers were government blocked. Her contact was able to link one of them with an address in Camberwell, South London. There she discovered a small warehouse, its windows barred and opaque, monitored by discreet cameras.

Convinced that she had found the headquarters of a state surveillance operation focused on gathering intelligence on civil society, she watched the building from the bar stool in a pub opposite, noting car number plates, terrified that, alone and exposed, she might be bumped off at any moment. Unbeknownst to her, she had in fact stumbled upon the headquarters of the Special Demonstration Squad.

Two days later, Jim 'ran into her by chance' in the Kingston book-shop where she had only recently started working. He confessed to her that he was a police officer who had been working undercover, though for some time he claimed his assignment was nothing to do with politics. He was now desperate to get out, he told her, but unable to find a way to extricate himself. He asked for her help, warning her not to be in touch with any of their activist friends for fear this would get back to his unit and jeopardize any escape from the police.

By that point, Rosa's life had been turned upside down. Disturbed, destabilized and frightened that she had inadvertently crossed the threshold of some parallel deep state, she didn't know who to trust. Truth and reality changed like the weather. One moment Jim would be mocking her for entertaining the idea that the British police spied on peaceful activists, the next empathizing over how this notion demonstrated the effects of the trauma his situation had caused her. But, whether his name was Boyling or Sutton, 'he looked like Jim and smelled like Jim', as she put it to me, and so she agreed to help him, badly wanting to believe in him. Any story would have been more plausible than the truth: that her life partner was in fact an actor sent in by the Met to spy on her.

Within two weeks of Jim's reappearance, Rosa was pregnant and soon found herself trapped in a relationship that grew increasingly abusive and controlling. Looking back, it was hard for her to escape the conclusion that the resumption of this relationship had been sanctioned by the SDS in order to contain her and prevent her from exposing their existence. She eventually fled with the children to a women's refuge, but Jim and his unit were, she told me, able to continue to manipulate her circumstances through their ongoing joint parental involvement with social services over the care of their disabled children.

Rosa knew from Jim that Helen Steel had also unwittingly been in a relationship with an undercover cop. Apparently, the SDS were aware that Helen had spent years searching for John Dines and had been tracking her activities. Rosa had been desperate to get word to Helen to warn her of what she had discovered. When she ran into a mutual friend of theirs, who indicated that Jim had been seen at a festival, Rosa felt she had to act, suspecting that he was once again spying on people, using his past relationship with her to shore up his cover story. She seized the opportunity to ask their friend to pass on a letter to Helen. As Jim had implied that this man might be an informant or another cop, she felt she was taking a huge risk, but saw this as her only chance. When the letter got through and Helen responded, the relief was overwhelming.

Among the discoveries Rosa wanted to share with her was that, according to Jim, Helen had also come into contact with another SDS 'spy', a man named Bob. Rosa recalled two colleagues of Jim's making a 'welfare visit' to the family home at the time their children's rare condition was first diagnosed. Although it was clear to her at the time that this was no welfare visit, it was only with hindsight that she realized they had been assessing the level of threat to the secrecy of the SDS. With the state about to become involved in the family's life, and all the questions that would be asked, there was an obvious risk that the unit could be exposed.

One of these men had been called Bob – Bob Lambert. She described him to Helen and found a photograph of him on the internet, now presenting himself as a terrorism and policing expert. At that stage, however, he rang no bells with Helen.

Amid the press frenzy precipitated by the Mark Kennedy revelations, Rosa felt obliged to speak out about Boyling and make it known that Kennedy was far from a lone rogue operative. In January 2011, the *Guardian* ran an interview with Rosa. It outed Jim as an undercover officer but could not, she felt, scratch the surface of the complexities of her life.

Soon after the piece was published, she arrived home to find two plain clothes police officers waiting for her. Assuring her that they were appalled by what had happened to her, they said they needed her help to investigate Jim for misconduct. While she was very keen for Jim to be held to account – even if it had to be by the police – not least because she feared that he was using his status as an officer of the law to control her through social services and cast her as mentally unstable, she had no idea whether she could believe these officers or whether she should or shouldn't go down this route. In the end, Rosa, now heavily pregnant with the baby I was soon to meet, agreed to make a complaint, with Helen's support. Helen sat with her while she gave her ABE interview.

Two more women, Ruth and Alison, came to see me through Helen Steel. Ruth, a Reclaim the Streets activist in the mid-1990s, had been in a relationship with Jim Boyling before Rosa. It had lasted about eighteen months and she had been the one to end it because she felt Jim could not commit. Since then she had moved on from political activism and had learned the truth about her former partner only when friends from those days alerted her that the *Guardian* piece was about to be published. Although there had been some rumours circulating in activist circles at the time Jim disappeared, Ruth had dismissed them as nonsense and the 2011 revelations had been a thunderbolt.

I would come to know Ruth as a private, thoughtful and perceptive person. She told me she had been in the middle of finishing a PhD when the news of Jim's deceit was confirmed.

It left me feeling devastated and confused and forced me to rapidly re-evaluate every aspect of our relationship, including past conversations, our sex life and our patterns of behaviour as a couple. I felt overwhelmed and distraught and I knew this would have a detrimental impact on my academic work. I

needed to somehow shut off from these events in order to finish
my thesis.

After allowing herself time to reflect, she said,

> I feel very angry at Jim. I feel conned, betrayed, emotionally and
> sexually manipulated and very much used by him. There is also
> something grubby and sordid about the way in which, unbeknown
> to me, the state (or a representative of the state) has interfered with
> the most intimate aspects of my life. I believe that these tactics
> have been utilized for politically cynical purposes.

Alison, unlike most of the others, had never been involved in
environmental protests or animal rights causes. She had met Helen
Steel some years previously after being introduced by a mutual friend
who recognized similarities in their well-founded suspicions about
the mysterious disappearances of their respective boyfriends. A
former teacher, she was outgoing and vibrant, with a great sense of
humour.

In the early 1990s, Alison had participated in a number of anti-
fascist and police-monitoring campaigns and projects based at the
Colin Roach Centre, a community centre in Hackney named after a
man shot dead by the police. In 1994, Mark Cassidy, a working-class
joiner from Birkenhead, joined the campaigners there. He drove a
red van (a van was apparently a standard feature of the UCO's kit:
offering lifts, or to bring placards to demos, helped them to assimi-
late quickly).

Within a few months Alison and Mark were dating and he moved
into her East London flat, where they would live together for the following five years. He became part of Alison's family and she was
keen to meet his relatives, too, but he seemed reluctant to introduce
her to any of them. He told her he'd had a difficult childhood: his

father had died in a road accident when he was a kid and he had a bad relationship with his mum. But despite their very different backgrounds, they were a well-matched couple and Alison saw Mark as her life partner. The only conflict between them was the question of parenthood: Alison wanted children and Mark did not. She persuaded him to attend couples counselling with Relate to try to work through this issue, but they didn't get very far.

As Alison began to withdraw to some extent from political activism, Mark was becoming increasingly involved, in particular with some of the more militant anti-fascist groups. He also showed an interest in Irish republicanism.

In December 1999, they were about to spend Christmas with Alison's family when Mark received a message that his grandfather had had a stroke. He dashed up to Birkenhead, and after he came back he didn't seem himself. In the new year he began a job on a site in Luton, which involved a long commute every day, and his depression worsened.

Then, one day while Alison was out, Mark removed all his belongings from the house and left a note saying he had gone. Alison, hysterical with shock, managed to reach him on his mobile and begged him to come home so that they could talk things through. He returned with only a small overnight bag and seemed incredibly twitchy, apparently fearing he was being watched. He stayed for about ten days before disappearing again, leaving Alison another note. A letter, and then a postcard, followed from Germany. After that, nothing.

Alison searched for him endlessly online. She called his ex-employer and the DVLA. She went to the Public Record Office to verify what he'd told her about his background. Unable to find a trace of him, she hired a private investigator. Mark Cassidy, it turned out, did not exist. Most friends and family in whom she confided her growing suspicions that Mark might have been a 'spook' told her not to be so ridiculous, interpreting her paranoid and obsessive behaviour as the emotional repercussions of a broken relationship and unrequited love. She was, she told me, quite mad for a while, taking to writing down car number plates and searching for hidden messages in spam emails.

Eventually, she started a new relationship with a man she had known since childhood – someone who couldn't conceivably pretend to be anybody else – and they had two children. She stopped actively looking for Mark but, with the mystery unsolved, it continued to preoccupy her. Sometimes she feared he was dead. She had wondered whether his real name might be Jenner, having once found a credit card in that name which he had explained away. It was not until the Mark Kennedy story, with its striking parallels, hit the headlines that she was provided with confirmation that she had been right all along.

In the meantime, I finally met the woman who had uncovered the truth about Mark Kennedy: Lisa, who had been in the process of moving the narrowboat on which she lived through the waterways from the Midlands to moor it in London. A 1990s veteran of the Faslane Peace Camp in Scotland, and of the tunnels and treehouses built by protesters in the battle to stop construction of the new Manchester airport runway that threatened ancient woodland, Lisa was warm, passionate and open, and clearly still completely devastated by her discovery that 'Mark Stone' had been a fraud.

When Lisa met him in 2003, he was living in Nottingham and involved with a friend of hers, Kate Wilson. Lisa and Mark got together in 2004. Fairly casual at the outset, the relationship became more serious about a year in. 'I guess you could say that Mark swept me off my feet as he was extremely attentive,' Lisa told me. 'I felt that we had a great deal in common.' Like her, 'he was really into outdoor stuff like mountaineering and climbing'.

For the following five years, they were to all intents and purposes a

couple. Like many others in her circle, Lisa believed that living a ful-
filled life meant remaining open to new experiences and intimacies,
rejecting the restrictions of conventional monogamous partnerships
and the possessiveness and connotations of ownership that went with
them. She encouraged Mark to be 'true to himself' and he had many
other sexual relationships. But Lisa was viewed by the world at large,
and, she thought, by Mark, as his long-term girlfriend.

After the Ratcliffe-on-Soar arrests and associated raids on activists' homes, Mark's mental health deteriorated and he told Lisa he
had to go away for a while. They stayed in touch by email but Lisa
was worried about him. In January 2010 he reappeared, announcing
that he had bought a narrowboat, which he moored alongside Lisa's,
and their relationship continued until the summer of that year. It
was while they were on holiday climbing in the Dolomites that she
found the passport in the name of Mark Kennedy and a second
mobile phone, which contained messages from two children to their
daddy. When she confronted him, he came up with a cover story, a
past as a drug-dealer he was ashamed of.

Lisa gave Mark the benefit of the doubt, but, back in England,
after hearing on the grapevine how Jim Sutton had been a long-term
spy in the environmental movement, she asked a friend involved in
genealogy research if he could check Mark out. This led to the exposure of his true identity as a police officer, married with two children
and living in Ireland.

By the end of June, we had five women who had been unwittingly
involved with four different UCOs. While they were at different points
in their own journeys, they'd had many eerily similar experiences and
all had believed themselves to be in serious relationships. It was an
extraordinary situation. The impact on them all had been life-changing.
But how could we use the law to bring these men to justice?

I thought it would be useful for the women to meet to share their
stories with each other and for us to begin to consider possible legal

remedies. Who were they most angry with? Their deceitful, manipulative exes, or the institution behind them that had facilitated, possibly encouraged, their actions? Did what had happened to them amount to rape? Were they targeted as individuals, or just used as a convenient cover for the officers to establish credibility among activists? What did they most want from a potential legal action?

The five women, plus Rosa's baby, crowded into the small meeting room at our office, where we'd provided food, along with Gareth, Sheila, my casework assistant, and me. These were an intense few hours. The women discovered just how much they had in common and cried, laughed and ate together. They were united in the view that the Met Police must be held to account and that they did not want this to happen to anyone else; that they needed to know why they had been targeted and how many of their intimate moments and communications had been shared with other police officers. There were some differences of opinion about the extent to which individual officers were culpable but, by the end of the meeting, everyone was agreed that we would explore the legal avenues jointly. For years they had suffered in isolation, and now they wanted to proceed with the support of each other.

We talked about bringing more women into the fold. One of the difficulties here for Lisa was the large number of sexual relationships in which Kennedy had indulged with women in the wider activist movement, a few of whom were now speaking out. While she believed it was only right that anyone affected should have the option of joining a legal action, the betrayal was still very raw for her and she was fearful of the potential of matters shared in meetings to continually re-traumatize her. She felt she needed the group to be a safe space for her, formed of people she trusted. She suggested I talk to two close friends who'd been involved with 'Mark Stone': Kate Wilson, with whom he'd been in a relationship when Lisa first met him, and Naomi, whose intimacy with Mark had overlapped with Lisa's in 2005.

Naomi, tall and striking, with dyed blonde hair shaven on one side and long on the other, had an academic background and a PhD. She now worked as a community gardener. She and Lisa had been in the same housing co-op and activists for similar causes. 'Many of us involved in the movement had a belief in open relationships and many of us, men and women, might have more than one sexual partner at any one time,' she confirmed. 'It was not a problem . . . provided you were completely honest about it, and it was not problematic, necessarily, to be good friends with somebody else your lover was sleeping with. Trust, of course, was critical to enable this challenge to conventional heterosexual relationships to work.'

That summer, Naomi went away on holiday with Mark and he accompanied her to a family wedding, but thereafter he seemed to her to become increasingly distracted and to be constantly changing his plans. Naomi sensed they were drifting apart and decided to end their nine-month relationship. He and Lisa were growing ever closer, he was also seeing a third woman at the same time and she felt that sustaining her friendships with both Lisa and Mark was more important to her than a sexual relationship with him. She was very surprised at his reaction: he seemed disproportionately distressed and sobbed in her arms. They stayed friends, and indeed did have a couple more sexual encounters. Naomi observed that Mark 'seemed to have this way of mimicking people that he was close with . . . When he was going out with me, I used to play the mandolin and he decided that he wanted to learn to play the banjo. When he was with Lisa, it was the drum and bass.'

By the time the true identity of this chameleon was revealed, Naomi had moved to London. In complete shock, she went up to Nottingham a few days later to be with others who had been friends with 'Mark Stone'. Amid the furore surrounding the collapse of the Ratcliffe-on-Soar trial, she spent a weekend away with Lisa. They read his self-serving story in the *Daily Mail* together and tried to process the photos of this short-haired, clean-cut man who was, and yet was not, the Mark they knew.

Kate, who was living and studying in Spain, emailed me to explain that it was therefore difficult for her to come to London to meet me but that she was happy for Lisa and Naomi to discuss her case with me. 'I was Mark's girlfriend from October 2003 to February 2005, when I left the country,' she wrote.

We remained close friends and political 'comrades' for many years after that. Mark made a point of getting close to my family, claiming they were like the family he never had and always wanted. He built up a relationship with my brother (around football) that continued for many years. He attended my grandmother's ninetieth birthday party.

I am interested in pressing a case against the police for a number of reasons. Foremost among them is that I just want to know what they did. I may have been specifically and operationally targeted by Mark . . . I believe it is extremely unlikely that the police did not know Mark and I were seeing each other. Obviously, I would like answers to the many questions that raises.

I have been deeply affected by the betrayal and loss of discovering that my close friend and lover never existed, and I am very wary of what it might mean to have to quantify that damage . . . My boyfriend and I have not had sex for almost six months, and I have had (and continue to have) attacks of paranoia about specific friends or colleagues that have been very difficult to handle. It has taken me two days to build up the energy to begin to write to you, and, writing this now, I feel physically sick.

The final woman to join our group was Belinda Harvey, who had been in a relationship in the late 1980s with Bob Lambert – the officer Rosa remembered from that 'welfare visit'.

Since looking at the internet image Rosa had found of Bob Lambert, Helen had racked her brain for fellow activists she had come across called Bob and thought of Bob Robinson, who had been involved with London Greenpeace in the 1980s – indeed, was one of the authors of the McDonald's leaflet that had led to her long legal battle. Were Bob Lambert and Bob Robinson the same man? Decades on, she could not be sure.

Rosa had told Helen that she believed Bob Lambert to have been a senior figure in the SDS. He had gone on to run the Met's Muslim Contact Unit (MCU), set up in 2002, in the wake of the 9/11 attacks, with the aim of thwarting 'extremist attempts to recruit young British Muslims to violent jihad by working with Islamic communities'. Jim Boyling had been part of that unit, too. By a strange coincidence, the name Bob Lambert was familiar to me as well. I had come across him during the Jean Charles de Menezes case, when we learned that he had been aware of the activities of Hussein Osman, the terrorist suspect for whom Jean Charles had been mistaken when he was shot on the London Underground.

It seems that through his work in the MCU, Lambert had built a reputation as an anti-terrorism expert and had gone on to establish a significant academic career in the field. As a result, very unusually for a former undercover officer, he had a public profile, which was how Rosa and Helen had found him online.

At the time Helen had known 'Bob Robinson', he'd left behind a serious girlfriend, Belinda, when he'd had to go 'on the run from the police'. Helen went to see Belinda and showed her a video from the internet of Lambert giving a lecture. It was Belinda who definitively confirmed that they were one and the same man. Helen asked her if she would like to join our case.

Belinda recounted to me how she'd met Bob at a party back in 1987. Twenty-four years old and from Cumbria, she'd been the first in her working-class family to go to university. After graduating, she had moved to East London, where she was sharing a house with other former students. Bob was 'very romantic and attentive' and she quickly fell for him. They spent the next twenty months together.

Bob talked to her about his involvement with London Greenpeace, Hunt Saboteurs and the Animal Liberation Front (ALF). She was not a political activist, although she was a vegetarian and had friends who campaigned for animal rights. But she admired Bob's idealism, his anti-materialism, his high principles. 'He was very charismatic,' she recalled, 'and all these young activists were quite in awe of him, I thought.'

That summer, Bob told her about an ALF plan he was involved in to plant incendiary devices in three branches of Debenhams – their department stores sold fur coats – in Luton, Harrow and Romford. 'I tried to persuade him not to do it as I thought it was wrong.' He reassured Belinda that nobody would get hurt. However, one of the devices did cause some serious damage. Two activists were arrested, prosecuted and sent to prison.

Meanwhile, the relationship between Bob and Belinda blossomed. She had introduced him to her family and, after about a year, she was ready to settle down and start a family of their own. But, to her distress, Bob resisted, claiming she deserved better than a life looking constantly over her shoulder. It was shortly after this that she endured a painful parting when, worried that the police had caught up with him, Bob went into hiding. He wrote to Belinda from Spain, a letter she had treasured for many years. 'I thought Bob had done something noble and that he was in a way being strong by cutting off from me. Of course, I hoped he would get in touch but he didn't.' Only now, over twenty years later, did Belinda know the truth. She felt violated and angry.

It would later emerge that by the time he met Belinda, Lambert had already fathered a child with an unsuspecting activist. The unravelling of his activities as an undercover cop would take a little while but it was Helen Steel and a few of her London Greenpeace colleagues who pulled at the first thread in October 2011 by publicly confronting him with his past as he gave a presentation on Islamophobia at a trade union conference.

It was time for our eight clients to instruct counsel. Phillippa Kaufmann, who had recently been made QC, and Charlotte Kilroy, an extremely sharp and capable barrister with whom I'd worked on a number of immigration detention cases, met the women that October and we explored a number of routes towards accountability. One idea was to push for a public inquiry, which could be ordered by a government minister. Should they take forward complaints against the individual police officers? How could they trust the police to investigate?

A civil action, as we've seen, has the advantage of putting the complainants in control of the narrative, and, all things considered, it seemed like the best option in this case. With the women keen to bring a joint claim, this would also give them a means of acting collectively. But what could we argue to be the causes of action? Nobody had ever before litigated a case concerning the police forming sexual relationships with women while spying on them and their friends and it was untrodden territory. The most obvious way forward, at first blush, was to use the Human Rights Act, which protects citizens from state violation of their rights to privacy and personal integrity. However, five of the relationships had been formed before the HRA came into force in 2000, which meant that this was available only to the three women deceived by Mark Kennedy.

But Lisa, Naomi and Kate faced another problem. When Parliament enacted the HRA, they made Article 8, the right to privacy, a 'qualified right'. In other words, there would be some circumstances in which an invasion of a person's right to privacy by the state would be justified and even necessary: for example, when the state undertakes surveillance of suspected criminals or terrorists. In order to ensure that any such invasion of privacy was proportionate, Parliament also enacted the Regulation of Investigatory Powers Act (RIPA), which requires any such spying-type activity to be carefully regulated and authorized.

If a person suspects that the state has violated their privacy in breach of their human rights through the use of surveillance powers, their complaint or claim must be made via the Investigatory Powers Tribunal (IPT). And the problem with the IPT is that hearings can be held in secret, with the complainant not necessarily having access to all or even any of the evidence. However, Phillippa and Charlotte thought there was a good argument to be made to circumvent the IPT. It was quite a complex argument, but in essence it came down to the premise that because Mark Kennedy's actions in relation to Lisa, Naomi and Kate were not, and could never have been, authorized, this was not conduct that was regulated in accordance with RIPA and it was therefore not appropriate for the IPT to consider the case.

Counsel advised that all eight women did have arguable common-law claims for damages and provided careful advice as to how these would arise. First, they might have a claim in assault, on the basis that any unwanted physical contact with another person could amount to a battery. Clearly that would include sexual contact. However, the difficulty here was that the women had not objected to sex at the time it took place, and consent is a defence to battery. The key question was whether the consent to sexual contact was vitiated by the police officers' deception – and the answer in the eyes of the law was far from straightforward.

Second, the women might be able to rely on the tort of deceit. This was a cause of action that had evolved in a commercial setting and was used mainly in circumstances where someone had suffered financial loss as a consequence of a fraudulent representation. Third, with the police officers all having abused their powers in ways that were likely to, and indeed did, cause the women damage, they could sue for misfeasance in public office. Both torts fitted the circumstances quite well, but they carried the requirement for the women to prove they had suffered material damage.

While they were all, naturally, very significantly affected by the discovery that men with whom they were in relationships were undercover police officers, in order to prove damage, they would have to demonstrate either financial loss or personal injury. Mental or emotional distress would not on its own amount to material damage, according to what some might describe as a traditionally sexist reading of the law, unless the level of mental distress met the criteria for a psychiatric diagnosis.

Finally, Phillippa and Charlotte thought it would also be worth considering negligence against the police force that employed the officers, because it had failed to put in place a safe system to ensure that undercover operatives did not cause foreseeable damage to the people they were spying on. Suing the police for negligence posed its own headaches as the law courts had repeatedly ruled that the police had immunity in this respect where criminal investigations were concerned. The question here was whether the activities of UCOs amounted to a criminal investigation.

Another legal issue we had to address was limitation. Any case brought under the Human Rights Act needed to be commenced within one year of the matter giving rise to the claim. For the common-law torts, it was three years where there was a personal injury. Obviously, some of the relationships went back a lot longer than that, but no one could be criticized for not bringing a claim if they were not aware that they had been wronged. However, where did that leave Rosa, who, despite having been continually spun lies by Jim Boyling throughout their relationship and beyond, had, on paper, been aware of his intial deceit for about ten years? The court did have the power to extend limitation if it would be equitable to do so and we felt there were certainly arguments we could apply. In the meantime, counsel thought it was important to issue a protective claim immediately for the three women who were bringing the HRA claim, given that it had been almost a year since Mark Kennedy had been unmasked.

And then there was funding. Most of the women had jobs of some sort, although none were well off. That put them in the all-too-common bind of being ineligible for legal aid but unable to afford to pay for the legal work required. The only real option was a conditional fee agreement – and it was not a great one for such a novel legal challenge. However, I reckoned there was a good chance the police would want to settle the case early on, given how much embarrassment had been caused by the all the news reports and in the light of public statements made by police leads that sexual relationships would never have been sanctioned.

Overall, we took the view that it would be worth setting out all the potential causes of action to see where they took us. Now that we had a strategy, it was over to me. I immediately issued a protective claim in the High Court for the three women deceived by Mark Kennedy. I also lodged the case with the IPT, inviting them to stay the claim until the conclusion of the case brought in the High Court, and wrote a detailed letter before claim to the Metropolitan Police on behalf of all eight clients.

My next task, to explore evidence that might support a claim for personal injury for all eight victims, was extremely hard for some of them. So much of their intimate lives had already been exposed in ways over which they had no control. The prospect that they might now have to lay open the inner workings of their own psyches to the scrutiny of a medical professional was a huge ask. As Kate had put it in her email to me a couple of months earlier: 'The idea of having to undergo psychological evaluations, and perhaps delve into things that I am frankly trying not to think about, makes me very nervous indeed.'

Helen, too, was strongly opposed to the intrusion of psychiatric assessment. She felt we should argue that one of the most significant aspects of damage caused was the loss of time. Most of the women had devoted years to nurturing a relationship that was never going anywhere, and some had spent many more driving themselves mad searching for a man who did not exist. All of the relationships had taken place when they were in their twenties and thirties, a point in their lives when they might well have been considering starting a family. Some felt that the time they had wasted, and the loss of their ability to trust another man, had cost them that chance.

Counsel, however, were clear that there was no precedent for this and a real risk that the failure to obtain evidence of psychiatric damage might undermine the claims. I proposed to Helen that we could instead instruct a psychologist, whose approach might be less medicalized and more trauma-focused.

Georgina Smith, an expert in rape-related trauma, assisted by her colleague Brock Chisholm, accomplished the mammoth task of assessing, in a short space of time, eight women whose experiences were unusual and whose psychological symptoms did not all follow a traditional pattern. The diagnostic criteria for PTSD, perhaps the most obvious diagnosis, require first of all the identification of a trigger event – a point where the person 'experienced, witnessed or was confronted with an event or events that involved actual or threatened death or serious injury, or a threat to the physical integrity of self or others' and that their response included 'intense fear, helplessness or horror'. That event also needs to be persistently re-experienced through, for example, recurrent and intrusive distressing recollections or dreams. The sufferer is also likely to avoid stimuli associated with the trauma and may manifest persistent symptoms of increased arousal, such as difficulty concentrating, hypervigilance or exaggerated startle response.

Brock and Georgina had found many of these symptoms in

several of the women, but the problem was pinpointing a trigger event. They felt that, rather than a single traumatic event, there had been almost a 'reverse explosion': a slow reveal whereby the more the victims learned, the more frightening the impact on their mental health became. This didn't quite fit the PTSD diagnosis in use at the time, although Georgina told us that modifications to diagnostic formulations for trauma- and stressor-related disorders that would correspond better were in the process of being agreed.

Unsurprisingly, a number of the women had experienced symptoms of paranoia. Some felt their sense of reality was so undermined that the diagnosis of delusional disorder, at least for a period of time, was applicable. Others became so focused on what had happened to them that they developed obsessional disorders. Most also suffered from severe anxiety, including panic attacks and depression.

The psychological reports put paid to counsel's concerns that we would not be able to prove material damage. Indeed, the diagnoses revealed the scale of harm caused by the activities of these undercover officers. Although these diagnoses carried the 'disorder' label, they were, ironically, for the most part natural responses to extraordinary events and to manipulation of their lives. Most of the women had been reasonably stable and secure prior to these relationships and there was nothing in their histories to suggest they would be vulnerable to such disorders if it hadn't been for the grotesque deceptions to which they had been subjected.

Meanwhile, I followed up my letter before claim on behalf of all eight claimants to the Metropolitan Police solicitors with more detailed individual letters before claim and invited the defendant to agree to our request for an extension of time for service of the formal pleadings in order to give them the opportunity to respond to the claims. The rather unexpected reply was to refuse my request. They also declined to provide any disclosure of documents, a standard part of the process.

When asked to reconsider, in the interests of avoiding the incurring of unnecessary costs, the police solicitor wrote back denying liability and indicating his intention to make an immediate application for summary judgment to strike out the HRA claims under the civil procedure rules 'as disclosing no reasonable grounds for bringing a claim', and to apply 'for an order that they are time-barred under s7(5) HRA'. Clearly my rather optimistic assessment of the prospects of early settlement was rapidly receding.

As the correspondence continued back and forth, the Met solicitor made some rather contradictory and confusing statements. In one letter, for example, he was intending to 'disclose as soon as I am able any relevant RIPA authorizations for Mark Kennedy whilst he was a serving Metropolitan Police Officer', and yet, a couple of weeks later, he was apparently minded not to provide 'inspection of the applications or authorizations prior to service of the Particulars of Claim'. The commissioner was 'not vicariously liable in respect of Mr Kennedy's sexual conduct as described in the letters of claim', but a couple of months down the line, 'the intimate and sexual relationship which it is claimed Mark Kennedy formed with your client was a "personal or other relationship" covered by RIPA authorizations and his conduct was therefore "lawful for all purposes" by virtue of section 27(1) of RIPA'. As the Commissioner for the Metropolis '"potentially" would be liable only for unlawful conduct', he concluded, 'it would seem that your clients cannot succeed with their claims'.

Given these inconsistent and obstructive responses, and, having issued a protective claim for the HRA women, we had no choice but to prepare and serve particulars of claim for Lisa, Kate and Naomi within the time limit. This, unfortunately, meant a separation of the claims. But at least there were still only two groups and the women continued to work closely together.

I convened meetings, for those able to make it, where they would

share insights from their personal experiences and discuss strategy.
They were incredibly supportive of each other and worked hard to
iron out political differences. Anyone who has been involved in
feminist and left-wing politics will know that uniting anarchist feminists with trade union socialists is no mean feat. Most of the women
held strong political opinions and were used to arguing these out in
meetings. Some shouted louder than others. Variations in approaches
to resolving conflict were also challenging, with some believing that
no decision could be made unless it had been reached by consensus,
whereas others found the lengthy going round in circles this entailed
frustrating. But, through it all, there was an amazing camaraderie
and commonality of purpose forged by some extremely rare shared
experiences.

So, if I felt on occasion as though I had metamorphosed from
solicitor into a cross between a convenor of a consciousness-raising
group and the chair of a rowdy political meeting, my overriding
sense was one of great privilege to be part of this tight band of brave
women who were essentially laying bare the dark underbelly of
police espionage methods and formulating a principled strategy for
holding those at the top accountable for tactics which, all were
agreed, amounted to institutionalized sexism.

On the way we were hitting a number of brick walls. After we
served the particulars of claim on behalf of the three clients who'd
had relationships with Mark Kennedy (the 'AKJ case'), the Met lawyers responded with their threatened application to strike out the
case. They sought a declaration that the High Court, where we had
issued the claim, had no jurisdiction to hear the claims brought
under the Human Rights Act, and moreover that the common-law
claims, which would normally be heard in the High Court, should
be struck out as constituting an abuse of process. We had, of course,
anticipated their argument in relation to the HRA, because human
rights claims come under the jurisdiction of the IPT, a creation of

RIPA. But we now had the opportunity to argue that RIPA could not have been intended to authorize conduct which amounted to the development of a sexual relationship.

In response to the grounds we set out for the claims of the other five women (the 'DIL case'), we were confident the police could not argue that the cases should be heard in the IPT. Or could they? With regard to the MKJ case, the Met solicitor asserted:

> The public interest consideration that lies behind our application [to strike out the AKJ case] is, as we have set out, that it is the MPS [Metropolitan Police Service] policy to neither confirm nor deny any allegation that one of its officers is a CHIS [Covert Human Intelligence Source], or the details of any undercover work, or to reveal any facts that may allow such information to be inferred. The reason for that policy . . . is that the work of undercover officers would be seriously undermined, and the safety of the public and others seriously put at risk, were it to become public knowledge that particular individuals had acted as a CHIS in the past.

The application made by the MPS in relation to the AKJ case had indeed raised the issue of 'neither confirm nor deny', known as NCND, which seemed particularly bizarre given that not only had Mark Kennedy himself, and half the world's press, confirmed his identity as an undercover cop, but so had the Met's solicitor. This letter from the Met went on to propose that the DIL case should await the outcome of the first application. However, for good measure, they then went on to attack as out of time on limitation all claims going back to the 1980s and 1990s and declared that 'more generally the claims for assault, deceit, misfeasance and negligence are simply unarguable'. They suggested that the deceit by undercover officers was no different from any man lying to his partner, which would not give rise to a claim in tort. 'Any claims pursued will be vigorously defended and costs applications pursued if appropriate. We reserve the right to apply to strike out the claims and/or to apply for summary judgment.'

The gloves were off. I convened a council of war at my office. My view was that, while we had strong legal arguments and the best counsel to advocate them, because we were in the hands of a cautious judicial establishment dealing with a novel action, we could not count on the moral strength of our case. We needed to keep up the pressure on the police in the public domain. Although there had been a lot of media coverage and no little public outrage following the Mark Kennedy revelations, similar stories were now causing less of a stir. Too often you'd hear people remark, much as the police solicitor was doing, 'It's not nice to be lied to in a relationship, but men do that all the time. What's the big fuss?' Others would dismiss those spied upon as 'unwashed anarchists' or suggest they must have been doing something dodgy to have attracted police interest in the first place.

For the police and their methods to be exposed and shamed we had to reach out beyond the world of left-wing and environmental activists to the general public. Only then would people begin to grasp the enormity of the state abuse that had been taking place. That meant engaging with mainstream politics and the mainstream media.

The police are, of course, funded by and accountable to local government and governed nationally by Home Office policy. We needed to galvanize politicians to get the scandal debated in Parliament and reported in the press. As most of the women were either anarchists or on the left of the Labour Party, there was some reluctance to work with politicians from the dominant parties. But people felt a little more comfortable with the Green Party, which had already raised concerns about the undercover policing of protest movements. Both

Caroline Lucas, the party's only MP, and Jenny Jones, an elected representative on the Greater London Assembly, were very keen to table the issue in relevant committees and meetings. Alison also arranged to see her local MP, Diane Abbott, who offered to discuss the matter with her colleague, Keith Vaz, chair of the Home Affairs Select Committee, which often scrutinizes issues relating to policing.

Most of the group had no experience of working with the mainstream media, and little appetite for it either. They knew that once their names were out there, they would be immortalized on the internet and defined for ever by these events and they very much wanted to preserve their anonymity where possible. I suggested radio as the best medium for providing first-hand accounts pseudonymously. One Radio 4 producer happened to be an old friend of Ruth's, and the women felt she could be trusted. Through that connection, some of them agreed to be interviewed for an edition of *File on 4*.

In the course of their long fight for justice, several spoke to the *Guardian*, where investigative journalists Rob Evans and Paul Lewis were responsible for much of the national reporting on undercover policing and were in the process of writing a book on the subject. One of the first to do so was Belinda, angry at being kept in the dark for over twenty years about what had been done to her, and at Bob Lambert's re-invented public profile as a liberal academic.

The women also established a campaign and support group, Police Spies Out Of Lives, raised some funding to pay an administrator and set up a website. To ensure good media coverage when the strike-out application was heard, they organized a protest outside the Royal Courts of Justice.

The hearing took place over three days in November 2012 before Mr Justice Tugendhat. We had joined forces with Tuckers solicitors and Heather Williams QC, who were representing three Cardiff anarchists with similar claims arising from their unwitting relationships with another undercover cop, Marco Jacobs. Between us we split the work and the arguments we would be making for the hearing.

The judgment was reserved and handed down in January. We lost our argument that the HRA claims should not be considered by the IPT, although we succeeded in establishing that the common-law claims had to be heard in the High Court. But the judge ruled that the HRA claims should be adjudicated by the IPT before the common-law claims were heard. We decided to appeal.

In February 2013, Keith Vaz convened a session of the Home Affairs Select Committee to examine the scandals surrounding undercover policing. Invited to give evidence were our clients and their lawyers, journalist Paul Lewis, deputy assistant commissioner of the Met Patricia Gallan and Mark Kennedy. Lisa, Alison and Helen volunteered to appear before the committee, accompanied by Jules Carey of Tuckers and me. We had hoped to see Mark Kennedy give his evidence but the session was carefully choreographed so that there was no chance of any encounter with him. Although some of the MPs' questioning of the women was insensitive at times, the interim report published a few weeks later was unambiguous.

We make no comment on the lawfulness or otherwise of the actions of the officers in these cases, but the terrible impact on the lives of those women who had relationships with undercover officers is beyond doubt ... One witness told us that, 'I have, for the last 13 years, questioned my own judgment and it has impacted seriously on my ability to trust, and that has impacted on my current relationship and other subsequent relationships. It has also distorted my perceptions of love and my perceptions of sex, and it has had a massive impact on my political activity.' Another witness described her feelings on discovering that her former partner was a police officer: 'It felt like the ground had shifted beneath me and my sense of what was reality and what wasn't was completely turned on its head.'

These cases raise troubling questions about public policy and the legal framework within which undercover police operations are authorized, which we believe require urgent action by the government.

While we appealed the AKJ judgment, we proceeded with the claims on behalf of the other five women. To provide the necessary proof of damage, we served the psychological reports and some preliminary schedules of loss where we sought to attribute financial loss to the damage caused. Where possible we claimed that the women's ability to work and advance in their careers had been affected by psychological damage and we also sought to claim damages for those who needed care from friends and family while suffering a breakdown.

Finalizing the wording of the particulars of claim proved to be a painstaking operation. I found myself caught between clients and counsel as I tried to ensure that all the women's wishes, and the articulation of their experience, were properly reflected, while at the same time respecting Charlotte's drafting expertise.

In the midst of this task, we were approached by a TV documentary team about participating in a programme for Channel 4's *Dispatches*, which, to our great interest, had secured the cooperation of a whistleblower – a former undercover officer who had been working with Paul Lewis and Rob Evans on background for their book. With television it is, of course, more difficult to remain anonymous, but by this time both Helen and Belinda had decided to waive their anonymity and they agreed to be interviewed and filmed meeting the whistleblower, Peter Francis.

In May 2013, two months after we served the meticulously pleaded particulars of claim, the Met served their defence. It was short and it

was contemptuous. In a nutshell, the police asserted NCND in relation to all the allegations we made and did not budge an inch on any
of their previous positions.

The next stage of civil proceedings would normally be to agree
directions for the future management of the claim, including a timetable for disclosure and exchange of witness statements. However,
the civil procedure rules encourage the parties to engage in alterna-
tive dispute resolution in an effort to avoid the escalation of costs.
The court therefore ordered a stay in the proceedings for options to
be explored. In this case, however, the women were adamant that
they did not want simply to walk away with some financial compensation but without the answers they so desperately needed, or even
any official confirmation that the men with whom they had shared
their lives had indeed been undercover police officers.

From the outset I had warned them about the Part 36 offer – the
device that can be used by either party to put pressure on the other
side to settle by making an offer of compensation calculated to be in
the region of a likely award of damages made by the court. This was
the tactic that was to work so well in our clients' favour, again
against the Met, in seeking damages for Fiona and Meena, the victims of John Worboys, in the case discussed in Chapter 4. In this
instance we were concerned that offers might be made that would
force the women to settle before they had achieved any of their
objectives on accountability.

At the end of the month's stay, the police duly made Part 36 offers.
Fortunately, they were relatively low, so while there was some risk
that we might not 'beat the offer' at trial, we felt we had a good
chance. It meant we could advise the insurance company that they
could continue to cover the risk to the women of having to pay the
police costs if they lost.

To prevent the police from endlessly stalling the claim, we asked
the court to list a case management hearing to set deadlines for the

pre-trial procedures required to move the case forward. It was sched-uled for a date in August, when all barristers seem to be on holiday. But with the women keen not to delay, I agreed to present our argu-ments myself, which is always slightly nerve-wracking when you get used to relying on counsel for advocacy. Alison and Helen came with me. Luckily, Master Leslie was presiding and, as I had learned over the years, he is never too impressed by obstructive lawyers repre-senting the state. He made an order that the police had to serve any application they intended to make within twenty-eight days or pro-vide disclosure.

In the meantime, the long-awaited *Dispatches* documentary was broadcast, on 24 June, to coincide with the publication of Paul and Rob's book, *Undercover*. As well as highlighting the stories of police spies forming relationships with women, the programme revealed a new atrocity: Peter Francis, the former undercover officer turned whistleblower, disclosed that he had been asked, as part of his deployment, to spy on the family of Stephen Lawrence, the black teenager killed in a horrific racist murder, and their campaign for justice. That case, and the extremely dignified campaign of Stephen's family, had become a cause célèbre, gaining the widespread support of the public and MPs across the political divide. The prime minister, David Cameron, announced in Parliament that there would be an immediate investigation into these serious allegations. Although the outrage in Parliament was primarily focused on the Lawrence case, references to the duplicitous relationships formed by undercover police were helpful to our cause.

Peter Francis, who had been a UCO with the SDS in the mid-1990s, had been tasked with infiltrating anti-fascist groups, which included gathering intelligence on a number of black justice cam-paigns. He became increasingly disillusioned with this aspect of his work, which he felt was undemocratic and an improper use of police resourcing, and, unable to reconcile his role as a police officer with the duplicity he was expected to practise, on returning to main-stream Special Branch duties he suffered a major breakdown. After being medically retired from the police, he successfully sued them for negligence.

At the time of his appearance on the *Dispatches* programme, Peter offered to meet our clients and me to answer any questions we might have. Because he was still bound by the Official Secrets Act, he had to tread carefully and could not divulge information of which we were not already aware, but he was able to confirm points put to him, which was invaluable in helping us to verify some of the SDS methods, the identities of the UCOs we were concerned with and aspects of their personalities. This information would also be very useful in dealing with the second strike-out application from the Met, which came in September, in response to Master Leslie's order.

The police argued that, because of their NCND policy, they could not defend the claim and should be released from their usual disclosure obligations. We now set about preparing evidence challenging the assertion that the police even had an NCND policy, and specifying some of the ways in which, if they did, that policy was not consistently applied. As far back as 2002, in a BBC documentary called *True Spies*, undercover police officers had revealed information about some of their operations. As well as the nonsense of citing NCND in the case of Mark Kennedy, and the confirmation Rosa had been given by the police investigating her complaint that Jim Boyling was an undercover officer, we pointed to the extensive self-disclosure made by Bob Lambert, who, having been outed, had publicly apologized for deceiving Belinda. We referred to the evidence discovered by Helen and Alison through their own detective work, which had corroborated the identities of John Dines and Mark Jenner.

Three judges reconsidered our submissions in the AKJ case in October at the Court of Appeal in a two-day hearing of complex legal argument about the operation of RIPA and the question of the legality of the undercover police conduct in the matter of forming sexual relationships. Three weeks later, they handed down their judgment. They rejected our arguments regarding the IPT but allowed our appeal over the High Court claim. This meant that the AKJ women could now have their case on the common-law torts heard before they had to take their case through the IPT. With luck, this would enable them to catch up with the DIL group.

In March 2014, just a week before the DIL case hearing on NCND was due to take place, the home secretary, Theresa May, announced in Parliament that there was to be a public inquiry into undercover policing in England and Wales. My immediate reaction was to wonder how on earth a public inquiry was going to function when the police were so determined to keep everything about undercover policing, past and present, a secret. This decision had been triggered by the publication of a report by Mark Ellison QC into spying and corruption in the Stephen Lawrence case. Theresa May described the revelations in his report as 'profoundly shocking and disturbing', declaring that 'policing stands damaged today'.

On the eve of the hearing of their NCND application, I received a letter from the Met: 'In the light of the recent developments,' it read, 'the MPS have undertaken a review and concluded that it would no longer be reasonable or appropriate for the claims to be struck out.' They were withdrawing their application and proposed we vacate the hearing date. But we pressed for the hearing to go ahead in order to set a timetable to progress the case. Days later, in court, it became clear that the police were in fact still intending to maintain their stance that they could 'neither confirm nor deny' our claims.

We were perturbed as to where this would leave us. Having felt the response we had prepared was so well evidenced that the MPS application would not succeed, we'd been hopeful that we might be able to make a real dent in their assertion of NCND and get some answers.

Counsel came up with an ingenious idea. We would lodge an

application at court to strike out the police's defence to our claim, on the basis that they were not entitled to rely on NCND to escape a proper response to our particulars of claim. In support of our application, we used exactly the same evidence we had prepared to defend their strike-out bid.

The hearing was listed before Mr Justice Bean in the High Court. He held that the police could not rely on NCND in respect of Jim Boyling, because he had previously been confirmed as an undercover cop by the police themselves, or Bob Lambert, who had already extensively self-disclosed. But in spite of the wealth of evidence suggesting that Mark Jenner and John Dines were both undercover police officers, that fact had not previously been confirmed by the police, or by them as individuals, and therefore the police could continue to rely on NCND – although, the judge warned, 'that may only postpone the day of reckoning'. He ordered that the police now needed to serve an amended defence, properly pleading to the claims made in relation to Boyling and Lambert.

The amended defence contained the first indication of responsibility the police legal team had ever made in this case: confirmation that Jim Boyling and Bob Lambert had been in sexual relationships with three of my clients. However, shockingly, they claimed those relationships were based on 'mutual attraction and genuine personal feelings' and denied any liability for the abuse and damage caused. As expected, they refused to confirm that Dines and Jenner were undercover police officers.

Belinda was extremely upset at the suggestion that her relationship with 'Bob Robinson' had been based on 'mutual attraction and genuine feelings'.

How can a relationship be genuine when it is based on a massive web of lies? He pretended to be a man with noble ideals and political commitments, when in reality he was a police officer spying on our friendship network. He pretended he was committed to the future when he always knew he would go back to his real job and wife and kids. That doesn't show genuine feelings; it is abuse, and I would never have consented to such a relationship had I known. This relationship was a total violation of me and my life.

The police now served a second Part 36 offer to each of the DIL women. This time the financial offers were considerably higher, approaching an amount that we could not confidently advise we would beat if we went to court, and it was therefore possible that if they did not settle, our 'after-the-event' insurance would be invalidated.

We all sat down with counsel to discuss strategy. I had informed the police that the women weren't prepared to settle for money alone. Now, as well as making monetary offers, the police had indicated that they might consider an appropriate 'non-financial remedy'. I asked the women what their bottom line was. What was the minimum redress it would take for each of them to feel the case had a satisfactory resolution?

Helen found the Bean judgment as it stood, with the police still declining to confirm that John Dines and Mark Jenner were undercover cops, unacceptable. She was angry that the police had been allowed to hide behind NCND, especially when she and Alison had provided such extensive evidence of the relationships and real identities of these men. For her it was vital to challenge the police use of NCND in this way. As a minimum she wanted a written apology acknowledging what had happened, so that the police could no longer deny it, and a clear statement that such relationships should never be formed again. She was prepared to risk any financial offer to fight on.

Alison and Belinda wanted to carry on but felt they were not in a position to take financial risks. Belinda was keen to see the case in court if the insurance would permit it and Alison's priorities were to get official acknowledgement that Jenner was a police spy and recognition of a culture of institutionalized sexism within these undercover units.

Rosa, too, felt that until the police understood that what they had done was fundamentally wrong, there was no guarantee it wouldn't happen again.

'We need it in black and white that this caused me damage,' said Ruth. 'I need my sense of balance restored . . . an acknowledgement that what the state did is profoundly wrong.'

The AKJ women, Lisa, Kate and Naomi, had not yet, of course, received any Part 36 offers. We had to try to move forward while getting the two groups realigned into a single united entity. I suggested that, rather than responding specifically to the financial offers made by the police, we should propose a formal mediation of the claims in which we could explore both financial and non-financial remedies.

In October 2014, I engaged in 'without prejudice' correspondence with the police solicitor about how this would work. I stressed how important it was to our clients to get across to the police the massive impact the conduct of the undercover officers concerned had had on their lives. That what they felt was a common playing down of their experience as little different from being deceived by a philandering man missed the key point of the role the state had played in the deceit and its cover-up. Since one of their main aims in bringing this litigation was to ensure that such gross abuses would not be repeated in the future, they did not want an empty apology but for there to be understanding and a real commitment to bringing about change.

I also expressed the claimants' wish, since they had been working closely together on this case and seeking accountability more generally, for the mediation to be open to all eight of them, even though, for the present at least, financial resolutions would concern only five of the claimants.

To mediate we wanted someone with gravitas who would command the respect of both sides. I proposed Dame Janet Smith, a retired High Court judge. The three-day confidential mediation duly took place under the oversight of Dame Janet in central London. I had not been overly hopeful that we would be able to agree terms to which all eight women would be prepared to sign up. Amazingly, we did arrive at provisional consensus, though we had to wait until we could consider monetary compensation in the AKJ women's case to conclude the process. Further mediation meetings took place the following year and we finally reached an agreement for seven of the eight women, which included substantial financial settlements and the delivery of a fulsome and extensive apology.

In November 2015 we timed a press conference to coincide with the video-recorded delivery of the agreed public apology by Assistant Commissioner Martin Hewitt, resplendent in full uniform with its brass-plated epaulettes, who had been present at the mediation to listen to the women.

The Metropolitan Police has recently settled seven claims arising out of the totally unacceptable behaviour of a number of undercover police officers working for the now disbanded Special Demonstration Squad, an undercover unit within Special Branch that existed until 2008, and for the National Public Order Intelligence Unit, an undercover unit which was operational until 2011.

Thanks in large part to the courage and tenacity of these women in bringing these matters to light, it has become apparent that some officers, acting undercover whilst seeking to infiltrate protest groups, entered into long-term intimate sexual relationships with women which were abusive, deceitful, manipulative and wrong.

I acknowledge that these relationships were a violation of the women's human rights, an abuse of police power and caused significant trauma. I unreservedly apologize on behalf of the Metropolitan Police Service. I am aware that money alone cannot compensate the loss of time, their hurt or the feelings of abuse caused by these relationships . . .

I wish to make a number of matters absolutely clear.

Most importantly, relationships like these should never have happened. They were wrong and were a gross violation of personal dignity and integrity.

And let me add these points.

Firstly, none of the women with whom the undercover officers had a relationship brought it on themselves. They were deceived pure and simple. And I want to make it clear that the Metropolitan Police does not suggest that any of these women could in any way be criticized for the way in which these relationships developed.

Second, at the mediation process the women spoke of the way in which their privacy had been violated by these relationships. I entirely agree that it was a gross violation and I also accept that it may well have reflected attitudes towards women that should have no part in the culture of the Metropolitan Police.

Third, it is apparent that some officers may have preyed on the women's good nature and had manipulated their emotions to a gratuitous extent. This was distressing to hear about and must have been very hard to bear.

Fourth, I recognize that these relationships, the subsequent trauma and the secrecy around them left these women at risk of further abuse and deception by these officers after the deployment had ended.

Fifth, I recognize that these legal proceedings have been painful, distressing and intrusive and have added to the damage and distress. Let me make clear that whether or not genuine feelings were involved on the part of any officers is entirely irrelevant and does not make the conduct acceptable.

One of the concerns which the women strongly expressed was that they wished to ensure that such relationships would not happen in the future. They referred to the risks that children could be conceived through and into such relationships and I understand that.

These matters are already the subject of several investigations . . . Undercover policing is also now subject to a judge-led public inquiry which commenced [on 28 July 2015]. Even before those bodies report, I can state that sexual relationships between undercover police officers and members of the public should not happen. The forming of a sexual relationship by an undercover officer would never be authorized in advance nor indeed used as a tactic of a deployment. If an officer did have a sexual relationship despite this (for example if it was a matter of life or death) then he would be required to report this in order that the circumstances could be investigated for potential criminality and/or misconduct. I can say as a very senior officer of the Metropolitan Police Service that I and the Metropolitan Police are committed to ensuring that this policy is followed by every officer who is deployed in an undercover role.

Assistant Commissioner Hewitt went on to acknowledge failures of supervision and management and to recognize that the necessary steps must be taken to ensure this can never happen again. He concluded the lengthy apology by acknowledging that the women had conducted themselves throughout 'with integrity and absolute dignity'.

This was indeed a momentous apology and a momentous victory for seven of the women. But it was by no means the end of the struggle for justice. They still had not received any disclosure from the police about the extent to which their intimate relationships had been authorized, reported on and known about by others in the force, including more senior officers. Ultimately, the terms of the settlement reached meant that they would lose their insurance cover if they wanted to fight on.

One woman found herself in a different position. In 2010, when Kate Wilson discovered the truth about Mark Kennedy, she had been training to become a doctor. The impact on her was so profound that this exceptionally academically able medical student felt forced to abandon her training. It therefore cost her a potentially lucrative career, for which the financial offers now being made by the police came nowhere near compensating her. In these circumstances, we were able to advise the insurers to continue cover in her case.

Kate's prolonged battle did not produce the desired disclosure either, and a year later she settled her claim, and received the same apology, but by pure chance the police omitted to insert the clause which prohibited her continuing with the IPT claim, as had been required in Lisa and Naomi's case. This allowed Kate to pursue a human rights claim via the IPT which, ironically, and contrary to our original arguments, eventually yielded significant disclosure and a historic judgment which held that her rights under Articles 3, 8, 10, 11 and 14 ECHR were violated.

After the settlement of the civil claim, I was approached by more women who had been in relationships with UCOs – one of them, Monica, with Jim Boyling, before Ruth and Rosa. Rosa's separate complaint against Boyling had been rejected by the CPS. She brought a victim's right to review, but the decision was upheld on grounds that Rosa and the other women found highly offensive, in particular the argument of the CPS prosecutor that 'the relationship was entirely genuine'.

Monica had also made a formal police complaint about Boyling's conduct and when she received a similar decision from the CPS, we decided to bring a judicial review. Unfortunately, in a judgment led by the lord chief justice handed down in 2018, our challenge was dismissed and we were refused permission to appeal. However, the case remains of significance in respect of the thorny issue of in what circumstances deception vitiates consent to sex.

The public inquiry that began in the summer of 2015 into the role of the SDS and NPIOU, and undercover policing in general, spanning an era of more than half a century, was intended to take three years. At the time of writing, it is not expected to be completed until 2026.

Proceedings have been prolonged by legal challenges from the police, who, as I anticipated, have strongly resisted the inquiry being held in public and, as a result, only parts of it are. But the interim report, covering the years 1968–82, of chair Sir John Mitting, published in June 2023, was damning, with the retired judge expressing the view that the majority of the SDS operations were disproportionate and unlawful and the unit should have been disbanded back in the 1970s.

As the lid continues to be prised open on these covert units, questions about this state-sanctioned assault on democracy remain to be answered. It has emerged that the majority of the groups on which they spied, and on whose members they gathered vast amounts of private information – which included the women's liberation movement of the 1970s, anti-Apartheid campaigners and trade unionists, as well as black justice groups and even the Jean Charles de Menezes family campaign – were never linked to any serious crimes.

While there is still much ground to cover, through the inquiry process lawyers and core participants have already exposed the misogynistic and racist culture that took root in these undercover units in the 1970s and which have been seen to infect other elite police units in subsequent decades.

To date, more than fifty women are known to have been deceived into intimate relationships with men they were unaware were undercover officers, and some of the further stories that are beginning to come out are mind-blowing.

Not only is there still no specific law in place to prevent this happening again, but the position has been exacerbated with the adoption in 2021 of the Covert Human Intelligence Service (Criminal Conduct) Act – known as the 'Spycops Act' – which provides a statutory process for public bodies to authorize undercover operatives to engage in criminal activities, not excluding rape, murder and torture, with impunity.

Although the government claims there are safeguards inherent in the authorization procedure, they failed to publicize their consultation on the accompanying code of practice. That has left people like the women in this story in the dark as to whether their experiences informed any such consultation and unable to ensure that they do. This could mean that future victims of undercover cops would be denied the right to bring a claim for compensation.

7

Women Who Kill: The Case of Sally Challen

IN THE WAKE OF Emma Humphreys' successful appeal in 1995, Justice for Women has, over the years, received countless requests for help from women either facing trial for murder or, more often, already found guilty and in need of support to appeal their conviction. Since embarking on my career as a solicitor, I have remained involved with the campaign group and have taken on a dozen or so such cases.

The women I have represented are not typical of any demographic. The one common factor is that they are all victims of male violence and abuse. They are working-class and middle-class; black, Asian and white; as young as seventeen and as old as seventy-three. Most have a diagnosis of some sort of mental disorder, usually, at least in part, caused or exacerbated by the abuse to which they were subjected. Many have used alcohol as a coping mechanism. None has killed for any ulterior motive other than being driven by their circumstances to respond in a way that is rare for women. Perhaps because it is so out of the ordinary, and contrary to every stereotype associated with what it means to be a woman, they are judged extremely harshly, portrayed as mad or bad and seldom get a just outcome from the criminal justice system.

In the summer of 2011, I took a phone call from a corporate lawyer,

Dalla Jenney, who had heard about my work on such cases. Dalla was married to the nephew of Sally Challen, who had been recently convicted of the murder of her husband of over thirty years, Richard. Dalla said that the offence had come completely out of the blue and was a huge shock to the family as Sally had seemed totally devoted to Richard, despite the fact that he did not treat her well. She felt that Sally's defence team had failed to highlight Richard's abusive behaviour and that a conviction for murder seemed wrong.

News reports of the trial described Sally as a jealous wife who had bludgeoned her husband to death with a hammer because he was having an affair. She had then driven to Beachy Head, the notorious suicide spot near Eastbourne in Sussex, to jump off the cliff. She had confessed to the murder to two suicide prevention negotiators who coaxed her back from the edge. 'If I can't have him, no one can,' she said. This immediately rang alarm bells with me. It is a classic refrain of the jealous and possessive husband who kills his wife when she is about to leave him.

This was not, on the face of it, an obvious Justice for Women case. But after decades of campaigning and representing women who had killed their partners, I was very familiar with the typical narratives shaped by the prosecution and promoted by the media. They needed to find a motive for the murder, and jealousy or gold-digging are usually the clichés of choice. In Sally's case, they had plumped for obsessive jealousy. Far easier to tell that story and get the woman convicted than to explore the reality of a response to relentless abuse. There would, I knew, be another story lying behind the headlines. But what was it? How had a well-to-do, middle-aged Surrey housewife suddenly come to take such dramatic action? I told Dalla I was willing to see what I could do to help but I would need to receive instructions directly from Sally.

It was not until May 2012 that I heard from Sally. Apparently, a letter she had written to me several months previously had failed to find me. She said she fully accepted that she was responsible for the death of her husband, but felt that 'I was simply not in my right mind at the time of my offence (nor for some time after), having been stretched to my absolute limit over decades, culminating in what I thought was evidence of a final act of betrayal which pushed me over the edge'. She had since participated in the Freedom Programme, a domestic-violence awareness course run in some prisons. 'They could,' she declared, 'have been talking about my life.'

I arranged a legal visit at HMP Bronzefield in Ashford, Middlesex, a purpose-built women-only prison run by a privately contracted firm, Sodexo, which can accommodate over five hundred inmates. After subjecting myself to the depressingly familiar bureaucratic process of producing three types of ID, placing all electronic items in a locker, putting my bag through a scanner and being patted down by an officer, I was led through a number of locked doors to a private consultation room.

I really didn't know what to expect of this woman with such an unusual story. When Sally was brought in, she seemed small and withered, her countenance sorrowful. I knew that her defence at trial had been based on a diagnosis of a depressive disorder, but often this is not apparent on a first meeting. It certainly was in Sally's case. I was surprised by her cold, limp handshake. I sensed that this was a manifestation of what psychiatrists would term 'depressed affect' – persistent sadness, hopelessness and a lack of interest in your surroundings.

I began by trying to relax her a little, asking about the prison, how she was finding it, whether she had made any friends. None, she told me. She kept herself to herself. In the limited time we had, we discussed her case: what she thought had led her to pick up a hammer and repeatedly strike her husband over the head until he was dead; why she felt a jury may have convicted her of murder and rejected the only defence she had – diminished responsibility, which would have resulted in the lesser conviction of manslaughter. I explained that I would need to obtain her papers from the solicitors who represented her at trial to understand a little more about the case against her and the strategy of her defence team.

On the advice of her family, Sally had instructed Kingsley Napley, a well-known London firm who describe themselves as the 'leading criminal defence solicitors in the UK'. This was not going to be one of those cases of a poorly resourced local duty solicitor turning up at the police station and hastily putting together a badly prepared defence. Kingsley Napley would have offered a state-of-the-art service and were highly unlikely to have missed anything obvious. This would undoubtedly make my job of finding grounds for appeal much harder.

Appealing a criminal conviction from the Crown Court is not easy to start with. As we have seen, the grounds on which even permission to appeal will be granted are very limited: essentially, unless you can produce fresh evidence, it comes down to being able to demonstrate a legal error in the judge's ruling or summing-up, or some material irregularity during the trial process, such as a juror having been nobbled by associates of the defendant. For fresh evidence that may cast doubt on the safety of the conviction to be admitted, you need to provide a reasonable explanation as to why it was not put before the court at the original trial – for example, new DNA evidence exculpating the defendant that is only now available thanks to the advancement of scientific techniques.

Kingsley Napley quickly furnished me, on Sally's signed authority, with several boxes of lever arch files of papers, all carefully organized and indexed. There was no doubt that her legal team had done a lot of work. They had prepared colour-coded schedules of phone messages and emails, complex timelines, a 'state-of-mind' chronology and a lengthy proof of evidence – a detailed account from Sally on which the defence would have relied at trial.

There were folders of medical records and psychiatric reports, dozens of statements obtained by the police, four volumes of prosecution exhibits, reams of disclosure, including 'unused material' from the police and a box of matrimonial papers from the solicitor who had handled an aborted divorce. There were DVDs recording the interview Sally gave on her arrest, videos and photos from the crime scene, including images of Richard's body lying on the kitchen floor, covered in blood. There were files of correspondence with the solicitor and written advices from counsel and their draft submissions.

It was going to take me a long time to read all this. To enable me to get started, my brilliant paralegal assistant, Cassie, and I indexed all the papers and put together a core bundle of the key documents which, from my experience of criminal appeals, I knew I would need to get my head round.

Birnberg Peirce had recently installed video-link equipment, which meant I could conduct legal visits directly from our video-link room in the dingy basement of the office with Sally sitting in a cubicle at Bronzefield. This saved hours of travelling, not to mention navigating all the security barriers, and allowed me, through regular meetings over the course of two years, to explore Sally's history more thoroughly in an effort to understand why she had acted in the way she had and to try to pinpoint some detail that might open up a route to an appeal.

Sally was only a few years older than I was, we were both from comfortable middle-class backgrounds and we had grown up less than thirty miles away from one another. But there the similarities ended. Her memories of her upbringing evoked a picture of a bygone age.

Her father had been a brigadier in the Royal Engineers and was involved in the partition of India. Her maternal grandfather was 'some sort of commissioner' in India. Her mother was well-educated and well-read but hadn't been sent to university. 'Both my parents were brought up in that upper-middle-class, ex-pat way in India with lots of servants.' They had returned to England to live in Walton-on-Thames, where Sally was born in 1954. Sally's parents were a lot older than those of most of her contemporaries – she was a late baby and the only girl. Three elder brothers, who would progress to high-powered careers, were already in their teens and away at boarding school, and she had one younger adopted brother.

Their father died when Sally was only six and she had no memory of him. She was sent to private school but as her mother 'did not think it was the thing for girls to go on to study', she didn't do A-levels or go to university. 'She thought I should do secretarial training, get a job and then get married.'

Sally met Richard just before her sixteenth birthday in 1969. He was twenty-two.

> I was really attracted to him. As soon as we started going out, I was immediately besotted. Richard was very sure of himself, perhaps even a bit on the cocky side. In the early years, he seemed so sophis-ticated and fun to be with. We used to hang out on the King's Road or go out for a meal in Surbiton, or we'd go out for a coffee. We used to go to discos and meet up with friends. He used to pick me up from school and I felt very special having a boyfriend with a car.
>
> When my family met him, they looked down on him slightly. He wasn't quite 'our class of person'. The fact that my family looked down on him only drew me closer. He didn't like my family, be-cause he felt he wasn't good enough for them. He mostly talked about himself.

After gaining six O-levels, Sally was dispatched to a finishing school in Brussels 'to become polished in the French language and learn cooking, dressmaking and that sort of thing'. She was not to discover until very recently that, in fact, this was an attempt by her family to get her away from Richard. But putting distance between them failed to break up the relationship, which had quickly become sexual. 'We used to drive into a car park and find a quiet spot. I was desperate to please Richard and felt that if I didn't fully please him he would leave me . . . I had never discussed sex with my mother, anything that I knew about sex was through my friends. I left the responsibility for contraception to Richard.'

It wasn't long before Sally became pregnant. Richard was horrified. Sally's mother arranged an appointment with a private doctor. 'The termination was quite traumatic. I had to be cut open as I was already eighteen or nineteen weeks' pregnant.' Her brothers were furious with Richard. 'They told him he should have taken responsibility. Richard was really pissed off that my brothers had had a go at him.'

Richard blamed Sally and refused to see her for a few weeks. By the time the relationship resumed, he had moved out of his family home and into his own flat. When Sally went round, she would cook and clean for him.

> I was never actually allowed to stay overnight. We used to have sex and then he would push me out and tell me that he wanted his own bed and I should go back home.
>
> When I was about eighteen or nineteen, I began to think that Richard was seeing another woman, but I didn't feel I could ask him about it. Eventually it became so obvious he was seeing her that I confronted him. He was angry and said, 'Don't make me choose, because I will choose her.' I started sobbing hysterically and he told me to leave, but I didn't want to go, so he dragged me down the stairs and pushed me out of the front door.

Sally took an overdose of aspirin and ended up in hospital. She was soon back with Richard but, increasingly, their relationship was conducted on his terms.

As Richard saw things, it was, it seemed, fine for him to date other girls, whereas he required Sally to devote herself to him alone. 'I remember an occasion when Richard was really angry that I had gone on an evening out with one of my cousins. He didn't want me to have any friends or do anything sociable apart from when I went out with him.'

With hindsight, she realized that he enjoyed having 'a plaything' who was totally subservient to him; someone who would come running whenever he snapped his fingers.

Although it was mystifying to me what made Sally want to settle down with such a man, I needed to try to understand what bound her to him. 'Richard was very charming and he could make me laugh,' she explained. 'He was very outgoing . . . a bit flash. People used to say he could charm the birds off the trees. He made me feel very special and made me feel loved. I also felt very safe with him and that he would look after me.'

In 1974, they spent some time in Australia, where Richard's brother had emigrated. Sally remembered this as a happy interlude, when they were able to live together and Richard was 'not distracted by other women'. But when they came home, Sally went back to her mother's house and he returned to his flat and his bachelor lifestyle, until they eventually married, in 1979.

Richard then became even more domineering and undermining. He didn't allow Sally to have her own friends and disparaged her appearance in front of others, often remarking that she looked fat. 'If I lost weight he would say I still had a long way to go. I never felt that I was completely right, even when I got really slim. If he saw a pretty woman on the television, he would always make a comment and he would eye up women in public. I felt very humiliated by that.'

Sally did all the domestic chores. 'I always felt that it was my place. Richard had always had everything done for him by his mother.' As the product of an upbringing geared to meeting a man and marrying him, 'that was very much the way I expected my life to be'.

Despite Richard's lack of enthusiasm for parenthood, they had two sons, James and David. 'Richard didn't like me being pregnant and he complained that I changed when I became a mother. I believe he was unhappy that my attention wasn't focused on him a hundred per cent. Richard never helped with the boys as babies.' David would later describe her as 'loving, kind, accepting, everything you'd want in a mother'. When he was about thirteen, she got an office job with the Police Federation and he would recall that, from then on, she was expected to pay all the household expenses out of her wages.

Although Sally, unlike other clients I had represented who had killed their partners, had not been subjected to a sustained campaign of physical violence, I was well aware that physical violence is only one facet of domestic abuse. Through my feminist connections with specialists working in the domestic violence (DV) sector, I became aware of the development of a new tool known as the 'power and control wheel', which represented diagrammatically the multiple tactics an abuser might use to achieve the subservience of his partner. In addition to physical violence, other typical components of a DV relationship include sexual violence, emotional and psychological abuse, financial abuse and the use of children, isolation tactics, minimizing, denying and blaming and male privilege. This was a big help as I delved with Sally into the dynamics of her relationship with Richard.

From early in our conversations, it was clear that Richard ticked most of the boxes on the power and control wheel. Since her teens, Sally had not been allowed a separate life or friendships. He didn't like her visiting her family, or friends or relatives coming to the house. He accused her of being disloyal if she engaged with anyone other than him. He kept control of the purse strings. She told me that she would never voice her opinions and he was never loving towards her in public.

'I didn't question him,' she said. 'Sometimes I got very upset, but I was always terrified he would leave me.'

Richard, later described to me by his friend Willie Noble as a 'fellow petrolhead', had his own car dealership, Westlake Garages. He was into fast cars, Formula 1 racing and treated himself to a Ferrari. 'Richard would always say, "I earn the money, I sell the cars – you do the rest,"' Sally told me. In the 1980s she inherited some money from an aunt and he wanted to invest it in his business to build up the stock. He then started getting Sally to do the books and she 'became aware that he was behaving in a fraudulent and criminal way. Sometimes he would make me do things I didn't want to do.' When he was investigated for an insurance fraud in relation to his Ferrari after crashing it on a racing circuit, he blamed Sally for not getting full insurance cover.

'In around 2003 or 2004, Richard had photographs taken of himself with his Ferrari and two naked busty models sitting on either side of him,' Sally recalled. 'He felt very proud of it and had the picture blown up, framed and put on display in the sitting room. He had Christmas cards made with it. He thought it was brilliant. That was humiliating.'

I had seen that picture. It was in the exhibits folder of the prosecution case. If any single image could encapsulate the provocation Sally had lived with year after year, I thought, this was it.

One element of abuse that often remains hidden at trial is sexual violation and humiliation, particularly when a woman charged with murdering her partner is represented by a male legal team. The sense of shame may discourage her from speaking out about it in detail. And yet it can hold the key to understanding the abuse and her ultimate response to it. Was there anything here that would help with grounds for appeal?

Sally said that sex, like every other aspect of their relationship, was always on Richard's terms. He would expect her to give him oral sex, for example, but never reciprocated. She invariably did what he wanted and never initiated sex.

She told me how, in 1998, they had gone to the US on holiday and stayed with Richard's old friend Del, who had been his best man at their wedding, in Los Angeles. 'One evening Del grabbed me and kissed me. Richard saw this and went completely mad, and when we went upstairs, he punished me by forcing anal sex on me. It was rape.'

After the Del incident, Richard became more sadistic towards Sally in the bedroom. He would make her do certain things to punish her. Sometimes he decided he wanted anal sex. He would also use pornography and sex toys.

'I didn't resist, I just let him do it. But it would have been clear that I didn't want it.'

Richard's treatment of Sally was becoming intolerable. Eventually she confided in her cousin Noel, who recommended she speak to a divorce solicitor. The solicitor wrote to Richard, whose response was simply to tear up the letter. 'He said to James, "Do you want to live in a hovel with your mother or stay here?" He told me he would not divorce me, but if I [divorced him], I would get nothing. He refused to answer the solicitor's letter and, in the end, I gave up.'

Richard was still seeing other women, although if Sally challenged him about it, he denied it point blank. He 'sometimes made me feel as though I was crazy, because I couldn't get an answer out of him. He often said I was paranoid or mad if I ever questioned him about anything, even when it was obvious.'

Then she discovered that he was using prostitutes. She followed him to a massage parlour in their local town. 'I actually waited outside, and when he came out, I confronted him and started shouting and yelling. Richard denied it all, although eventually he had to confess that he had been there. I felt really devastated by that. I'd done everything for him – cooking, cleaning, being his dutiful wife.' The fact that the massage parlour was only a few doors away from the office where Sally worked added insult to injury. It seemed to her that he was deliberately rubbing her nose in it.

Not long after this incident, she learned from a local TV news report on a prostitution ring that this massage parlour had been staffed by victims of sex trafficking. Sally lost it then, and dialled 999. The recording of her hysterical phone call would be played at her murder trial. She had been drunk and full of rage when she made it, and the recording didn't do her any favours, undermining the picture her defence were painting of a meek, subservient housewife.

By 2009 the marriage had become untenable. Sally's younger son, David, was by this time twenty-three and going through a breakdown. James had left to live with his girlfriend. Sally used an inheritance from her mother, who had died a few years earlier, to buy a house locally and moved out of the family home with David. Richard asked her not to leave, but he didn't beg her to stay.

And yet, having mustered the considerable courage it must have taken to break free, Sally floundered. She was simply not used to living outside Richard's control and, desperately unhappy, was starting to give up on living at all. 'I just felt I could not cope on my own and I wanted Richard back at virtually any cost.'

She sent him an email: 'I want to be with you, I am sorry I left. We are soulmates, we have been together so long, I can't see a future without you. You are my life. I love you.' He replied imposing conditions on any reconciliation, at the same time insisting that she proceed with the divorce she had instigated.

Sally, it has been a difficult time since you left me, a choice you made without discussing with me, after 30 years of marriage, I think I deserved more . . . Now you want to destroy me by taking half my money and my livelihood and business away from me . . . I will consider your return only on these terms. You will continue and complete the divorce with a £200,000 settlement. That when we go out together it means together. This constant talking to strangers is rude and inconsiderate. We will agree to items in the home together. To give up smoking. To give up your constant interruptions when I am speaking.

So great was Sally's anguish that she promised to abide by these unconscionable terms. In return, he apparently agreed that they would see each other once a week, while he assessed whether 'she had changed'.

I found it very hard to understand why Sally, having managed to extricate herself and her son from this toxic domestic set-up, would once more subjugate herself so completely to her abuser. She would stop and start the divorce at least five times during their separation. Her divorce solicitor said he had never seen anything like it.

Richard's views on how their property should be divided were perhaps predictable. He told Sally she wouldn't get any of Westlake Garages because it was his business, or an equal share of the house, because he had paid the mortgage. 'He wouldn't recognize all the help I had given him over the years. It was as though I had not contributed to the marriage at all.'

Richard then came up with the idea of a post-nuptial agreement, again drawn up very much in his favour, rather than a divorce. Sally believed this was a tactic to ensure that she wouldn't try to divorce him again. 'I could see that ... but I didn't really care, I just felt so desperate.'

At the original criminal trial, Sally had been portrayed as obsessively jealous. Copious evidence was produced to show that she was spying on Richard. She had asked her neighbours to report on his movements and she tried to log into his computer when he was out so that she could find out who he was seeing. Such behaviour might

be characterized as stalking and supported the prosecution narrative. Sally tried to explain it to me.

> Seeing Richard again gave me some hope but I was on tenter-
> hooks when I was with him, frightened that if I said something or
> did something that might upset him, it would all fall away. In
> retrospect, I think Richard was toying with me. He wanted me to
> believe that we would be together so that I would sign the post-
> nuptial agreement and stop the divorce. My mind was in turmoil;
> I was desperate to believe that Richard wanted to be with me, and
> I was terrified to confront the possibility that he was going to
> drop me in it. I was clinging on to the idea that he wouldn't do
> such a thing to me.

I guided Sally through what happened in the weeks, days, hours,
minutes and seconds that led her to pick up a hammer and rain
repeated blows on the head of the man she still insisted she loved.

By August 2010, it seems that Richard had proposed renting out
the family home while they made a fresh start with a trip to Australia
for a few months. 'We began emptying the family home and storing
things in mine. I noticed that he was only storing old things at my
house that he wouldn't need, and I had a feeling he was setting me up
for a fall.'

She was suspicious of why Richard was in such a rush for her to go
to a lawyer and get the post-nuptial agreement signed. She recalled
Willie Noble urging her: 'Don't sign it, don't go back to him. He will
ruin your life.'

> Willie knew that Richard was seeing prostitutes and other women.
> I realize now that Richard didn't actually want to get back together.
> I realize that now, but I'm not sure if I knew it at the time . . . He

was all I knew, and he was my life since the age of sixteen. It was like losing a part of me. I could not imagine existing without him.

On Saturday 14 August 2010, Sally went to the family home to continue clearing the house ahead of the planned trip to Australia. 'It was pouring with rain. Richard said he wanted something to eat and was insistent that I go out to buy some bacon and eggs from the supermarket.'

When Sally returned, she noticed that the portable phone handset was sitting on the sofa. It hadn't been there before. She immediately suspected that Richard had wanted her out of the house so that he could ring the woman she knew he was seeing. The last number dialled displayed on the handset confirmed it.

Then I asked him, 'Am I going to see you tomorrow?' He responded angrily, 'Don't question me, don't question me.' It felt as though this was never going to stop and he would never have me back. I was anxious and distraught. Something flipped inside my head. That was when I picked up the hammer and hit him on the head repeatedly. I don't know why I did it. I don't know why I had the hammer in my bag. I don't actually remember putting the hammer in my bag, but I accept I must have done. I couldn't stop hitting him. I think I took him by surprise.

After Sally had killed Richard, she was, she said, 'on autopilot'. She covered him with some old curtains and then went upstairs and changed her clothes. Mechanically, she washed the dishes. 'I got a piece of paper and wrote "I love you" on it. I left it on Richard's body.'

Then she went back to her own house, resolved to throw herself off the top of the Marks & Spencer car park in Kingston. She typed out a note for David. Then she remembered that Richard had always said if he ever lost his mind, he wanted to be strapped to his motorbike and pushed off Beachy Head. Sally decided instead to drive there the next day, after dropping David at work, and to jump off the clifftop.

'I felt this wasn't happening. I don't think I thought about what had happened. I just thought I wasn't going to be around much longer. I wasn't panicking: I was calm, because I was going to be with Richard again.'

On the way to Beachy Head she called her cousin Noel to tell her what she was doing. Her sons needed to know and she didn't want them walking into the family home and discovering their father dead on the floor. Noel alerted the police.

When Sally got to Beachy Head and walked towards the cliff edge, she was greeted by a police officer and a chaplain, with whom she talked for a couple of hours. 'One of them said to me, "What about your sons?" That's what made me agree to come back from the edge. Up until then, I'd felt like an utterly worthless person and I didn't want to live. I somehow just hadn't considered the boys. I hadn't thought about them when I killed Richard, or when I was going to jump.'

After hours spent listening to Sally's account and trying to make sense of her actions, what ammunition did I have? There was no question that Richard was a deeply selfish man who had no respect for Sally. To say that he treated her as a doormat would be a massive understatement. He was an archetypal male chauvinist pig. Many of the witness statements obtained by the police and used at trial confirmed this impression. His behaviour towards her was undoubtedly a form of cumulative provocation, but could it really provide a rationale for her extreme response?

At her trial in June 2011, her defence team called a psychiatrist, Dr

Tim Exworthy, who had spent several hours with Sally considering her state of mind at the time of the offence. He concluded in his report that she had suffered periods of depression and there was evidence to show that she was suffering from a depressive disorder when she killed Richard. He went on to say that this diagnosis was capable of and, in his opinion, did 'substantially diminish her responsibility' for the offence. If the jury had accepted his opinion, they would have concluded that Sally was guilty of the lesser offence of manslaughter, not murder.

But it seems they preferred the view of the psychiatrist instructed by the CPS, Dr Paul Gilluley. While he could see that there were occasions when Sally had suffered symptoms of depression, he noted that at the time of the offence she was still holding down a job and concluded that she did not meet the criteria for a diagnosis of depressive disorder. In his opinion, her actions were motivated by anger when she discovered Richard was seeing another woman.

The jury took several days to consider the evidence, including the competing psychiatric explanations. Ultimately, they came back with a majority verdict finding Sally guilty of murder. There was one juror who disagreed.

I pored over Sally's account of what had happened after she was arrested, how she felt her defence team approached the case and what she thought the jury made of her.

When I was interviewed by the police, I felt like I was talking at a hundred miles per hour. At some point during the questioning, I realized the enormity of what I'd done. Everything seemed surreal, as though it wasn't actually happening to me.

Two to three months before the trial I lost masses of weight and dropped to rock bottom. I felt as though contact with my solicitors tailed off as the case went on . . . I can barely remember [the trial] . . . I hardly bothered. When asked questions, I responded, 'I suppose.' I felt flat and disconnected emotionally. Both my sons felt that there were things that they wanted to say but weren't questioned about in evidence.

James and David had provided detailed statements to the police and were called as witnesses for the prosecution at trial. Despite their mother having just killed their father, their continued support of their mother was conspicuous. James said in his statement: 'I just can't believe this has happened. It is so unlike my mum to do anything like that. She is not violent at all . . . I disliked his character, but it's hard to hate him – he's my dad.' David had told the police: 'I am very shocked at what has happened. I feel angry at my dad for pushing her so much.'

David contacted me quite early on to see whether and how he could help. A young gay man, he was, understandably, given the environment in which he had grown up, quite tortured. I was surprised by the degree of anger he expressed towards his dad and his forgiveness of his mum.

I always felt there was something wrong with my dad. I felt he was a 'bad apple'. He had no interest in me. He used to make my mother think she was going insane. He wanted complete control. He didn't care about us, he just wanted to do what he wanted. He didn't respect my mum in any way. If my mum ever confronted him about anything, he would just say, 'It's a man thing.' My impression was he was deliberately sending her round the bend and was manipulating her almost for the fun of it.

I feel that he constructed the whole situation and pushed my mother around her whole life. I think he was deliberately destroying her and she was desperately trying to hold the family together. My mother's life was totally constructed around Richard and she was pushed to the limit.

I asked him about the trial. He was frustrated that he hadn't had the opportunity to explain when he gave evidence more about the dynamic of his parents' relationship and how it impacted on his mum. He also had questions about the tactics of the legal team and their policy 'not to speak ill of the dead'. 'They made a decision to focus on her state of mind, but only from 2004 onwards. I felt they really needed to look at her in the context of the whole period of her life because she was so moulded by my father.'

During my video-link consultations with Sally, she frequently told me she missed Richard, still loved him and thought about him all the time, every night. It seemed as though her own sense of identity was completely dependent on and defined by him. She literally couldn't conceive of herself as separate from Richard. David strongly corroborated this impression.

While this interpretation of Sally's state of mind at the time of the offence provided an explanation of sorts, it did not open up any avenues to appeal her conviction. I spent hours scratching my head, researching the law and chewing it over with colleagues, members of Justice for Women and others. I feared this was a case I was not going to be able to crack, but I wasn't ready to give up. I kept in touch with Sally and spoke to a counsellor she was seeing in prison, who was also convinced that her murder conviction was too harsh.

When I'd first started talking to Sally, she was very low and I found it difficult to relate to a woman whose life choices and ambitions were so different from mine. But gradually we connected, a warmth began to permeate our meetings and we laughed about things. We discovered we both enjoyed Zumba. Sally was going to classes every day in the prison when she could. I started to notice a marked shift in her demeanour. She seemed to be very 'high', talking at speed and sometimes speaking nonsensically. She took to sending me reams of notes about her relationship with Richard. She was aware herself of this change in mood and spoke to prison healthcare about it. The prison psychiatrist prescribed medication to calm her down, including a mood-stabilizer.

I had picked up on references in some of the statements on file to similar behaviour by Sally in the months leading up to the killing. Her friend Sarah Noble said she thought Sally had bipolar disorder. Her divorce solicitor remarked specifically on her manner when he first met her, describing her as 'excitable'. In the police interview after her arrest, she spoke, as she herself remembered, in an almost uninterrupted stream-of-consciousness torrent. Might these have been indications of an as yet undiagnosed problem that had slipped through the net at the time of the trial which could strengthen Sally's defence of diminished responsibility?

I decided to instruct Dr Gwen Adshead, a highly respected consultant forensic psychiatrist, to produce a new report. Dr Adshead had considerable experience of both male and female perpetrators of domestic homicide and other forms of intimate partner violence, as well as significant expertise in trauma and the diagnosis and treatment of personality disorders.

After visiting Sally in May 2015, Dr Adshead concluded that Sally

> suffers from a personality disorder of moderate clinical severity, and has had symptoms of a severe clinical mood disorder: most probably bipolar affective disorder . . . People with personality disorders characterized by dependence and self-defeating traits tend to efface themselves and rely entirely on others, allowing those others to exercise dominance and control, even if this makes them unhappy.

These diagnoses amounted to an 'abnormality of the mind', a criterion of the diminished responsibility test, and they were relevant to the dynamic of Sally's relationship with her husband and the state of mind she reached at the time of the offence.

Dr Adshead's opinion was going to be helpful in formulating grounds of appeal, but I wasn't sure this would be enough. As I pondered her report, another possible path began to suggest itself: legislation was being debated in Parliament to introduce a new offence of coercive and controlling behaviour.

This concept had been developed by an American professor of social work, Evan Stark, in his seminal text *Coercive Control: How Men Entrap Women in Personal Life*. The theory had coalesced around frustrations with a criminal and family justice response to domestic abuse which focused primarily on individual incidents of physical violence and did not reflect the reality that an abuser will use a range of tactics to subjugate his partner. The definition of coercive control as set out by Professor Stark was explicitly political. It recognized structural inequality between men and women and that this bespoke form of abuse was less about a series of incidents and more about trapping the victim in a relationship and removing her humanity and autonomy. This specific formulation seemed a much closer fit with the experience of Sally Challen.

Theresa May, the home secretary, was very committed to improving the government response to domestic abuse and supported the proposals to introduce a new offence of coercive and controlling behaviour (CCB) as an amendment to the Serious Crime Act. This was duly passed into law in November 2015.

Although coercive control was familiar to specialist practitioners working in the field, beyond that it was an unknown concept to most people, including a majority of the legal profession. This was set to change with the arrival of the new legislation. Of itself, CCB was not a defence to murder, but I thought the new criminal offence was something we might be able to use, perhaps to construct an argument along the lines that this advance in our understanding of domestic abuse constituted a form of fresh evidence which would meet the stringent Court of Appeal test. Essentially, we could assert that coercive control represented a new framework for interpreting the dynamics of an abusive relationship. It was like placing a powerful new lens in front of the existing facts and everything suddenly becoming clear.

I discussed this idea with Clare Wade, a fellow member of Justice for Women and a barrister with whom I had worked on previous criminal appeals. She agreed that it might give us an opening. We could demonstrate how the evidence that Sally had been subject to CCB was already present, and that there was a 'reasonable explanation' as to why this context had not been advanced at trial: namely that coercive control was not a behaviour that was widely understood in 2011.

We decided to bring in an expert to advise us. Davina James-Hanman was the obvious choice and happy to help. It was Davina who had first made me aware of coercive control. She had worked with Evan Stark to educate policy-makers and been involved in bringing about the new legislation. A tireless advocate for victims of domestic abuse, with an expert grasp of policy and implementation, she trained senior police officers, advised the Home Office, was the specialist adviser on DV to the mayor of London and, most importantly, understood the experience of survivors.

Davina identified many of the features of coercive and controlling behaviour in the relationship between Richard and Sally. She also helpfully indicated that Sally's obsessive spying behaviour might be interpreted less as stalking and more as a form of reality-checking in an individual who was being gaslit by her partner.

We went back to Tim Exworthy, the psychiatrist who had assessed Sally for the previous defence team, to explore whether this new evidence might have affected his conclusions. He told us that it would. The concept of coercive control, he said, offered a clear, overarching framework for various possible manifestations of abusive behaviour.

'In addition, it provides a mechanism as to how the effects of abuse are cumulative rather than specific to a particular incident.' He also considered, and agreed with, Dr Adshead's diagnosis. He felt the new evidence, in combination, helped to explain why Sally had stayed in the relationship and thought this new understanding opened a door to the defence of provocation as well as strengthening the diminished responsibility argument.

With these new reports, I formally instructed Clare Wade to draft grounds of appeal and an application for permission to appeal out of time. These were lodged at the Court of Appeal in December 2016.

David Challen was very taken with Davina's report and impressed by the argument we were putting forward. It felt, he told me, as if suddenly there was a language to describe the atmosphere in which he had grown up.

Serendipitously, at around this time, the issue of coercive control was being aired in a slow-burning storyline on *The Archers*, the BBC's long-running and much-loved radio soap, which had culminated in the character of Helen stabbing her husband Rob and being charged with attempted murder. The media coverage and climate of general public discussion around coercive control provided a useful backdrop to Sally's case.

I was feeling hopeful of our chances until I heard that the papers had been allocated to a single judge, Mr Justice William Davis, not known for his sympathy towards women. In June 2017, he refused us permission to appeal, suggesting that Davina James-Hanman was not a proper witness and that we were simply 'expert shopping some years after the event'. It was a crushing blow for Sally, who had recently been moved from HMP Bronzefield, where she had built up some support and friendships, to HMP Send. She had found the move unsettling and her mood dipped significantly.

We had one final opportunity to renew our application before the full court. This would involve a short oral hearing with three judges. There was no question that we were going to take it.

As we prepared for Sally's last chance to appeal, Justice for Women looked at ways to step up their campaign. Once we had a date for the hearing, I put Fiona Hamilton, crime editor of *The Times*, who was interested in writing about the case, in touch with David, who was very eager to do what he could to support his mum. Fiona's news story – run under the eye-catching headline 'MY MUM MURDERED MY DAD. IT WAS HIS FAULT' – was published on 17 February 2018, drawing on her interview with David, who described the extreme controlling behaviour to which his mother had been subjected. By the time of the renewed hearing two weeks later, considerable media interest had been galvanized.

On 1 March, as Justice for Women campaigners stood with their placards in the snow outside the Court of Appeal, Clare set out the case in brief. The trio of judges appeared interested in the arguments made regarding the relevance of coercive control. Lady Justice Rafferty, in her short judgment, granted Sally permission to appeal, noting: 'It should be plainly understood that the application today is but one step in what it is hoped might be a full, detailed exploration of the position based on scholarship, learning and clinical expertise which should now assist a jury to reach a verdict on the basis of an understanding which, it is said, was not available in 2011.'

The judges had made clear that we needed a more academic, peer-reviewed expert in place of Davina. When I received an unsolicited email from Evan Stark in the US, asking how he could help, I was thrilled. If there was any expert who could meet the stringent requirements of the court, the professor emeritus at Rutgers University, widely acknowledged as the world's leading academic authority on coercive control, was the one.

Professor Stark lived in Woodbridge, Connecticut, where news of our appeal had reached him. He was, I estimated, in his seventies and had recently suffered a stroke which had left him with a slight speech impediment. We connected by Skype.

He asked me to tell him about the defences we had explored and then questioned why this wasn't a case of self-defence. 'But she was not responding to any attack or threat of violence when she attacked her husband,' I responded, not sure whether he was kidding.

'Did she not face an existential threat?' he said. I was to discover that Evan approached issues from left field and also had a cheeky sense of humour.

He agreed to write a report. Would he be able to do this without meeting Sally? Video-link was now not available to us as HMP Send, infuriatingly, didn't have the equipment. As Evan lived in the USA, we decided he would work from the papers and provide me with any additional questions or clarifications he needed, which I would check with Sally.

Clare Wade, by this time a QC, and her experienced junior, Lucie Wibberley, began amassing and absorbing the growing literature on coercive and controlling behaviour and moulding an argument that would combine it with the psychiatric evidence on which we would have to rely if we were going to persuade the Court of Appeal to overturn the conviction.

In his report, Professor Stark explained coercive control:

Abusers deploy a broad range of non-consensual, non-reciprocal tactics over an extended period to subjugate or dominate a partner, rather than merely to hurt them physically. Compliance is achieved by making victims afraid and denying basic rights, resources and liberties without which they are unable to effectively refuse, resist or escape demands that militate against their interests.

Like Sally Challen, many abuse victims profess love for the persons who are hurting them, hoping against mounting odds that the abuse will end but not the relationship.

Applying the theory to the facts of the case of Sally Challen, he cited statements and other sources of evidence, concluding:

SC returned to the home apparently willing to accept RC's terms for their reconciliation, however unfair and self-serving these were. She had been dependent before; the arrangement to which she was agreeing would merely further erode her rightful claims to their joint properties. What she had not considered were the psychological costs entailed when he not only confronted her with a new deceit, but demanded she not question him about it; that she would not be allowed to 'know what she knew'. To SC, at that moment, having to choose between being 'safe' and 'accepted' and being a 'nobody' (a person who doesn't know their own reality) threatened her survival. When she struck, it was against the gigantic imago of RC she carried into the kitchen and with the cumulative rage of thirty years of hurt.

One problem we felt we needed to forestall was the fact that Evan Stark's pioneering book had been published in 2007, over three years before Sally's original trial, when our grounds relied on the argument that the understanding of coercive control was effectively fresh evidence which had not been available in 2011. Of course, a book published in the United States did not of itself constitute evidence of a wider appreciation of the subject on this side of the Atlantic, and it had not been until 2015 that the offence of CCB was passed into law in the UK, but to bolster our argument I instructed Professor Marianne Hester to submit a report setting out how, and the extent to which, coercive control had been promulgated in academic, social and legal circles in the UK over the previous seven years.

The appeal was eventually fixed for a date almost exactly a year after the hearing where we had been granted permission. To my consternation, this fell at the end of a long-planned winter holiday in the Caribbean. I felt I had no choice but to cancel the holiday. The case was just too big to miss.

So, instead of lying on a beach sipping cocktails, I spent much of February reviewing final skeleton arguments, visiting Sally in prison and arranging conferences with experts, including Evan Stark, who had flown over from the United States to give evidence in court.

The first day of the appeal was eventful. It was heard by Lady Justice Hallett, vice-president of the Queen's Bench Division, Mr Justice Sweeney and Mrs Justice Cheema-Grubb in a courtroom jammed with supporters and press. The Court of Appeal had recently introduced televised hearings for selected cases and this was one of them. During the morning session, as messages reached Lady Justice Hallett that many members of the public had travelled some distance to attend and could not get into the courtroom, she asked her clerks to investigate whether a larger one was available.

We had arranged for all our expert witnesses to be present. But Dr Gwen Adshead was nowhere to be seen and her phone was going to voicemail. I set my two paralegals, Zizi and Hattie, the task of trying to get hold of her by any means necessary. Sally would be attending by video-link (my request for her to be brought to court having been refused), which meant she'd had to be taken to HMP Bronzefield, where they had the facilities. Lucie and I spoke to her from a small room along the court corridors before the hearing began. Although nervous, she was reasonably calm.

The judges made it clear that they had read all the reports and any evidence should be limited to highlighting particular points. Evan Stark was first into the witness box. The judges said they did not want to hear from him regarding how the theory of coercive control applied to Sally Challen and questioned whether his evidence was admissible. But his testimony gave us the opportunity to clearly set out the context for what was to follow.

Caroline Carberry QC, appearing for the Crown, had prosecuted Sally at the original trial and was seeking to uphold her conviction. In cross-examination she attempted to discredit the expertise of Professor Stark by pointing out that he was not medically qualified and hadn't assessed Sally in person. The judges eventually stopped her on the basis that her cross-examination was not necessary as he was not giving evidence on Sally's state of mind.

With Dr Adshead still AWOL, we called Dr Exworthy, who explained that when he assessed Sally before the trial, he had not been aware of any hypomanic episodes but rather assessed her as clinically depressed. Bipolar disorder had only come to light through the two manic episodes Sally had experienced and been treated for since she was in prison. When asked to consider if some of the evidence available at the time of the trial might have indicated that Sally had been suffering from a manic episode in the lead-up to the offence, he agreed that, in retrospect, her behaviour was consistent with that.

By lunchtime the clerk had arranged for us to move to the more capacious lord chief justice's courtroom to accommodate more members of the public and press, and Zizi had managed to track down Dr Adshead at one of the hospitals where she worked. There had been a muddle about dates, but she was now rushing to get to the court before the afternoon session began.

With Dr Adshead still en route when the hearing resumed at 2 p.m., the judges decided that they should hear from the prosecution psychiatrist first. As it turned out, this was to work in our favour.

At the original trial, Dr Gilluley had considered that, while Sally had some depressive symptoms, she did not meet the criteria for clinical depression as she had been able to hold down a job. When he was asked by Ms Carberry whether, in light of the new evidence and

Dr Adshead's diagnosis, he still held the view that Sally was not suffering from any mental disorder, Clare got up to complain that this was the first time we were hearing his evidence and he had not provided a report in advance, as he should have done.

In the meantime, there was a dramatic commotion in the public gallery behind me. An elderly member of the public – one of Sally's sisters-in-law, it transpired – had passed out. The court was cleared. Fortunately, after lying down for a bit, she recovered and everyone trooped back.

Clare started her cross-examination by drawing Dr Gilluley's attention to Sally's medical records and the manic episodes that had required treatment with medication. He suggested that they had been caused by her incarceration and insisted there was no indication that she was suffering from either bipolar or a dependent personality disorder prior to the offence. He claimed that Sally had only suffered two very brief episodes of manic depression. In fact, as Lady Justice Hallett pointed out to him, the medical records showed that each episode had lasted several months.

I was enjoying the way things were going. At last, Dr Adshead arrived, and she was able to explain how the coercive and controlling behaviour impacted on Sally's pre-existing mental disorder, with the latter determining how she responded to the former. The judges were beginning to appreciate how interconnected Sally's diagnosis was with the history of abuse and were clearly impressed by Dr Adshead's evidence.

By the end of the day, I sensed the judges were leaning towards quashing the murder conviction. But the danger that they might order a retrial, rather than reducing it to manslaughter, which would ensure Sally's freedom because of the time she had already served, filled me with some dread.

With all the expert witnesses heard, day two would be about the legal arguments. The following morning Clare tackled the pertinence of coercive control and how it needed be understood as a whole series of behaviours which, taken together, amounted to a significant form of abuse, often tailored by the perpetrator to exploit the victim's individual weaknesses. This was how the psychiatric diagnosis became relevant.

Clare fielded a series of questions and interruptions from the judges on why we wanted to admit the evidence on coercive control when we already had evidence of psychiatric harm. As Lady Justice Hallett disappeared down the rabbit hole of suggesting that 'battered women's syndrome' was about physical violence and coercive control about psychological violence, I passed Clare a note asking her to clarify that this was not correct.

But the course the judges' questioning was taking reinforced my hopes that they were going to allow the appeal.

Caroline Carberry now endeavoured to undo the damage to her case and reverse the direction of travel. She challenged the psychiatric diagnosis made five years after the offence and pointed to evidence that, at the time, Sally was functioning well, despite being somewhat stressed and drinking too much. Lady Justice Hallett, however, remarked upon the elements of Sally's behaviour that suggested the opposite.

We were on shakier ground on the question of the hammer Sally had in her bag, which she accepted she must have brought with a conditional intent to use it. This had been particularly problematic for the provocation defence, which required a 'sudden and temporary loss of control'. The final shot across the bows from the prosecution was to suggest that Sally may have embellished her account to suit the analysis provided by Professor Stark. This didn't go down well with the judges and eventually the Crown QC dropped the 'bad point'.

It was almost lunchtime. To my surprise, Lady Justice Hallett announced that when we returned at 2.30 p.m. she hoped to provide an ex tempore judgment – an immediate decision delivered orally.

This was unusual in such a case and I was not expecting it. Evidently they had more or less decided on the outcome and did not need to reserve judgment. My best guess was that they were going to allow the appeal, but on a limited basis focusing on the psychiatric evidence. The suspicion that the fast decision might point to a retrial tightened the little knot of dread in my stomach.

We headed off to lunch, and to discuss with David, James and his partner Jen, and Sally's wider family, who had turned up in force, where we thought this might be going. We talked to Sally on the video-link about our options in the event that the judges ordered a retrial. If that happened, we could try submitting an application for bail.

We returned to the court for the judgment at 2.30 p.m. The court was packed and the reporters sat with pens poised. As Lady Justice Hallett read the judgment, my adrenaline surged. Coercive control was recognized as context and Dr Adshead's evidence proved critical: the judges found that the murder conviction was unsafe and were allowing the appeal. On the video-link, Sally burst into tears of joy. Cheers from the public gallery behind me were quelled by a stern look from the judge before she concluded by ordering a retrial on the charge of murder.

Reporting restrictions were ordered as a new jury would be required. Although there had been considerable coverage of the case in the lead-up to the appeal, little could now be said in the public domain about the judgment beyond that an appeal had been allowed. It also meant that, for the present at least, Sally would have to remain in prison. The disappointment in the public gallery was palpable.

We focused on the positives: Sally was naturally hugely relieved that her conviction had been quashed. We would apply for bail swiftly. But hanging over it all was the risk that she could be reconvicted of murder.

The retrial was listed at the Old Bailey. At a plea and directions hearing, we made an application for bail, having obtained a further psychiatric report on risk and a safe address where Sally could stay. Bail was granted and, the following day, Sally was collected by James and Jen and taken to their home in Essex.

In the meantime, I made detailed written representations to the CPS that it was not in the public interest to pursue a second prosecution for murder when Sally was willing to plead guilty to manslaughter. She had already spent nine years in custody; there was compelling psychiatric evidence supporting her defence of diminished responsibility and compelling evidence that she was a victim of abuse; nobody in her family, or Richard's, supported a conviction for murder and a retrial was an unnecessary burden on the public purse. It all fell on deaf ears. The prosecution insisted that they wanted their own psychiatric evidence and informed me they were instructing Dr Philip Joseph.

This was bad news: Dr Joseph had a reputation as a prosecution hired gun, particularly in cases where women were accused of murder. It looked as if we were definitely heading for trial. However, after Dr Joseph assessed Sally, and much to my surprise, he diagnosed a completely different psychiatric disorder, but one that nevertheless supported the defence of diminished responsibility. Finally, the CPS conceded that they would accept a plea from Sally of guilty to manslaughter and we would avoid the uncertain outcome of another trial by jury.

At a hearing before Mr Justice Edis at the Old Bailey, Sally entered her plea and submissions were made on sentence. The judge handed down a sentence which allowed her to walk free from the court.

'Many other women who are victims of abuse, as I was, are in prison today serving life sentences,' she told the press after the hearing. 'They should not be serving sentences for murder but for manslaughter ... Getting an appeal is very difficult. I was turned down on the first attempt. The justice system needs to listen.'

This landmark victory would lead to the Criminal Cases Review

Commission sifting through some 3,000 murder cases to identify possible unsafe convictions. And in 2023, in a new law dubbed 'Sally's Law', the government announced changes to the legislation that will ensure judges must take into account coercive and controlling behaviour as both an aggravating factor when abusers kill, and a mitigating factor when victims of abuse kill their tormentors.

For Sally herself, freedom meant not only liberation from prison but, at the age of sixty-five, the freedom to make her own choices for the first time in her adult life, with the support of her loving sons and her extended family.

8

Releasing a Serial Rapist: A Risk to the Public?

IT IS JANUARY 2018, AND I am sitting round a table with about fifteen other lawyers in a meeting room in Gray's Inn Road. We are discussing the interminable intricacies of the undercover police inquiry and the proposed rules and protocols that would govern its practice.

My phone, switched to silent, suddenly starts to vibrate repeatedly. Glancing at it, I see a host of calls and texts coming in from mainly unknown numbers. I step out of the meeting for a moment to find out what is going on and discover that I am being pursued by journalists seeking a comment on the news that serial rapist John Worboys is about to be released from prison.

As luck would have it, Phillippa Kaufmann, with whom I worked on the case against the Metropolitan Police over their failed investigation into Worboys' crimes, was in the same meeting. As we wrapped up, I took her to one side to tell her what was happening. Before Phillippa branched out into actions against the police, she had primarily specialized in prison law and was extremely knowledgeable about the parole process and the types of assessment that would need to be made before a prisoner was recommended for release. Given what we knew about Worboys' prolific offending from the civil claim, we were both astounded by the decision to free him so soon after his conviction.

I called back a couple of the journalists, mainly in the hope that they could provide some further explanation or context for this extraordinary development rather than out of any wish to comment – for the present I told them I would need to ask the two Worboys victims I represented whether they wanted me to do so on their behalf. Birnberg Peirce was, of course, a leading light in the field of civil liberties, and my experience of the targeting of some of our clients by the tabloids, as well as my personal commitment to those civil liberties, made me feel slightly queasy about speaking out against the release of any prisoner who had served a sentence imposed by a court and met the requirements of further judicial process.

I gathered from the journalists that one of Worboys' victims who had given evidence at his trial had been informed by the probation service of the Parole Board's decision. Up in arms, it was she who had alerted the press.

The Parole Board is responsible for making decisions about the release of prisoners who have been given an indeterminate sentence, whether it is a life sentence or, as in the case of Worboys, an indeterminate sentence for public protection (IPP). When a judge passes an indeterminate sentence, he or she will also set a minimum term, a fixed period of imprisonment before the offender can be considered for release. If parole is granted thereafter, licence conditions will be set and the individual will be subject to supervision by probation. They will remain on licence for the rest of their life, or indefinitely, and can be recalled to prison at any time if they breach any of its conditions.

When considering a prisoner's release or progression to lower-security conditions, a parole panel will need to evaluate whether they still pose a risk to the public and, if so, whether that risk can be managed in the community. The panel will also need to be satisfied that the offender has accepted responsibility for their crime and taken genuine steps to learn how to deal with the circumstances or impulses that led to it. But the priority overriding all else is the protection of the public.

Worboys had been eligible for review after serving eight years. However, the judge passing sentence had been very clear that he would not be released until the Parole Board decided he was no longer a threat to women. Given what I knew about his crimes and the trauma he had caused so many victims, it seemed inconceivable that he could be assessed as no longer posing a serious risk. My feminist instinct told me that the decisions taken on both sentencing and release might have more to do with the sexism endemic to the criminal justice system and a failure to understand the risk inherent in so many sex offenders.

My own experience of Parole Board decisions was largely based on my work with women who had killed abusive partners and been convicted of murder, for which a life sentence was mandatory. I was seeing some of these 'lifers' being turned down for parole long after serving their minimum term on the strength of factors like mental health concerns that, if anything, probably made them more of a risk to themselves than to the public.

This had been apparent to me from the start of my legal career, when I discovered that Emma Humphreys had already served her minimum term of eight years. I was told that she was not considered safe for early release because of her self-harming and 'unstable mental health'. Emma spent ten years in custody before she was freed on appeal.

Another woman whose murder conviction for killing her wealthy boyfriend I challenged later, in this instance unsuccessfully, was refused parole twice before she was eventually released on licence several years after the expiry of her minimum term. She had been coping well with her custodial sentence, and had been moved to an open prison – until she suffered a mental breakdown on learning that a penfriend she had acquired, a man she believed had romantic intentions towards her, was a fraud. She walked out of the prison in what a psychiatrist would subsequently describe as a 'fugue-like state', triggering a massive police hunt. She soon contacted her parents and was returned the next day to secure conditions, but as a consequence of 'absconding from prison', and concerns about her susceptibility to forming new attachments, she was deemed high-risk.

I have never come across a case where a woman who killed her violent partner seriously assaulted another person, let alone killed again, after being released from prison. Yet parole panels continually exercise extreme caution over recommending release for such female prisoners, even where there is little empirical evidence that they represent any risk to the public. It seemed to me that risk-assessment criteria and protocols, and indeed the whole prison, parole and probation system, were founded on a model designed for the male offenders who constitute the vast majority of the prison population.

All of which raises the question of what type of offender, in general, the system is geared to identifying as a public risk. Serial sex offenders fall into a category of their own. Their crimes usually rely on clever manipulation and grooming to gain the trust of their victims (techniques that may, moreover, stand them in good stead when it comes to attempting to game the parole system). Which kind of prisoner is most likely to pose the bigger risk? A woman suffering the long-term mental-health consequences of coercive control who finally, fatally, lashed out at her abuser, or the sex offender who has attacked time and again, without compunction, solely for his own gratification?

But at this point I was not in possession of all, or indeed any, of the facts of this new situation with John Worboys. I decided my response to the media needed to be informed by my clients' perspective. It was on their behalf that the press wanted me to comment, after all.

Although it had been five years since the original trial of the civil claim against the Met, I remained in touch with Fiona and Meena because the police kept trying to appeal the outcome. The Supreme Court hearing had taken place only nine months previously and we were still waiting for the judgment. Generally, I avoided contacting either woman unless I had to because I knew that a call from me could be triggering. They both wanted to try to bury their horrible memories and get on with their day-to-day lives. But Worboys had reared his head again and they were soon going to hear about it if they hadn't already.

Meena and Fiona were shocked and disgusted. They hadn't been informed by the probation service, as they should have been, that a Parole Board decision had been made to release Worboys. They were not even aware that such a decision was in the offing. And yes, they did want me to make their feelings known.

As I was already in Gray's Inn Road, a few doors down from ITN headquarters, I agreed to record an interview for their six o'clock bulletin and, somewhat nervously, to speak to *Channel 4 News* live in their studio later on. Before Channel 4's 7 p.m. programme, Cathy Newman, the anchor that night, asked me whether there was a way of legally challenging the Parole Board decision. I honestly wasn't sure. I had never heard of such a challenge being made by a prisoner's victim rather than by the prisoner concerned.

I rang Phillippa. She had been involved in many battles opposing decisions *not* to grant parole, but didn't know whether a case had ever been brought to try to prevent the release of an offender. She told me that it would be a very difficult challenge to make because, whereas a prisoner questioning a Parole Board decision would have been given the reasons for it, a victim would not. It wasn't at all clear whether Worboys' victims would even have any 'locus standi', the legal right to bring such an action.

On air I explained that the first my clients had heard of this had been on the news earlier in the day and expressed how sickened they both were. Asked by Cathy if I considered Worboys safe to be released, which appeared to be the view of the Parole Board, I speculated that this could have been due to his risk being assessed only on the basis of the sample of offences against twelve women for which he had been convicted, rather than the attacks on 105 different women for which he had been reported.

Hurrying out of the building afterwards, I had a distinct sense of déjà vu. As my phone continued to ring and ping, I was waylaid by the BBC in the shape of Daniel Sandford, asking for an interview, which I gave across the street. Hopefully, in the twelve and a half years since ITV had revealed the details leaked from the IPCC about the shooting of Jean Charles de Menezes, when I had appeared in front of television cameras in the same places and in the same sequence, I had become more practised in not accidentally becoming a news story myself.

The journalists really wanted to hear from my clients. As neither Fiona nor Meena was comfortable with talking directly to the media and I could not deal singlehandedly with all the incoming enquiries, I put out a press release to make their reactions known.

Fiona said that since learning the news, she had been in a state of complete shock and panic. 'How can a prolific sex offender be rehabilitated in such a short space of time when he has never admitted to his guilt or shown any remorse?' she asked.

I read on Friday that the Parole Board are 'confident' he will not reoffend . . . I do not share their confidence and I am convinced he will. I truly hope for the sake of every mother, daughter, wife and sister out there that I'm wrong.

When we took the police to court regarding their huge and cata-strophic failings to investigate and stop Worboys, it was noted that lessons needed to learned. We won that court case but since that time the police seem incapable of accepting the judgment . . . Clear-ly no lessons have been learned as everyone involved in this case is more interested in Worboys' rights and has no regard whatsoever for any of his victims. When do we get parole? When do we get to have a clean slate and walk away from the nightmare he has created?

Meena added that she was 'appalled and haunted' by this latest horror. 'I can't watch the news or read the papers. My heart freezes when I hear his name. Seeing his face makes me feel unwell. He's ruining my life all over again.'

Both women were prepared to be involved in a legal challenge to the Parole Board decision if we could find a way forward. I was dis-covering from various sources a little more about Worboys' history in prison. It seemed that after he was found guilty of multiple offences of sexual assault and administering a noxious substance, he tried to appeal those convictions. When that failed, he lodged a claim with the Criminal Cases Review Commission. So much for accepting responsibility for the attacks or showing remorse.

I also learned that, in 2015, Worboys had been denied a transfer from the high-security HMP Wakefield to a lower-security open prison on the basis that he posed an 'unacceptable risk'. And yet, just over two years later, it seemed he was deemed suitable for parole? Since Worboys apparently decided to accept responsibility for his offences around the time this move was refused, and when it looked as though his appeal was going nowhere, I suspected that this was a cynical strategy to clear a path forward through the parole process.

During the civil trial of the Metropolitan Police, I'd had dealings with Richard Scorer, a solicitor based in Manchester who has acted for hundreds of victims of historical child sexual abuse. He and his colleague Kim Harrison had also represented eleven of Worboys' victims (including Fiona and Meena) in a claim for compensation directly against Worboys and knew a bit more about his time in prison. Worboys had fought the claim for compensation, and, even when he eventually settled, refused to accept liability for the harm done to the women he assaulted.

Richard told me that, because Worboys didn't have a lawyer, it had been necessary for one of his solicitors to visit him in prison to discuss some terms of settlement. Worboys did, however, have a 'McKenzie Friend', an unqualified advocate there to provide advice and support, with him at the meeting. It turned out that this McKenzie Friend was Levi Bellfield, the notorious serial killer and rapist convicted of three murders, including the killing of thirteen-year-old Milly Dowler.

One of the women Richard had represented in the civil claim was Carrie Symonds, head of communications for the Conservative Party (and later the wife of prime minister Boris Johnson). Carrie had courageously waived anonymity at the time of Worboys' original arrest in order to encourage more women to come forward. Although she was reluctant to be a claimant herself, due, perhaps, to her position in the Conservative Party, she was keen to lend background support to any legal action against the Parole Board.

Such a challenge still looked like an uphill struggle, not only because it was unprecedented, but mainly because of the lack of access to the evidence the panel had considered – or even, as Phillippa had noted, to their reasons for reaching their decision – because Parole Board rules prohibited the disclosure of details of individual cases. We reckoned our only option would be to issue a judicial review in court and to seek an order for disclosure of their file.

Another significant barrier where Meena and Fiona were concerned was that they were not in a position to take a financial risk.

They had, of course, been in the same situation when we mounted the civil claim against the police, but since then LASPO (the Legal Aid, Sentencing and Punishment of Offenders Act 2012), which reformed funding for legal actions, had become law. We could still bring a case on a conditional fee agreement, but new rules excluded the recovery of after-the-event insurance premiums, which meant insurers were unwilling to support these sorts of claims. Without insurance, the claimants were at risk of having to pay the other side's costs if they lost.

There was one other, still quite innovative, option which, coincidentally, I had only recently been discussing with a woman who had approached me on behalf of a newly established organization called CrowdJustice. Jo Sidhu was trying to encourage legal firms to consider crowdfunding as a way of financing legal action. The idea was to put out a public appeal for donations to support bringing or defending a particular case. The funds raised could be used to cover costs, disbursements and, potentially, lawyers' fees in the event that you lost. If you won, the pledges could be transferred to support another similar case or cause.

In general, I was pessimistic about the likelihood that tens of thousands of pounds could be drummed up from altruistic donors to fund a legal challenge. However, given the public outcry over Worboys' release, if there was any kind of action that might attract the necessary level of popular support, this was probably it.

Jo's advice on achieving maximum sums was to get as many individuals and groups as possible on board who were in a position to spread the word widely and promote the CrowdJustice appeal. Sarah Green and Rachel Krys, co-directors of the End Violence Against Women coalition, one of the organizations that had intervened in Fiona and Meena's Supreme Court case, were eager to assist with fundraising and gathering support. Richard Scorer and Kim Harrison, who were talking to the press on behalf of other Worboys victims, also agreed to endorse the action. Carrie Symonds spoke to George Osborne, the former chancellor of the exchequer who, having resigned from the government after a Cabinet reshuffle in the wake of the Brexit referendum, was now the editor of the London *Evening Standard*. The *Standard* agreed to publicize the campaign. All extremely helpful, although, as my politics have always been on the left, I was slightly uneasy about some of the alliances we were making on this issue.

But with the parole decision already made, we had to move quickly. It might only be a matter of days before Worboys was released. Phillippa suggested we boosted the team with a colleague from her chambers, Nick Armstrong, who was an expert in prison law and would be an asset on both strategy and the detailed work we would need to undertake to bring the challenge.

Nick and Phillippa got down to work on the letter before action. They decided we would need to bring a claim against not only the Parole Board, for its apparently perverse decision, but also the secretary of state for justice, in order to challenge Rule 25 of the Parole Board regulations, which prohibited the sharing of information about any of its decisions.

On 14 January 2018, *The Sunday Times* reported that David Gauke, the justice secretary, was also taking legal advice about bringing a judicial review. He would have had access to the reasons for the decision because the secretary of state, or, more precisely, an official acting on his behalf, plays a role in the Parole Board process. It seemed odd to me that such a legal challenge could be sought by a government office that was part of the machinery that had produced the decision in the first place.

A couple of days later, Professor Nick Hardwick (last encountered as chair of the IPCC at the time of the Jean Charles de Menezes case, who now chaired the Parole Board), put out a public statement welcoming the decision of the lord chancellor to judicially review the board. 'I hope such a review will provide assurance that the Parole Board itself has acted in accordance with the law and the evidence,' he said, going on to express concern that many of Worboys' victims reported not having been kept informed or consulted about licence conditions as they should have been, although, he pointed out, this was the responsibility of the National Probation Service, not the Parole Board. He also stated, helpfully, that he did not agree with the rule preventing the disclosure of details about a Parole Board decision. 'Justice needs to be seen to be done. If the parole system is closed and secretive, we cannot complain if people do not understand it.'

Later the same day, I sent our letter before claim to the chief executive and chair of the Parole Board, requesting a stay on the release of Worboys pending the resolution of the threatened judicial review proceedings. In the letter, which was also copied to Worboys and the justice secretary as 'interested parties', we argued that, first of all, Rule 25 was 'ultra vires', in that it went beyond its legal authority by prohibiting the provision of information. Second, we said, the decision itself to direct Worboys' release was 'irrational'.

I notified the board that I acted for the two victims of Worboys who had brought the civil claim against the Metropolitan Police, pointing out that Meena had given evidence at the criminal trial, and that, although Fiona had not, this was not because her allegation did not pass the evidential threshold but because 'the CPS did not wish to overload the indictment'. Both claimants, I emphasized, had been assured Mr Worboys would not come out of prison for a very long time.

We asserted that the decision was ultra vires in essence on the grounds that Rule 25 offended the fundamental common-law principle of open justice – particularly blatantly where there was an overriding public interest, as there was in this case. The total restriction was inconsistent with the rules governing other judicial proceedings, such as mental health tribunals, which determined issues relating to the denial of liberty to psychiatric patients. We referred to Nick Hardwick's statement calling for an amendment of the rules.

We knew we would have a huge uphill struggle with our second ground. The test for assessing the rationality of a decision by a public body was established in a legal case in 1948, *Associated Provincial Picture Houses v. Wednesbury Corporation*. For a court to quash a decision as irrational, it had to meet the test that it was 'Wednesbury unreasonable', later defined by Lord Diplock as 'a decision which is so outrageous in its defiance of logic or of accepted moral standards that no sensible person who had applied his mind to the question to be decided could have arrived at it'.

While it appeared that most of the general public and the media regarded the decision to release Worboys after only ten years in prison as insane, it had nonetheless, as Nick Hardwick spelled out in his press statement, been made by a three-member panel 'chaired by one of our most experienced women members'. Another was a Parole Board psychologist. They had considered a 363-page dossier and heard evidence from four psychologists as well as prison and probation staff responsible for Worboys. The secretary of state had been represented and Worboys himself had been 'questioned in detail'.

How were we going to argue that such a three-person panel, having carefully evaluated a comprehensive dossier of evidence, had taken a decision that no reasonable parole board could have reached – especially when we had no idea of what this evidence was or what explanations they had given? We said that the decision was 'prima facie irrational', citing the scale and seriousness of Worboys' offending; the fact that, until recently, he had shown no recognition of his guilt; the assessment made only two years previously by the Parole Board, when refusing his transfer to open conditions, that he posed an 'unacceptable risk'. And, because he had remained through-out in high-security custody, we contended, the risk to the public had not been tested in lower-security settings, as was normally required for prisoners serving long sentences for sexual offences.

Then I issued a press release announcing that we had threatened judicial review and launched the CrowdJustice campaign.

Two days later, it was reported that David Gauke would not be pursuing judicial review proceedings to challenge the decision, apparently on legal advice. Given that the justice secretary's lawyer would have had access to the Parole Board dossier and their reason-ing, this was worrying, but to deal with a further flood of media enquiries, I issued another press release confirming that we were still at this point pursuing the judicial review option. 'The decision by the secretary of state does not weaken our case at this stage,' we announced. 'Firstly, because the Parole Board is the MoJ's creation and he cannot therefore challenge his own rules.' It was possible, we speculated, that Ministry of Justice officials may have contributed to the Parole Board decision.

In its response to our pre-action letter, the Parole Board confirmed the conclusion of the panel convened in November 2017 that 'it was no longer necessary for the protection of the public that the prisoner should be confined'. On the matter of the ultra vires grounds, it claimed to have no power to determine that question, which needed to be directed to the justice secretary, who was ultimately respon-sible for the rules. The board was not able to provide the reasons for the decision but stated that it was one the panel was entitled to reach on the evidence before them, and that it did not have the authority to agree to stay the release of Worboys, also a matter for the justice secretary, or to reconsider the decision, which would require a court order.

Next we wrote to the government lawyers acting on behalf of the justice secretary expressing our intention to issue judicial review proceedings against both him and the Parole Board and inviting them to delay Worboys' release until an application to the court for 'interim relief' (a temporary remedy to preserve the status quo until a legal matter has been decided) had been considered.

They indicated that they agreed with our application and that, if the court granted us permission for the judicial review, the case should be heard expeditiously. They did not agree, however, that our challenge in relation to the open justice principle needed to be dealt with so urgently. They proposed instead that the court could order the disclosure to us of the reasoning for the Parole Board decision, subject to a strict undertaking of confidentiality.

In the three weeks since the news of Worboys' imminent freedom had been leaked to the press, I had been receiving phone calls from other women he had attacked who were extremely alarmed by this incomprehensible development. They wanted to know if there was anything they could do to prevent it. Some of them had never reported him to the police and asked whether, if they did so now, he might have to be arrested again for what he had done to them. Others who had made complaints wondered whether their evidence might help the legal challenge. I took brief accounts from all the women I spoke to and their stories bolstered my understanding of Worboys' coldly manipulative methodology.

Rachel, from Bournemouth, was certain there would be lots of victims in this area as well as around London – it was known that Worboys owned a flat in nearby Poole – and indeed, other Bournemouth women were coming forward. Rachel had got into his cab at a taxi rank one night sometime between 2000 and 2002 after an evening out at a club. A black cab was not, at that time, a common sight in a town where the local taxis were yellow. When the driver told her he'd had a win at the casino and passed a white plastic cup of champagne back to her through the window, Rachel, like so many of Worboys' victims, was pressurized to drink it and found it easier to take a sip than not, just to be polite. It had a horrible, bitter taste and she didn't drink any more. The driver was really chatty and 'off-the-scale' charming: in retrospect, it felt to her that she was being intensively groomed. They sat outside her drive for ten minutes or more as he tried to persuade her not to get out of the cab. She could not remember doing so.

When Rachel heard that Worboys was about to be freed, she was extremely troubled. She told me she was convinced he was incredibly dangerous because of his adept use of a 'puppy dog' manner and his deliberate targeting of lone women in vulnerable situations. She had not reported the incident but was willing to do so now if it would make a difference: whatever it took to stop him attacking more women.

Marion, too, got in touch to voice her concerns about the risk Worboys posed to women. She had testified at his trial and he had been convicted of administering a substance with intent to sexually assault her. Marion had been attacked in 2005, after Worboys picked her up outside a nightclub in London. She felt he approached her in a 'carefully calibrated way': he was 'respectful' and, she sensed, good at reading people and intuiting how to get round them.

Marion should have been kept informed through the victim contact scheme, but she was never contacted at any stage of the parole process. Like Fiona and Meena, the first she heard of the decision was from the media. She felt there were a lot of inadequacies in the overall procedure. Even if this decision could not be reversed, she wanted to see change in the future.

On 25 January I lodged an application for judicial review, together with an application for urgent consideration and for interim relief in the High Court. We asked the court to grant a stay preventing the imminent release of Worboys (who had now changed his name to John Radford) and for an urgent hearing to decide on whether we should be granted permission to proceed with the challenge and, if so, for the court to order disclosure of the Parole Board dossier.

In the accompanying statement of facts and grounds, we developed the arguments we had set out in the pre-action correspondence. In support of the thorny ground that the Parole Board decision was 'irrational', we acknowledged the high threshold but maintained that this was a special case. The board had decided to direct the release of a man with a long history of cold, deliberate, highly planned and very serious sexual assaults of a very large number of women. He had acknowledged his guilt only two and a half years before, having been refused a transfer from high-security custody. It was difficult to know what could have changed since then that was capable of satisfying the board that the statutory test for release had been met.

We noted the significant public interest and the sheer scale of Worboys' offending: that between 2002 and 2008, he was thought to have committed in excess of a hundred rapes and sexual assaults but had been prosecuted and convicted on counts involving only twelve victims, even though a great many more offences had been reported to the police. We quoted the CPS lawyer who had been intent on 'not overloading the indictment so that the case could be presented to the jury in a simple way'. Victims were assured that the indictment properly reflected the range of Worboys' criminality and would enable the trial judge to impose a sentence that would adequately protect the public from him. We asserted that the Parole Board would have needed to take into account not only the offences of which he was convicted but the totality of assaults for which there was evidence he committed.

While the claimants had limited knowledge of Worboys' conduct, attitude or potential rehabilitation in custody, we argued that since, from what we did know, he had been maintaining his innocence until at least May 2015, he could not have completed any meaningful therapy to address his proclivities and offending behaviour – something that would be regarded as essential for the Parole Board to assess his ongoing risk.

Even if he had subsequently participated in the prison service's Sexual Offences Treatment Programme, there was no indication that this would have reduced his risk – indeed, it may even have increased it, according to an impact evaluation of the programme in 2017. A Ministry of Justice report found that 10 per cent of criminals who had completed SOTP 'treatment' in prison had gone on to commit at least one sexual offence after their release, compared with 8 per cent who had not received treatment. It had been suggested that the group therapy format and the sharing of stories may have had the effect of normalizing criminal behaviour and even facilitated the exchange of sources and contacts.

The following day a judge considered our urgent application, together with a separate one made by the mayor of London, who, we discovered, had also launched a judicial review challenge of the Parole Board decision. The judge ordered that the release of Worboys be stayed pending an application for permission for judicial review and that the oral hearing should take place on a date between 6 and 8 February. He also ordered that any application by our clients be heard together with the application from the mayor of London and that, at the hearing, the Parole Board be given the opportunity to set out reasons why they opposed the disclosure of the decision and the dossier.

I put out a fresh press release announcing our victory in the first phase of the challenge, aimed at encouraging more donations to the crowdfunding appeal, and rallied more support through the media. On LBC radio, I was interviewed by Nick Ferrari alongside a representative of the Licensed Taxi Drivers' Association, who was concerned about protecting the reputation and livelihoods of his membership. He pledged £5,000 on behalf of his organization. The

Evening Standard ran an editorial and published a link to the crowdfunding appeal with its news coverage. We were on course to raise sufficient funds to ensure that there would be no financial risk to Fiona and Meena if we lost the case. In the end, we raised in excess of £60,000. The chance I had taken that this might be precisely the sort of high-profile case where crowdfunding could work looked like it was paying off.

The permission hearing took place on 7 February before Lord Justice Leveson, president of the Queen's Bench Division, and Lord Justice Garnier. Fiona decided she would like to be there, but wanted to remain incognito if possible. Meena couldn't face it. Court 5 of the Royal Courts of Justice was heaving, not just with press and public, but with a plethora of lawyers representing the different parties to the proceedings. As well as my team – Phillippa, Nick, my paralegal Alice and me – there were teams acting for the mayor of London, the Parole Board, the justice secretary and News Group Newspapers: the *Sun* newspaper, we discovered, had also issued proceedings to argue in support of the principle of open justice. The only party not represented was the man whose entitlement to liberty was the subject of this hearing: John Worboys.

We had anticipated that Worboys would appear by video-link from prison, but Lord Justice Leveson began the hearing by explaining that, because the court equipment had not been working effectively the previous day, and because 'John Radford' was an important participant whose interests were crucially affected, he had requested that 'Mr Radford' be brought to court in person. We had not expected to encounter Worboys in the flesh. I checked that Fiona, who was in court as planned, was OK with this. Since she had not attended his criminal trial, it would be the first time she'd had to occupy the same space as this man since he drugged and assaulted her in the back of his taxi fifteen years earlier. She seemed resigned to dealing with whatever she had to confront.

While we waited for Worboys' prison van to arrive, practical matters about the proceedings and the scope of legal challenges were
discussed. It was almost eleven o'clock before he was brought up
from the cells below the court to stand in the dock. Having spent so
much time across so many years concentrating on the crimes of this
sexual predator, with a picture of him in my mind's eye based solely
on the single mugshot that had been shared with the newspapers, it
was strange to finally come face to face with him. He looked notice-
ably older but also smaller, slightly stooped and very unassuming.

Lord Justice Leveson was concerned that Worboys had no lawyer.
He noted that he'd had a solicitor with him at his Parole Board review,
but it seemed she was not representing him now. He told Worboys
that the issues involved complex points of law and, as someone who
would be significantly impacted by the outcome of the proceedings,
he was entitled to legal representation. Worboys confirmed, quietly,
that he would like the assistance of a lawyer.

To our frustration, this looked likely to spell a delay – until a man
sitting in the public gallery stood up to say that he was a prison law
specialist and was willing to step in. The court was adjourned for
half an hour to enable Worboys to meet Dean Kingham, who, we
discovered during the break, was chair of the Association of Prison
Lawyers and an expert on Parole Board reviews. There were some
mutterings in court about the audacity of a lawyer standing up and
offering his services mid-hearing, but I, for one, was pleased that
someone appropriately qualified was available to provide meaningful representation and ensure that the process was fair.

After the adjournment the judges considered a series of directions
that needed to be made to enable the case to proceed to a full hearing
and permission was granted for all three cases to go ahead on both
grounds argued, although the issue of whether the mayor of London
had 'standing' was still to be determined. We would be provided
with the reasons for the Parole Board decision, together with a copy

of the full dossier of evidence the panel had considered, upon signing strict confidentiality undertakings. The court then set a tight timetable of further steps to be taken so that everyone would be ready to argue the claim at a hearing beginning on 13 March.

We waited with bated breath to receive the dossier, anticipating that surely there must be some plausible explanation for the decision to release Worboys. Perhaps he was dying and it had been made for compassionate reasons? We had warned our clients that, while the open justice challenge had a chance of success, winning the rationality argument was highly unlikely. Nick had set aside a few days to go through the dossier carefully and kept us up to speed with a string of emails as he read it. Every page, it seemed, was bringing him closer to the conclusion that the decision really was crazy, and we might have a chance of succeeding on that ground after all.

The court had ordered that once we had reviewed the dossier, we could amend our statement of facts and grounds to take account of the new evidence we had seen. An open and closed version of our amended statement had to be filed with the court and served on the other parties by 21 February.

While Nick and Phillippa reviewed the dossier and drafted amended grounds, I explored further evidence that might support our argument. Still more Worboys victims were getting in touch. I prepared a statement summarizing their accounts and offered to connect any women who had not previously reported their assaults with a dedicated Met Police team which had been set up to look at fresh allegations. My thinking was that, if we failed with the judicial review, another way to keep Worboys off the streets might be to prosecute him for further offences. All the women described being given spiked drinks and losing consciousness; all were in no doubt that he would do it again. The more of them I talked to, the more convinced I became that not only was Worboys a highly manipulative sociopath, he was one who could probably never be rehabilitated.

Many of the victims who hadn't reported their attacks, like Lesley, who had got into Worboys' cab in 2007 with a friend, thought they wouldn't be believed because of the gaps in their memories. Lesley's friend had a lucky escape – he pressed drinks on them both – thanks to being dropped off first. When the taxi pulled up outside Lesley's house, Worboys 'looked like a spoiled child who had not been rewarded for the effort he had put in', she recalled. After that, her mind was a blank until she woke up in her bed with her arms crossed over her chest (a position in which she never slept). Lesley was 'completely shellshocked' and just tried not to dwell on what might have happened to her that night. But after the recent news coverage, she had decided she did not want to allow this 'pathetic man' to 'keep me in fear or silence for one minute longer'.

I wanted to find out more about how prisons conducted the process of evaluating prisoners as safe to be released and the disputed science around the specific risk assessment of sex offenders. I talked to my colleague in the prison law department, Sally Middleton, who had always helpfully taken on any parole or prison law matters relating to the appeals I'd been involved with on behalf of women convicted of killing violent partners.

Sally directed me to some of the relevant rules, legal framework and literature on risk assessment. I discovered that, while the volume of literature on the subject is huge, very little of it is tailored to promoting an understanding of sex offending, still less of rapists. Risk-assessment tools are based on indicators taken from large aggregate populations and their known offending patterns. This produces statistical probabilities, but it is unclear how accurate they are for any individual – especially for someone like Worboys, who, with his unusual modus operandi and the scale of his crimes, was less likely to be typical of a wider group of offenders.

An important distinction between sex offences and most other crimes to bear in mind is that the number of sex offences actually recorded is only the tip of a very big iceberg. Most sex crimes are not reported. Rape Crisis England & Wales estimate that 1 in 4 adult women have been raped or sexually assaulted but only 1 in 6 who have been raped report it. They say that, in 2022, fewer than 2 in 100 cases of rape recorded by the police resulted in a charge in that same year, let alone conviction.

So, if risk is assessed on the basis of the number of convictions an offender has, the scale of the threat is unlikely to go anywhere near the reality. Worboys had been found guilty of multiple offences within an eighteen-month period and we knew of five times that number across six years or more which either hadn't been reported prior to his trial or with which he had not been charged. How many attacks might he have committed in the course of his lifetime? Probably many hundreds, if not thousands. Yet, as I suspected and would soon have confirmed, the Parole Board had only taken into account the relatively small number of offences of which he had been convicted.

The contents of the Parole Board dossier of evidence were grippingly revealing. Worboys had been a Category A (maximum security) prisoner for his entire sentence. He had maintained his innocence until 18 May 2015, when he had approached the Assessment and Intervention Centre at HMP Wakefield to tell them that he had 'changed his stance' before withdrawing his case from the Criminal Cases Review Commission. Therefore, as we had surmised, he had done no work to address his offending behaviour before that date. On 10 September, the Parole Board decided he was too high-risk to be suitable for transfer to open conditions. Indeed, every year until September 2017, it was considered unsafe for even his Category A restrictions to be relaxed.

The Parole Board was required to assess not only whether the offender had accepted his responsibility for his crimes, but whether he had gained an understanding of what led him to offend so that he could work on avoiding those circumstances ever arising again. The dossier detailed Worboys' claim that the break-up of a relationship in 2005 had been the trigger for his first offence.

Of course, a considerable number of women, including Fiona, had reported attacks well before 2005. It appeared that Worboys was indeed seeking, or had been asked, to account only for the offences of which he had been convicted and not the complaints of the other ninety-three women. Nor had his narrative been challenged by the psychologists or others who had prepared reports for the Parole Board.

Phillippa and Nick noted other features of Worboys' account and behaviour which seemed to have been accepted or overlooked by the board. These included his 'significant minimization' of the offences of which he had been found guilty. For example, in April 2017 he told the offender manager that the rape of which he was convicted was the only rape he had committed, and that it lasted only four seconds. Since 'changing his stance', Worboys had participated in the SOTP programme. Given that this was decommissioned a few months later, as a result of the study indicating that it actually increased offending rates, how could it have been viewed as helping him to reduce his risk? It also appeared that Worboys had links with at least one other high-profile and dangerous sex offender from his time in prison.

Perhaps most concerningly, the Parole Board seemed to have per-ceived his own analysis of his offending as somehow persuasive of his insight and ability to change. This 'evidence' was in the form of 'new me' diaries and records described by Phillippa and Nick as self-serving assertions that his reformed attitudes towards women 'would make it much harder for him to offend against them'. Yet even in these diary entries, references to 'young highly sexed women' and the 'natural, primal instinct' of being attracted to scantily clad women revealed the opposite: a deep-rooted, problematic view of women.

The decision was based primarily on the views of three psychologists who assessed Worboys as having a low risk of reoffending. This conflicted with some of the internal prison staff reports, which stressed that Worboys should undergo testing in lower-category prison conditions before being considered ready for release.

But the Parole Board concluded that Worboys took 'full responsibility' for his offending and had learned to be 'open and honest'; that his triggers for harmful behaviour were 'well known' and he had 'good insight' into his risk factors. Contrary to some of the concerns expressed, they said, an increase in risk was not inevitable and would be readily detected.

Counsel now felt we had a respectable argument to put on rationality and they were able to refine the legal basis for the challenge. The key question to be determined was whether it was no longer necessary for the protection of the public that the prisoner be detained and we asserted that there were two reasons why the Parole Board's decision was wrong.

First, the board had failed to take into account evidence (and police conclusions) that Worboys had attacked at least 105 women over a six-year period, a fact that rendered the psychological evidence unreliable. We were able to set out in detail the available evidence from our clients, from the other victims who had contacted us and from disclosure we had obtained for the civil claim against the Metropolitan Police that spoke to both the extent and scale of Worboys' crimes as well as to the 'clinical and conniving' manner of his offending.

Second, the Parole Board's decision was in any event irrational. Here we relied on the paucity of evidence and lack of adequate testing that could have led any reasonable person to the conclusion that Worboys now accepted full responsibility for his offending, had gained insight into his risk factors and was open and honest with professionals. A rational Parole Board, we said, having proper regard to its duty to give preponderant weight to the need to protect innocent members of the public against any significant risk of serious injury, had to take a very cautious approach and not direct release straight from a Category A establishment unless the evidence that the prisoner no longer represented a more than minimal risk of dangerous reoffending was compelling. No such compelling evidence concerning John Worboys had been presented to the panel.

As counsel were finalizing their grounds, I was informed that the Supreme Court was at long last ready to hand down its judgment on the appeal by the Met Police it had heard nearly a year previously in the case we had brought against them on behalf of Fiona and Meena. The court had refused the police appeal. We were all delighted to have seen off this challenge and established the important binding precedent that the Human Rights Act provides a remedy for victims of serious sexual and violent crimes when the police are found wanting. And, with the Parole Board challenge imminent, the timing couldn't have been better.

The defendants in the judicial review, as well as Worboys himself, now filed their response to our claim. We discovered that Dean Kingham had brought in Ed Fitzgerald QC to act on behalf of Worboys. Ed was perhaps the most experienced and renowned prison law barrister. He had been Phillippa's pupil master and they had a long and close working relationship. I had instructed Ed in the past and had the utmost respect for his work in this field. Worboys was going to be well represented.

The foundation for the legal resistance to our claim was that the Parole Board had no proper basis on which to treat Worboys as guilty of offences other than those for which he had been sentenced. 'They were provided with no evidence to justify such a course,' Worboys' counsel argued. 'But even if they had been, it would have been wrong in principle to embark on a wide-ranging exercise of determining guilt in relation to other alleged historic offences in circumstances where the CPS had declined to prosecute.'

Accompanying their submissions was a short statement from Worboys in which he claimed to be innocent of every offence of which he was accused other than those of which he had been convicted. Perhaps such a claim was logically necessary in order to maintain the argument that the Parole Board decision was safe. However, the deeply unpalatable implication of this statement was that the ninety-three other women who had come forward must have been lying, or at the very least fundamentally mistaken.

On 13 March we all trooped into court for the two-day hearing. There were, unusually, three senior judges sitting to hear the judicial review, with Lord Justice Leveson presiding. The court had to consider arguments from three sets of lawyers in support of the judicial review and three sets of lawyers who were, in varying degrees, opposing it.

The judicial review lobby agreed to divide the oral submissions. Phillippa would focus on the rationality issue while Dan Squires, for the mayor of London, and Gavin Millar, for News Group Newspapers, on behalf of the *Sun*, dealt with the ultra vires challenge in support of open justice. It was ironic, I thought, that the *Sun* should be relying on the Human Rights Act to bolster their argument when they had led public campaigns calling for its repeal. Then we heard from the representatives of the Parole Board defending the Worboys decision, and the team acting for the secretary of state for justice opposing the claim that Rule 25 of the Parole Board rules was ultra vires.

The High Court judgment was handed down a fortnight later. To our great relief, and that of the legion of Worboys' victims and doubtless most of the country, we had won. The decision to release Worboys was quashed and would have to be reconsidered by a newly constituted parole panel operating to revised guidelines. Rule 25 of the Parole Board rules was declared ultra vires and was required to be reformulated by the secretary of state.

The written judgment acknowledged that this was an unprecedented and wholly exceptional challenge. Although the court found that, on the extremely high threshold for irrationality challenges, we had not succeeded in establishing the decision as irrational, they did find it was irrational that the board had failed to consider evidence of Worboys' wider offending and other factors that could have been used to test his account of his crimes and the likelihood that they would be repeated.

That same day, it was reported that Nick Hardwick, chair of the Parole Board, had been forced to resign by justice secretary David Gauke. 'You told me that you thought my position was untenable,' Hardwick wrote in his resignation letter, but 'I had no role in the decision of the panel in the case and believe I am capable of leading the Parole Board through the changes, many of which I have advocated, that will now be necessary.'

A couple of months later, the justice secretary announced that reforms would be made to the parole process and, in 2019, the government published a series of initiatives aimed at ensuring that mistakes made in the Worboys case could not be repeated. These included the publication of a new decision-making framework for Parole Board members, the introduction of a new mechanism for victims to challenge Parole Board decisions and improvements to the victim contact scheme.

In August 2018, we heard that Worboys wanted to make a legal bid for his release and that he viewed himself as a 'political prisoner'. In November, the fresh parole panel decided not to direct Worboys' release. This time, the reasons for their decision were made public, among them 'risk factors associated with Mr Worboys, including sexual preoccupation, a sense of sexual entitlement, his attitudes towards women (including a need to have sexual contact with women and to control women), a belief that rape is acceptable, alcohol misuse and problems with relationships'.

Further prosecutions were brought against Worboys and, in 2019, he was convicted of attacks on four other women between 2000 and 2008. He was given two additional life sentences. Apparently, he now admitted to having targeted ninety victims, motivated by a 'hostility towards women'. A probation report that summer had concluded: 'He is potentially just as dangerous now as at the point of his first sentence.' The judge, Mrs Justice McGowan, told Worboys: 'I do not know when, if ever, you will cease to be a risk.'

9

Fighting the Legacy of the Sex Trade

AS WE CELEBRATED EMMA HUMPHREYS' appeal victory and release from prison in June 1995, I imagined we had liberated her from a lifetime of male violence and institutionalized injustice and that this would be the start of a new life for her.

At the party that evening we had organized for Emma and her supporters, Gareth Peirce, whom I'd recently got to know after she offered to take on Sara Thornton's second appeal, warned me not to expect it to be plain sailing. Gareth was aware that Julie and I, and our housemate Sarah Maguire, had offered Emma a room until some suitable and supported accommodation could be found for her. She told me how Judith Ward, wrongfully convicted in 1974 of the IRA M62 coach bombing in what has been described as one of the worst miscarriages of justice in British legal history, had come to stay with her on her release because she had nowhere else to go. She recalled Judith turning the light switch on and off repeatedly, marvelling over her agency to do so after eighteen years of being denied even this most basic form of personal control.

We were soon to learn that Emma was going to have to overcome a great deal more than a fascination with lights or unlocked doors. For us, it would be a precipitous learning curve in confronting the legacy of institutionalization for people with a history of severe abuse.

Emma had been so badly damaged that she found it hard to manage her life without the strict boundaries she was used to and nose-dived into self-destruction. Within days of her release, she was trading sex for drugs and we had to call an ambulance when she overdosed. The deep-seated sense of worthlessness rooted in her childhood and exacerbated by abuse, street prostitution and incarceration, combined with the weight of the guilt she felt for taking a man's life, may all have played a part in her defaulting to the only way she knew how to survive: self-harm, anorexia and becoming involved with violent and abusive men.

This rapid unravelling of our hopes of a new beginning for Emma left me in such despair sometimes that I wondered if it was actually possible for a woman who has been so utterly degraded ever to be able to enjoy her freedom.

For the next three years we constantly explored ways to provide Emma with stability and a road to recovery but she seemed set on proving to herself, and to us, that she was just a bad person, or that her only value was as a vessel for men's sexual use.

In 1996, Julie was employed by Professor Jalna Hanmer of Bradford University as press officer for an exciting feminist venture: the first-ever international conference in the UK on violence against women, to be held that November at the Brighton Conference Centre, best known as a regular venue for the annual conferences of our three main political parties. Julie persuaded me to go to the conference – headlined Violence, Abuse and Women's Citizenship – for the whole week and it was a memorable and hugely educative experience. Over 2,500 women from 137 countries attended, with many of the world's leading feminists, such as Andrea Dworkin, speaking at plenary events.

I met Norma Hotaling, an American survivor of prostitution who had, among other projects, been instrumental in establishing the 'john school' in San Francisco aimed at deterring men who used prostitutes by educating them in its inherent harms. I was introduced to Fiona Broadfoot, a young woman, by then heavily pregnant, who had walked into the conference press office at Bradford University one day and been recruited by Julie to speak at the event and share her experiences in a workshop.

Fiona had only recently freed herself from prostitution and she was angry: about how she had been exploited, about the violence to which she had been subjected and about how the police had done nothing to protect her from being put on the streets of Leeds at the age of fifteen by a predatory pimp. Instead she was repeatedly arrested for soliciting or loitering by the police (as they exchanged friendly greetings with her pimp) and left with a long history of criminal convictions. She was looking for a way to harness that anger constructively to bring about change.

Meeting these women who had survived the same sort of violence and degradation as Emma and come out fighting gave me renewed hope at a time when I felt so helpless to prevent her from being sucked back into a life of self-abasement.

And Emma was, albeit slowly, showing signs of recovery. She remained painfully anorexic and physically frail, but, after about eighteen months of craziness, her life began to stabilize. She reconnected with her father and her half-brother, Matthew, in Nottingham. With the help of social services, we managed to get her a flat a mile down the road from us, and she would visit regularly for Sunday lunch. The following year, Julie and Jalna organized a national conference on prostitution and violence against women and girls and invited Emma to speak there. As she started to accept requests for interviews to talk about her experiences, she began to find a voice. In one documentary dealing with the harms of prostitution, she said:

> I ran away from home when I was twelve and the only way I could
> get a room for the night was to sleep with a man. Then I met this

other girl and we started doing it for money. It could be a judge, could be a mechanic, could be an unemployed bloke. There was abuse, rape, muggings, you name it, everything happened to me. I don't care what anyone says, there is no such thing as a happy hooker. Three-quarters of the women who walk the streets are out there not because they want to be there, but because they are made to be there. Like a piece of meat, they are there to be bought and sold.

After ten years of regularly being dosed in prison with chloral hydrate, a medicine otherwise known as the 'chemical cosh' that was given to inmates displaying disturbed and traumatized behaviour to keep them calm, Emma was addicted to it. She was now prescribed this drug by her GP and used to take it in liberal quantities when she was feeling agitated and to help her sleep. One day in July 1998, unable to reach her on the phone, Julie and I went round to her flat. We found her in bed, dead. She had died in her sleep. An inquest later determined that the cause of death was an accidental overdose of chloral hydrate.

Emma's life and death had a profound impact on us both. It was outrage at what had happened to Emma that led me to find my vocation in the law, where I have been able to stand up at the heart of the justice system for other survivors of male violence and state-sanctioned discrimination. It was outrage at what had happened to Emma that had drawn Julie into investigating and challenging the violence endemic in the sex trade.

I gained further insight and understanding into the lasting damage wreaked by prostitution, and about the experience of survivors, through Julie's writing and research on a host of issues – trafficking, the men who use prostitutes, the growing abolitionist movement and the way prostitution is viewed and handled by different legislative regimes worldwide – and through meeting activists and survivors in other countries when I travelled with her.

One key area identified by a major research study to which Julie contributed, later published as a book, *Exiting Prostitution: A Study in Female Desistance*, was the huge stumbling block often posed by the past criminal convictions that were an occupational hazard of street prostitution.

Although the act of selling sex is not a criminal offence in itself, standing on a street corner with the apparent intention of doing so is. Section 1 of the Street Offences Act 1959 stated: 'It shall be an offence for a common prostitute to loiter or solicit in a street or public place for the purpose of prostitution.' It was a very minor criminal offence, normally resulting only in a small fine, but the criminal conviction would remain on a woman's record until, bizarrely, she reached the age of a hundred. The objectionable term 'common prostitute', which dated back to the Vagrancy Act 1824 and was applicable solely to women, was not removed until 2009, when the offence itself was amended, at which point 'common prostitute' was changed to 'person' and could apply equally to men and women.

Like Fiona Broadfoot, most women who had been involved in street prostitution, usually as a result of having been pimped as teenagers, were regularly arrested by the police and had accumulated a string of minor criminal convictions. They were now finding that if they wanted to apply for a job working with children or vulnerable adults, or to volunteer in these sectors, they would first have to obtain a certificate displaying their criminal record under the Disclosure and Barring Services (DBS) scheme, which they were required to show to a prospective employer or relevant authority. Although the presence of such minor convictions was not necessarily a bar to being given a job, having to disclose them would reveal a former life in prostitution – a deeply embarrassing and stigmatizing prospect which, for many women, was a real psychological barrier to getting, or even seeking, work.

Julie asked me if I could look into whether there was any way of legally challenging mandatory disclosure of such records. Debaleena Dasgupta agreed to help me with this and Julie introduced us to Janice, one of the women she had interviewed for her research, who was keen to take a legal challenge forward.

Janice's story was horrific and by no means atypical. She had been born in Leeds in the early 1970s to a mother who suffered from serious mental illness and was sectioned several times. When her father began sexually abusing her from the age of around nine, she told no one. She started running away from home, shoplifting and becoming disruptive at school. Her mother couldn't cope, and handed her over to social services. Janice was taken to Shadwell, a children's home where she was bullied and beaten up by some of the other children. She complained to a male staff member, who told her she was 'promiscuous' and a 'slag'. Many years later, that same staff member was convicted of sexually abusing some of the children in the home.

When Janice was twelve or thirteen, she was raped by two of the boys at Shadwell. She told staff and the police were called, but the boys denied the allegations and nothing further came of it. Although one of the boys was moved to another home, the other was still there, right under her nose. Janice's behaviour became more and more destructive, she truanted constantly from school and was dismissed as a 'delinquent'.

At about fourteen, she and another girl ran away and ended up at an after-hours party at a 'blues house' in Chapeltown, the local red-light district, where they danced with older men and were given alcohol and spliffs. It was here that Janice met Kevin, in his late twenties, who offered her a place to stay, had sex with her and was soon referring to himself as her boyfriend. Kevin would buy her clothes, make-up and other gifts and picked her up regularly from Shadwell to take her out. Janice told the children's home staff that he was her boyfriend. They warned her that he was too old for her but never called the police.

Kevin was not the only pimp who used to sit in a parked car out-side the home after school and at weekends. Mainly men in their twenties, they would play music on the radio, chat up the teenage girls coming in and out and offer them cigarettes.

Before long, Kevin persuaded Janice to go to London with him, where they 'could be together and wouldn't be hassled by police or social workers'. He took her to a flat which she was surprised to find already occupied by several women. Kevin told her that they belonged to him, and so did she. She would have to pay him back for all the clothes and gifts he had been buying for her. Janice was stricken. 'How can I? I don't have any money.' He said that if she slept with some of his friends, they would pay for it, and, if she loved him, she would do this to help him out.

It was when she insisted that she didn't want to, and only wanted to be with him, that she saw his nasty side for the first time. He beat her black and blue with a bicycle chain. With no other option but to have sex with Kevin's 'friends', she gave in. The other women at what she didn't really grasp at the time was a brothel, some of whom were a lot older than Janice, kept an eye on her and dealt with the money that she wasn't aware at first was changing hands.

After a while Kevin took Janice back to Leeds, where he made her have sex with men who came to his house. Then he put her to work on a street corner in Spencer Place, at the heart of the red-light area, with some other girls. She was instructed to offer sex in exchange for money, told how much to charge and given condoms. If she agreed to have sex without a condom, she learned, she would be able to charge a lot more. Kevin kept a tight rein on the cash. She was still having sex with him, still regarded him as her boyfriend and still believed she loved him, even though she was now frightened, too, of the violence that would erupt if she didn't do as he wanted.

Janice was frequently stopped by the police for soliciting and loiter-ing. Sometimes they would call her mother to collect her or take her to Shadwell themselves. The staff there cannot have failed to realize that she was selling sex and being controlled by Kevin, and yet she was treated not as an abused child but as if she was doing this out of choice. Sometimes Janice was given a caution; other times she was arrested, charged and taken to a juvenile court in Leeds, where she would plead guilty. Kevin was never arrested or investigated by the police.

The only intervention the police made was to take Janice to a semi-secure children's home, Westwood Grange, probably as a result of somebody reporting her plight. Increasingly distressed and despairing, she had told one of her punters that she lived in a children's home and guessed it must have been him.

At Westwood Grange, Janice was punished rather than helped. She was grounded for four weeks and, if she misbehaved, she would be locked in the 'Orange Room', which was devoid of any facilities or furniture, not even a bed. Once she was allowed out, she soon fell back into Kevin's clutches. He put her back on the streets at Spencer Place and beat her up if she did not comply. The police would pick her up and return her to Westwood Grange, where the staff would merely ask her, 'Are you stopping or going?' and she would run off again.

And so the cycle continued until eventually Janice decided to tell one of the female staff members about what Kevin was doing to her. The police were called and she provided a statement giving them the whole story. Even now Kevin was not arrested. The police said they would look into her complaint but that, in order to prosecute a man for pimping, they would need her account to be corroborated by statements from at least three 'working girls'. They later informed Westwood Grange that they would not be taking the case any further. Kevin punished Janice by beating her up especially savagely and making her walk around Spencer Place in the snow on a bitterly cold winter day in her bra and pants. She was still only fifteen years old.

A few weeks after she and another girl from Westwood Grange were offered a 'business opportunity' by two men in their forties – they were coerced into being filmed having sex with one of the men and with each other – the police came to the children's home and arrested the girls. The officers treated the whole thing as a joke. 'Are you the girls from the video?' they asked. 'Well, you're famous now.' Janice learned later that the men were part of a paedophile ring producing child pornography. The staff at Westwood Grange blamed the girls.

When Janice turned sixteen, she walked out of Westwood Grange for good and went to Bradford, where she was befriended by a succession of predatory men involved in the only kind of life she knew. It was not long before her next boyfriend was pimping her. After she became pregnant by him she moved out to try to look after the baby, but the child was taken into care and Janice went back on to the streets. A new boyfriend, Ahmed, with whom she stayed for several years, proved to be a gangster as well as a pimp and introduced her to heroin. They had a baby together, but that child, too, was removed by social services.

By the time Ahmed was imprisoned for attempted murder, Janice was hooked on heroin and saw no option but to continue selling sex to fund her habit. After giving birth to a third baby, she worked really hard to show herself capable of caring for her but, once again, her child was taken away. Finally, with a little assistance, Janice found the strength to turn her life around. She completed a methadone programme and came off heroin, began counselling, put prostitution behind her and, when she became pregnant for a fourth time, by which point she had access to some support, she was able to keep her son.

Janice had no training and no work experience, but although she lacked the confidence to apply for a regular job, she was encouraged to volunteer and to share her experiences with other vulnerable women and girls. She was offered some paid assignments to talk to social work students to help them understand some of the signs of sexual abuse and grooming. She was also invited to visit New Hall prison to raise awareness among young offenders. This role gave her some sense of self-worth: it was an opportunity to play a part in preventing others from suffering as she had done and to move on from her past.

But suddenly the shutters came down. Owing to new, more stringent regulations that required her to provide disclosure of her criminal convictions, she was told she would no longer be able to visit New Hall prison. Neither, she learned, was she allowed to work with children or travel outside the European Union. But what upset her more than anything else was that she was not to be permitted to enter her son's school unless accompanied by a teacher – not even to take him inside in the mornings or to discuss his education, let alone volunteer to go with her child and his classmates on school trips as other parents did.

The change in the legislation had come about in the wake of the shocking murders in 2002 of ten-year-olds Holly Wells and Jessica Chapman by a school caretaker, Ian Huntley, and the public outcry after his conviction, when it emerged that not only had the police failed to pursue numerous previous allegations against him of sexual assaults on underage girls and young women, but he had been able to secure a job, and free access to children, at the primary school in Soham, Cambridgeshire, attended by Holly and Jessica.

The Bichard inquiry set up by the home secretary made recommendations for the introduction of a mandatory registration scheme for people working with children and vulnerable adults, as well as the tightening up of various procedures within the Criminal Records Bureau system, including compulsory records checks on anyone applying to work with children and others at risk.

It was an important protective measure for the vulnerable, but it appeared that it was screening out not only abusers but also survivors of abuse.

Under the Data Protection Act, Debaleena applied for Janice's criminal records as listed on the Police National Computer (PNC). They showed that, between 1990 and 2005, she had a total of sixty-four convictions, of which all but seven were for either soliciting or failing to surrender. The convictions that were not specifically for soliciting related to offences committed under duress in the context of being pimped and involved in prostitution. There were more convictions she had received at the juvenile court before the age of sixteen that did not appear on the criminal record.

Janice was a victim of the most horrific child sexual abuse, violence and exploitation. She had been forced into prostitution as a child and left unprotected by children's home staff, social workers and police. That she had, eventually, managed to save herself, having grown up equipped with so few tools to do so and with so little support, was a minor miracle. When she came to see us in 2014, she had recently turned forty. She was a lovely woman, but lacked self-esteem. Her one source of pride was that she had managed to keep hold of her son and to apply herself to giving him a good upbringing, and now her history was casting a shadow even on that. I felt this was a grave injustice and that there might be avenues to legally challenge at least the mandatory disclosure of her criminal convictions under the DBS scheme.

Debaleena and I approached Karon Monaghan QC, a public law specialist and a lead expert on discrimination law. Karon provided a written legal advice exploring the very complex statutory framework that had evolved in this area and set out a number of potential routes to mounting a challenge to the current law.

A huge number of survivors were affected by this discrimination. It seemed to me a good idea to pull together some more testimony to strengthen the legal challenge by demonstrating that Janice was by no means an isolated or extreme case.

I immediately thought of Fiona Broadfoot, who, in the eighteen years since I'd met her at that Brighton conference back in 1996, had remained committed to using her knowledge of prostitution and its repercussions to influence change and had been vocal about the impact of carrying lifelong criminal convictions. Fiona agreed without hesitation to become another claimant in the action we were preparing.

Although she had spoken publicly many times from personal experience of the damage caused by prostitution, it was clear that having to recount her deeply private history to me in detail was very painful for her.

Fiona, a few years older than Janice, was from Bradford, and had a similar story to tell, one of a troubled childhood and being groomed at fourteen by a 'boyfriend' who first lavished attention on her, then forced her into prostitution and kept her in line with violence. On being 'rescued' from the first pimp by a second, she was sent out on to the streets, where she came to the attention of the police, appeared at juvenile court and was remanded to the same semi-secure children's home, Westwood Grange, to which Janice would later be taken. Her pimp, who was allowed to visit her there, soon persuaded her, with promises of the bright lights, to go with him to London, where she was made to sell sex on the streets and in brothels around Paddington Green and Sussex Gardens.

Fiona tried to escape back to Leeds or Bradford several times, only for the pimp to find her and beat her up. Eventually, at the age of twenty-one, she succeeded in getting away and went back up north. She applied for a childcare course at college and absolutely loved it. Allocated a placement at a local primary school, she had already started working there when the criminal records check she'd been asked to apply for arrived. The headteacher called her in, told her that the school wasn't an appropriate environment for her and had her frogmarched off the premises.

Utterly humiliated, and with her new life in tatters, Fiona decided she might as well go back to selling sex. For several more years, she endured this existence, and the violence and rape that went with the territory – on one occasion, she told me, after being kidnapped and repeatedly raped by a terrifying man, she got away with her life only by spraying perfume into his face and running off down the street naked – until the shock of a terrible murder convinced her that she had to get out for good. The victim was her cousin's daughter, Maureen Stepan, also groomed from the age of fourteen. She had been introduced to heroin, and with it dependency on prostitution to support her habit, and then, finally, killed in her home by a notorious punter. She was seventeen years old.

Fiona's resolve was strengthened by the discovery that she was pregnant with her son. It was now no longer just about her: she had someone she could love and who needed her. She had something to live for.

She rebuilt her confidence by speaking at meetings, working on the kerb-crawlers' rehabilitation scheme (the British take on the 'john school'), helping to train police officers and advising girls at risk of sexual abuse and exploitation. She wanted to apply for a course to train to be a social worker but they told her she wouldn't get a placement because of her criminal convictions for 'sexual offences'.

Fiona was a powerful communicator and effective trainer but for much of the kind of work she wanted to do, and in which her past experience was a valuable asset, she had to apply for a DBS certificate. She gave me a sense of just how severe an impact this had on her life. 'Every time the DBS has been delivered to me, I go to bed for several days. I stop washing and go back into the memories of when I felt degraded and inhuman. At these times, I can't eat, I can't sleep and I knock myself out with alcohol. I am traumatized by it.'

That trauma was echoed by other women who had experienced street prostitution from whom I took additional statements to support the claim. All had come to be there as coerced and exploited teenagers after abuse and neglect in childhood, and all had survived the experience only through their own courage and determination.

Women like Martha, who had been employed as a social worker by the same local authority for fourteen years before she was required to apply for a DBS certificate. Highly respected by her colleagues, Martha felt that not only had she succeeded in putting behind her everything she had suffered as a young woman, but that what it had taught her made her more empathetic and effective in her job.

She had been controlled by her pimp boyfriend for eight years from the age of eighteen until she gave birth to her baby. When she refused to return to the streets afterwards, he brutally assaulted her, and this time she pressed charges. The respite offered by a women's refuge had helped her to take charge of her life and gain an understanding of self-esteem and male violence. She stayed there for a year with her son and often returned as a volunteer after moving on and earning a place at university to study social work. On qualifying, she started her job supporting people with mental health problems and had never looked back – until she came up against the changes ushered in by the Bichard inquiry.

When she was shown her list of convictions by her manager, it was the first time she had ever seen them. 'I was really shocked. Suddenly, my whole history was in front of me, presented as a long criminal record. While I had a context for that history, someone not knowing that context would make all sorts of assumptions. I felt really disgusted, horrified and ashamed.' Although her manager was supportive, the shame was too much for Martha. It began to overwhelm her to such an extent that she eventually left her job, and her profession, and spiralled into depression.

Sam had never had a job, despite applying for many vacancies through the Job Centre. After she disclosed her criminal convictions, no offers were forthcoming. The shame that dogged her meant she also avoided getting involved in any of her children's school activities for which a DBS check was required. Sexually abused as a child by adult men, she had ended up in street prostitution at the age of fifteen and became addicted to the heroin that offered her the illusion of escape from the pain of her existence.

Eventually, with the help of social services and the motivation of having two sons to take care of, she came off drugs and got out of prostitution. 'I feel that I am more a victim of crime and can't see why I am being punished for this,' she said. 'The only person I harmed was myself.'

The common perception that Section 1 soliciting offences were classed as sexual offences, Karon Monaghan advised, was incorrect. She suggested that the misunderstanding might stem from confusion with the separate offence of soliciting under the Sexual Offences Act 2003, which criminalized kerb-crawlers. This form of soliciting *was* classified as a sexual offence, and required those convicted to be recorded on the sex offenders' register. However, the misinterpretation was clearly widespread and persistent, as both Janice and Fiona, along with many other women who had contributed to the research, believed themselves to be categorized as sex offenders.

Karon thought there was a potential legal argument that the requirement to disclose these 'spent' convictions in specified circumstances amounted to an interference with the women's rights as protected under Article 8 of the European Convention of Human Rights, namely the right to privacy. A case concerning the disclosure, many years after the event, of minor cautions and convictions (one of them involving the juvenile theft of a bicycle) had gone all the way to the Supreme Court, which had held that the ongoing disclosure was an unjustified interference in the private life of the individual. The court made a declaration of incompatibility under the Human Rights Act which led to the government modifying the operation of the DBS scheme to accommodate the filtering out of single minor spent convictions from the disclosure certificate. Karon felt we could build on this case to argue similarly in respect of our clients.

She also suggested there might be a sexual discrimination claim under Article 14 of the ECHR on the basis that, first, the vast majority of those who held convictions for soliciting and loitering were women, and, second, the majority of posts for which disclosure of spent convictions was required were likely to be jobs caring for children or other vulnerable people – jobs disproportionately performed by women.

Through my work on immigration detention cases, I was aware of the development of human rights law around the protection of victims of trafficking and wondered whether Article 4 ECHR, which provided for a duty by the state to protect its citizens from forced labour and servitude, might have a bearing.

The signature in 2006 of the Palermo Protocol, a Europe-wide treaty aimed at safeguarding victims of trafficking, had paved the way for the recognition that such victims who are forced to commit crimes should not be criminalized. Non-penalization provisions had been introduced, enhanced by European law directives, and, as a result, victims of trafficking, whether for sexual slavery or forced labour in illegal activities – working in cannabis farms, for example – were able to appeal criminal convictions if the link between the offence and their servitude could be shown.

Although 'sex trafficking' is commonly understood as the transporting of victims from one country to another for the purposes of sexual exploitation, it does not require movement across borders. The essential element is the subjection of an individual to commercial sexual activity through force, fraud or coercion. Much more recently, Parliament had passed the Modern Slavery Act 2015, which introduced a defence in circumstances where an offence was committed as a consequence of coercion through slavery or exploitation as defined by the legislation. While this Act did not apply retrospectively, it was a powerful indicator of contemporaneous attitudes towards those whose criminal convictions were incurred in this way. Karon agreed that this was another argument we should deploy as part of our grounds of judicial review.

With Janice and Fiona as claimants throughout what would turn

out to be a marathon process, and with the backing of witness statements from several other women in the same situation, we fired the
starting gun. The appropriate defendant was the home secretary, who
was ultimately responsible for the Disclosure and Barring Service,
and accordingly, in May 2016, I submitted our letter before claim to
the government legal department, setting out how the recording,
retention and disclosure of our clients' criminal records violated their
human rights as protected by Articles 4, 8 and 14 EHCR.

We did not hear back from the government lawyers until some two
months later, when they invited us not to issue proceedings because
there were several other cases due to be decided by the Court of
Appeal which dealt with the same issues. It was clear that these cases
concerned individuals with more than one minor criminal conviction for entirely different offences, and that the legal matter to be
determined related only to whether the statutory regime for disclosure of criminal records was in accordance with the law and
proportionate with regard to the human right of those individuals to
privacy. They did not raise issues of discrimination or trafficking.

I pressed for a proper response that addressed our legal arguments,
pointing out that our claimants were suffering from significant and
ongoing stigmatization and shouldn't be required to wait indefinitely.
After another delay, the government solicitor wrote back challenging
our sex discrimination argument by citing a range of other offences
subject to the statutory regime, such as rape, which were either exclu-
sively or disproportionately committed by men. As far as trafficking
was concerned, she asserted that the recording of offences, as opposed
to their prosecution, did not constitute a 'penalty' within the meaning of the anti-trafficking instruments.

I talked it over with Karon and we felt we could counter these
arguments and should proceed with the judicial review. To support
the claim for sex discrimination, I needed to assemble any context-
ual factual evidence available to show how women were subject to

discrimination. I made a Freedom of Information request to the Disclosure and Barring Service to find out how many convictions for soliciting and loitering appeared in DBS certificates as disaggregated by sex. The answer told us that between 2012 and 2017, 3,337 certificates containing these convictions were provided for female applicants and a mere 26 for men.

Further probing of the total number of offences under Section 1 of the Street Offences Act enabled us to set out in our grounds how they were overwhelmingly likely to be committed by women. Between 1984 and 30 April 2004, when the offence was still gender-specific, 190,045 convictions or cautions were handed down or given to women. For the same period, the figure for men was 1,595: less than 1 per cent. In the ten years from 1 May 2004 to 2014, it was 2 per cent: 11,341 for women and 213 for men.

We also wanted to look at the types of jobs for which a DBS certificate was required and to confirm, as was our impression, that they were roles performed principally by women. My paralegal assistant, Paul, researched the gender breakdown of all the 'excepted' professions, appointments and occupations for which a certificate was needed. Some were predominantly male, judges and police officers, for example, but far more were disproportionately taken up by women, such as teaching, social services and care work. Overall, from the data we were able to capture, the picture revealed that approximately 70 per cent of the jobs for which a certificate had to be supplied were more likely, by a significant margin, to be carried out by women than by men.

Also relevant to these convictions was the fact that most women who had been in street prostitution would end up with multiple convictions for soliciting and loitering, because of the nature of this activity and the way in which it was policed. As all the women told us, they would be picked up by the police while standing on a street corner and charged with a Section 1 offence, for which the penalty was customarily a small fine. The women would then go straight back

on to the streets to earn the money to pay it. Unusually, repeat offending under Section 1 did not generally lead to more severe penalties, as
would be normal with other types of law-breaking. What it did mean,
though, typically, was a very long list of criminal convictions.

Another woman whose story we were using to support our claim
had been prostituted before she was fourteen and moved around
from city to city. It had taken her sixteen years to break free. In that
time, she had accumulated ninety convictions. As Martha had
pointed out, any employer seeing their DBS certificates would be
given the impression they were dealing with career criminals. But
the multiple conviction rule, which required the disclosure of all
convictions, whatever the circumstances, for more than one offence,
prohibited the women from arguing that any of these convictions
should be filtered from the certificate.

We contended not only that this impacted with unfair severity on
those who had committed offences under Section 1 of the Street
Offences Act, but that the disclosure regime was itself unlawful, and
so was the criminalization in the first place of 'soliciting and loitering', because it discriminated against women. 'It is in the nature of
"public nuisance"', we stated in our grounds, lodged with our evidence at the administrative court, and, invariably, those penalized
were the most vulnerable, 'typically in circumstances of great sexual
exploitation and commonly trafficking. It does not pose a risk to any
person (other than the woman engaging in such conduct). It also
impedes a woman's ability to exit prostitution.'

In response, the lawyers acting for the home secretary informed
us that they would be applying for a stay in the proceedings pending
the Court of Appeal judgment in the case of *R(P) v. Secretary of State
for the Home Department and Others*, which concerned the effects of
the multiple conviction rule on disclosure of some minor criminal
offences of a different type.

I knew from Debaleena, who had recently moved from Birnberg

Peirce to the legal charity Liberty, where she had been assigned this very case and was therefore familiar with both actions, that this Court of Appeal hearing had just taken place and they were waiting for the judgment. I told the government lawyers that we would be opposing their application for a stay, once again drawing their attention to the distinction between our case and this one.

The hearing of the application for the stay was eventually listed for July 2017, by which time the judgment in *R(P)* had been handed down. The decision was largely in favour of the claimants and therefore helpful to us. However, the government had been granted permission to appeal it in the Supreme Court, and was now arguing that our case should wait until that appeal had been heard. In my experience, that might easily take another couple of years.

When the application for a stay was heard at the Divisional Court, I was encouraged by the comment of one of the judges, Lord Justice Simon, that there had been 'a change of approach in the last quarter-century – now women such as the claimants are viewed as victims'. This was precisely the sort of recognition of a shift in public attitude that could help carry our argument in court. The judges refused to grant the stay, and ordered the government to file their full response to our claim. It would then be for a judge to decide whether our grounds were 'arguable' and whether permission for the judicial review should be given.

After the government filed their summary grounds of resistance, Mr Justice William Davis granted us permission on some of our grounds but refused on others. We applied to renew and the court agreed to a 'rolled-up hearing', whereby our procedural application for permission would be heard immediately before our substantive arguments, to take place in January 2018.

At last we would have the opportunity to assert in court that the criminalization of victims of sexual exploitation and their consequent stigmatization through the retention and disclosure of their criminal records was unlawful. In preparation for the hearing, while counsel honed her legal arguments, we took our landmark legal challenge to the media. Fiona, who had waived her right to anonymity, made herself available for interview. On the morning we were due in court, she and I appeared on the *Today* programme. Before the interview, Fiona made it clear to the producer that she did not wish to be referred to as a 'sex worker', the label that had now been widely adopted by the media on the basis that it was viewed by some organizations as less stigmatizing than 'prostitute'.

Fiona was a direct and impressive speaker. When she was asked on air why she objected to the term 'sex worker', she said: 'It's not sex and it's not work. I have been an activist for twenty-three years since I exited prostitution and I can tell you now ... I have never met a woman who is empowered by prostitution. So for me "sex work" does not describe what it is really about. I bet the person who coined that phrase has never had to have sex with up to ten or fifteen men a day.'

As we left the studio, John Humphrys, the veteran *Today* presenter, ran out after us to shake hands with Fiona and commend her on her articulate response.

In court we were joined by some of the women who had provided witness evidence for the case, campaigners and supporters and a smattering of journalists. Karon was assisted by Keina Yoshida, a young barrister with a legal academic background and an excellent knowledge of international UN treaties, including the Convention on the Elimination of All Forms of Discrimination Against Women. In our grounds we were relying on important CEDAW provisions on violence against women and sex trafficking. Karon's task involved a very complex exposition of the statutory framework and she did a marvellous job with a clear and calm presentation of the legal arguments. The two (white male) judges informed us at the end of the day that they would reserve judgment.

Six weeks later, we learned that we had won in relation to the arguments under Article 8, the right to privacy. Their lordships explained that they were bound by precedent to accept the Court of Appeal decision in the *R(P)* case. However, they went on to say: 'We would have reached the same conclusion even if not bound by *R(P)*, in particular because the facts of this case vividly illustrate the fact that the multiple conviction rule operates in circumstances in which any link between the past offending and the assessment of present risk in a particular employment is either non-existent or at best extremely tenuous.'

In other words, the automatic disclosure of these convictions under the DBS scheme was unlawful. It was a massive victory for the women mired in this pernicious bureaucracy.

'Finally, I feel like a weight has been lifted off my shoulders,' Fiona told the press. 'It's a vindication. I have carried these convictions around – eight pages of them – all my life and it's a disgrace. Not one of those men who bought and used and abused me – even the ones who knew fine well I was a child when first put on the streets – has ever had to face the consequences of his actions. It has been a long fight but worth it.'

From the legal point of view, though, it was a mixed bag of results. The judges went on to reject our grounds with regard to sex discrimination, trafficking and the criminalization of the Section 1 offence itself. Their reasoning was disappointing and we felt it was worth applying for permission to appeal the decision on those grounds. The government, meanwhile, applied for permission to appeal the ground upon which we had won. The judges considered written submissions from both parties and, to our dismay, ruled that our grounds had 'no merit' whereas the defendant should be granted permission to appeal.

That meant the potential win, and the benefits we needed to see flow from it, would be put on hold until the Court of Appeal hearing, which could be more than a year away. We fired off various further written submissions and another judge decided there should be an oral hearing – in the end there were two – for us to argue for permission to appeal all of the decisions we were challenging. In between, the *R(P)* case went to the Supreme Court, where the judgment was upheld, which we thought would make the defendant's appeal in our case unarguable. Yet the home secretary's lawyers did not withdraw it.

We pressed on with a second, short oral hearing to argue for permission to appeal on our trafficking and sex discrimination grounds before two Court of Appeal judges, Lady Justice King and Lady Justice Rafferty. In court, alongside our legal team, were Fiona and Sam, who wanted to see the whites of the government's lawyers' eyes, hear counsel's arguments and enjoy the theatre of the courtroom. They would not be disappointed.

As Lady Justice Rafferty walked in, it did not escape notice that she was sporting a pair of extremely high heels. She sat down and surveyed the court, doing an almost comic double-take when she saw me. Lady Justice Rafferty was the judge who had granted us permission in the Sally Challen appeal in a different court the previous year. Before the hearing commenced, she said: 'I see that Ms Wistrich sits before me in this court. May I please extend my congratulations to you on the outcome of the Challen appeal? You must be very proud.' Everyone looked round and smiled. I just sat there blushing.

Permission was granted to argue our additional grounds before the full Court of Appeal at a hearing that finally took place in January 2020. Shortly beforehand, the defendants at last announced that they were withdrawing their appeal in the light of the Supreme Court judgment in *R(P)*, which meant the government was no longer opposing the basis of the victory we had achieved two years earlier. The Court of Appeal was therefore now considering the other challenges from our side.

The judges decided against us on some points but ruled that the so-called 'hundred-year rule' merited further consideration. This concerned the length of time that a record of criminal convictions could be retained on the Police National Computer. The rule specified that they would remain until the offender reached the age of a hundred. So, while the women's DBS certificates could now be filtered of their soliciting and loitering offences, which would not be seen by prospective employers and others, a full record of their convictions would still be available to a number of agencies, such as the criminal courts, on the PNC.

The argument regarding the retention of convictions on the police database was remitted back to the High Court, where the National Police Chiefs Council was joined to the case as a second defendant. As this hearing took place during the Covid lockdown, everyone was participating online. We created a WhatsApp group to give our clients and the other women involved in the case a forum in which to ask questions and make observations on proceedings. The punctuation of the solemn and complex legal arguments by their commentary, littered with emojis and by turns infused with dark humour and downright fury, added to the surreal atmosphere of the virtual courtroom.

'100 years seems rather long! That's another 52 years for me.'

'What a fucking joke . . . the amount of coppers, military and tax men who bought sexual access to our teenage bodies . . .'

'Crazy we are lumped in with sex offenders.'

'Probably a blessing it is virtual. I have a feeling Fiona would have probably jumped the benches by now!'

There were domestic encroachments of the kind people all over the country were experiencing as they tried to do their jobs from home. During the court lunch break, Julie's key got stuck in our front door and I had to climb out through the front-room window into the street to get it open. Although their lordships were none the wiser, the story was shared in the WhatsApp group, where it provided more light relief. 'Could Harriet refrain from breaking and entering,' posted one member. 'The police disapprove.'

Judgment was again reserved. When we eventually received it, the application of the hundred-year rule to these Section 1 offences stood. The judges said they readily accepted that the claimants felt fearful, angry and degraded by having convictions on record for the rest of their lives, despite decades having passed since they had offended. But the High Court took the view that the public interest in having a comprehensive record of all criminal convictions outweighed the personal interest of the claimants.

As counsel did not think our arguments strong enough, taking into account legal precedent, to appeal this judgment, we had reached the end of the road with the English courts. We have now taken the outstanding issues in this claim, those relating to the criminalization of the soliciting and loitering offence itself, and the hundred-year rule on the retention of convictions, to the UN committee that monitors the international implementation of the CEDAW treaty, and, at the time of writing, we await the result of their deliberations. Meanwhile, Fiona and Sam set up a new campaign, HOPE (History of Prostitution Expunged), to fight for these objectives.

The easiest solution could be a political one. The Section 1 offence is seldom used now, and the police rarely arrest women on the streets. If Parliament simply repealed Section 1, 'soliciting and loitering' would no longer be a crime and therefore no longer recorded on the PNC. A separate mechanism could then be put in place to expunge historic convictions from the record, along the lines of a similar process established recently to address offences dating back to when homosexuality was a criminal offence.

In a society where attitudes have changed since the far-off days when this legislation was enacted, an organized lobby of Parliament might produce the result that has to date evaded us in the courtroom.

10

The Centre for Women's Justice

By 2015 I HAD BEEN a solicitor for twenty years. The work was challenging and intense, often rewarding, but relentless. I was fifty-five and my beloved father had just died after a long period of deteriorating health, while my fiercely intellectual mother's engagement with reality was declining as her Alzheimer's advanced. I needed a break to reflect and take stock. Did I want a change of pace? Did I want to do something different? Explore film-making again, maybe?

I took a three-month sabbatical and travelled with Julie, who was researching her book on prostitution, to Canada, South Korea, Cambodia and Vietnam. In our last port of call I had arranged to meet Sasha, an old friend from my university days. She had done some training in life coaching, and offered herself as a sounding board. In leisurely conversations by the banks of the Mekong River, we sifted through possible future directions and I raised an idea I had been contemplating for a number of years but had never had time to take further: my vision of a legal charity that would tackle state accountability for all types of violence against women by undertaking litigation specifically aimed at bringing about systemic reform.

Justice for Women was by design a single-issue campaigning group that had deliberately remained unincorporated, and largely unfunded, to preserve its independence. What I wanted to create was something more stable and substantial that, through legal action, could influence policy to bring about changes in the law and ensure that existing legislation was properly implemented. Charitable status would open the door to applying for funding and seeking donations to take on cases for which legal aid was unavailable and to mount high-risk but potentially game-changing legal challenges.

Sasha had no training in or experience of the law, but she thought I had a clear concept of what I wanted to achieve and how I might go about achieving it. She encouraged me to spend the last month of my sabbatical formulating a project plan and conducting a feasibility study. I distilled the objectives of the organization I envisaged into a summary that fitted on to one A4 page and could be easily shared with potential stakeholders to seek their feedback. I then identified and contacted some key people in the women's sector, legal NGOs and other institutions in the field to explore whether they thought there was a place for a legal charity like this. When my proposal met with widespread enthusiasm, I decided to take the plunge.

A couple of the women I spoke to pointed me in the direction of a funding stream being offered by the Baring Foundation for projects with the goal of strengthening civil society through the use of law and human rights. I was delighted: this could have been designed with my vision in mind. I applied through the foundation for seed funding and was awarded a small grant, which I put towards setting up the charity that would become the Centre for Women's Justice.

I invited three women to be its founding trustees: Sasha, Sarah Ricca, a fellow solicitor practising in the same field as me at another firm, and Davina James-Hanman, who, having worked for decades on DV policy and with women's charities, knew all the principal players in the women's sector.

By this time my sabbatical was over and I was back at my desk at Birnberg Peirce. With the support of the partners, and in particular

Marcia Willis Stewart, with whom I had worked closely for so many years, I reduced my working week to four days to carve out the time I needed to get the Centre for Women's Justice up and running.

In our first year we concentrated on arranging outreach events across the country to bring together survivors, activists, lawyers, academics and journalists committed to combating violence against women and girls. Our launch, in Manchester in 2016, was attended by over a hundred people, and we held additional gatherings in Cardiff, Newcastle and Bristol, where we exchanged information and initiatives on holding the state to account by using legal tools to address bad practice and decision-making and agreed the principle of collaboration in instigating legal challenges.

The following year I was back in Manchester to speak at an International Women's Day event hosted by Doughty Street Chambers. I had just spent two days in the Supreme Court defending the judgment against the Metropolitan Police in the John Worboys case, which had established that the police had a duty to conduct effective investigations into rape and other crimes of serious violence.

After my panel, I was approached by Maggie Oliver, a former detective constable with Greater Manchester Police. Maggie had resigned in disgust over the way her force had failed so many young women caught up in the child abuse ring that eventually resulted in the first high-profile criminal trial, in 2012, of members of a Rochdale 'grooming gang'. These men, mainly of Pakistani origin, had targeted and sexually exploited working-class, socially excluded young girls – forty-seven victims were identified during the police investigation. Nine men were convicted of offences that included rape, sex trafficking and conspiracy to engage in sexual activity with a child.

Maggie had been brought in to assist the investigating team to build bridges with a number of the young victims who had been badly let down by both the police and child protection services. She

had experience of how victims like these had been handled in a previous disastrous investigation, and agreed to join the team only after
she was assured by the police and the CPS that things would be very
different this time. Maggie worked closely with two sisters, gradually
gaining their trust and helping to instil in them the confidence to
provide critical information which was instrumental in identifying
some of the key perpetrators.

The elder sister, while still a child herself, had been used by the
paedophile ring to ensnare younger girls. In spite of the assurances
of the police and the CPS that she would be treated as a victim, this
young woman had, without her knowledge, been listed on the original indictment as one of the conspirators to the abuse. Appalled at
how investigators had ridden roughshod over a vulnerable witness
to suit the way they wanted to frame their case, Maggie was determined to speak out publicly about how it had been mishandled and
that her own force should be held accountable. For months her
attempts to be heard by the justice system – by the chief constable,
the IPCC, the Home Office – had been ignored and she had been
told by local lawyers suing social services over their safeguarding
failures that it was not possible to sue the police. Encouraged by our
hard-won success against the Met, she asked if I could find a way.

I arranged to meet Maggie to discuss this properly a couple of
months later when I was up in Sheffield at another event. She told
me that the prosecution had barely scratched the surface of an
entrenched organized crime scandal and recounted a catalogue of
horror stories: of testimony buried by the police; of how victims
were neglected, mistreated, dismissed as unreliable witnesses and
criminalized. A TV dramatization of the case, *Three Girls*, on which
Maggie had advised and which would tell some of the story, was, she
mentioned, due to be broadcast shortly.

This harrowing account of how the gang used and abused teenage
girls won a clutch of BAFTAs and other awards the following year.

Though pleased that the series had been made, Maggie was unhappy with its portrayal of Amber, the character based on the young woman whose trust had been so utterly betrayed. She had never been charged or prosecuted, but, as if she had not suffered enough, the dramatization of her role in the trial led to her being stigmatized in the press as 'the honey monster', a cruel nickname they picked up from another damaged victim.

Grooming gangs were being talked of as a recent phenomenon but the Rochdale offenders were just the latest in a long line of abusers preying upon disadvantaged children: the close parallels with the experiences of women like Janice and Fiona, forsaken by the care system, pimped and prostituted as teenagers twenty and thirty years before, struck a chord with me. I told Maggie I would do whatever I could to get some justice for this new generation of victims.

By now I had raised enough financial support at CWJ to employ a smart young solicitor, Kate Ellis, to help set up our litigation department so that we could start taking on our own cases. Kate launched a civil claim for damages on behalf of three of the victims of the Rochdale grooming gang, the girls on whom two of the characters in *Three Girls*, Amber and Ruby, had been based, and Daisy, who had regularly been arrested as a young teenager, the worse for drink, in the company of adult men, while the men themselves went about their grubby business untroubled by the police. Over three years we prepared a claim against both Greater Manchester Police and the CPS, relying on the precedent set in the Worboys case. In April 2022, we finally settled the claim and the new chief constable of Greater Manchester Police met our clients, who were given a personal apology for the way they had been treated. In the meantime, in 2019, Maggie Oliver set up a foundation to support and fight for justice for survivors of abuse.

CWJ was expanding in a number of directions. Another solicitor I had collaborated with previously, Nogah Ofer, who had recently decided to leave private practice and litigation and wanted to put her legal skills to use in the women's sector, joined our small team. Nogah was instrumental in establishing a scheme offering legal training and advice to organizations working on the front line with victims and survivors of male violence across the country, geared to helping them identify where police and other criminal justice agencies are falling down in their legal duties so that they can better challenge such failures.

Where their advocacy on behalf of survivors does not achieve the right response, we can supply legal advice and representation as necessary through a panel of lawyers we have set up to consider specific cases, or specific issues within cases. Our work with organizations at the sharp end helps us to build up a picture of the national pattern of failures and malpractice which, in turn, feeds into the decisions CWJ takes about potential strategic litigation and other remedies.

In 2018, the government opened a new avenue for police accountability in the form of super-complaints, whereby complaints about a particular policing issue, as distinct from the conduct of individual officers, could be lodged by a designated body. If accepted, these super-complaints would be investigated by three national agencies with the authority to make recommendations for change: HM Inspectorate, the College of Policing and the Independent Office of Police Conduct. CWJ swiftly applied to become a designated body, enabling Nogah to draw on evidence gathered from our front-line partners to put forward specific systemic issues for scrutiny. Our first police super-complaint concerned the failure of forces across the country to make proper use of the powers they have to protect women facing domestic violence. The second addressed police-perpetrated domestic abuse.

Both turned out to be extremely timely and, as a result, our detailed, evidence-based reports were picked up by the media, which gave CWJ a platform to comment publicly and authoritatively on these issues. In March 2021, a year after our second super-complaint was lodged, the news broke that Sarah Everard, a thirty-three-year-old woman who had disappeared while walking home from a friend's house in South London, had been kidnapped, raped and murdered by a serving police officer. He had used his warrant card to 'arrest' Sarah, claiming that she had breached Covid-19 regulations. It later emerged that PC Wayne Couzens, who had worked in the Parliamentary and Diplomatic Protection branch, a specialist armed elite unit of the Met, had previously been reported on several occasions for indecent exposure and was known among his colleagues as 'the rapist'. Nothing had been done to deal with his conduct or these allegations.

The disappearance, rape and murder of Sarah Everard precipitated a public outcry about the safety of women and lifted the lid on a prevalent misogynistic culture in policing. The person in charge of the Met at the time was, ironically, the first-ever female and openly lesbian commissioner of police for the metropolis, Cressida Dick, with whom I was only too familiar as the commander in charge of the operation that had led to the fatal shooting of Jean Charles de Menezes sixteen years earlier. Her characterization of Wayne Couzens as a 'bad apple' brought to mind the 'rogue officer' claim made a decade before about Mark Kennedy, the first of what would turn out to be a significant number of undercover police officers to be exposed for having sexual relationships with women on whom they were spying.

This flew in the face of what our super-complaint was bringing into the light: alarming numbers of women disclosing abuse by police officers. Other depraved police conduct being reported by the media included the sickening story that officers tasked with guarding the bodies of Bibaa Henry and Nicole Smallman, two black sisters murdered in a London park, had taken selfies with the dead women and shared the pictures with colleagues.

The findings of an investigation into police bullying and harassment at Charing Cross police station, which revealed, through the examination of texts and WhatsApp chats, that deeply racist, misogynistic and homophobic messages were being exchanged between a number of officers, was the last straw for the mayor of London, Sadiq Khan, who was ultimately responsible for policing in the capital. He called a meeting with Cressida Dick and her resignation soon followed.

More shocking police-perpetrated abuse surfaced, particularly within the Met. The case of David Carrick, who, over a period of twenty years as a Met officer, formed relationships with women he controlled, raped, degraded and tortured, was next to hit the headlines. Carrick, we learned, had worked in the same specialist unit as Couzens, where he was nicknamed 'the bastard'. Both men had been cleared through vetting procedures. Carrick used his police badge initially to gain the trust of women and subsequently to convince them that they would not be believed if they attempted to report him. Many of those he victimized had indeed been too terrified to try; those who did were stonewalled. It was not until after the conviction of Wayne Couzens, when a separate police force finally began taking the allegations against Carrick seriously and opened an investigation, that women felt able to come forward and the scale of his abuse became clear. CWJ have been working with several of his victims to explore a claim for damages against the Metropolitan Police.

Another high-profile issue on which we took action was a disturbing plunge in prosecutions for rape. In 2018-19, statistics were showing that the number of rape cases being charged and prosecuted had declined by a massive 53 per cent from two years previously. Less than 1.5 per cent of reported rapes were ending up in court. Through our work with Rape Crisis and other organizations supporting victims, we were being inundated with requests for help to challenge CPS decisions either not to charge or to discontinue prosecutions.

One woman, Rebecca, told me she had been raped at knifepoint and held prisoner for two days by a man she had recently started dating, a man known by the police to be violent. Despite an abundance of evidence, the CPS prosecutor dropped the case on the eve of trial, on the basis that WhatsApp messages Rebecca had sent to placate her attacker were open to misinterpretation by the jury.

Lexy Topping, a journalist with the *Guardian*, got in touch to tell me that she had spoken to a CPS whistleblower who attributed the collapse in prosecutions to a deliberate change in policy or approach on the part of senior leadership within the CPS. If that was what was going on, we thought, there might be scope for a legal challenge against the director of public prosecutions, the head of the CPS. The EVAW coalition, who were also in contact with the whistle-blower, told us that, in 2017, Gregor McGill, the CPS director of legal services – together with Neil Moore, the DPP's principal legal adviser, whom I'd last come across in the de Freitas case – had conducted a series of training sessions for all specialist rape and sexual offence prosecutors with the key message of encouraging them to remove 'weak cases' from the system in order to achieve a higher conviction rate.

With EVAW as the claimant, and Kate Ellis at the helm, we put together a crack legal team to bring a judicial review of the DPP. We assembled a dossier of over twenty strong cases of rape that had been referred to the CPS by the police but were then dropped. The whistle-blower gave us a detailed statement about the alleged change in policy and methodology. The crucial shift was a retreat from the previous 'merits-based' approach to decisions to charge, which stipulated an objective assessment of the evidence and not one influenced by guessing how a jury, potentially prejudiced by rape myths and stereotypes, might perceive it. We also instructed a statistician to analyze the various statistical evidence available to see if that could help us link the onset of the fall in charging rates to the adoption of new training steering prosecutors away from the merits-based strategy.

As we have seen, when deciding to prosecute, the CPS must follow the Code for Crown Prosecutors and consider, first, whether the case passes the 'evidential test', namely that there is sufficient evidence to provide a reasonable prospect of conviction, and, second, whether the prosecution is in the public interest. Rape is a notoriously difficult crime to prosecute because of the persistence of a victim-blaming culture awash with misconceptions and assumptions about how a victim should behave. The merits-based approach – introduced some years earlier during Keir Starmer's tenure as DPP – was one of a number of measures incorporated into the guidance for Crown prosecutors to help prevent investigations and prosecutions of rape from being swayed by such fallacious bias.

Our client, EVAW, as the claimant, were vulnerable to having costs ordered against it if we lost what was going to be a complex and novel legal action. It was, though, like the successful challenge to the decision of the Parole Board to release John Worboys, a matter of widespread public interest, and another case, we felt, where crowdfunding might be the answer. The CrowdJustice campaign we launched attracted a huge level of support, mainly from thousands of women across the country who felt themselves failed by the criminal justice system. Vera Baird, with whom I had first worked all those years ago on the Emma Humphreys appeal, had recently been installed as the government's victims' commissioner for England and Wales, and in that capacity she was a tremendous help in highlighting the lamentable handling of rape complaints. In concert with women's sector voices, she was pushing the government to initiate an 'end-to-end' rape review to examine the plummeting number of prosecutions, among other issues.

During the crowdfunding campaign we locked horns with Max Hill, DPP since 2018, who adopted an increasingly defensive approach. The hotly contested legal case went up to the Court of Appeal, where it was considered by the lord chief justice. Despite the strength of our evidence, the court dismissed our claim, in essence because they didn't want to get into arguments over disputed facts and chose in this instance to rely on the principle of deference to the state body, in other words, to favour the DPP's framing of the evidence. Costs were ordered against EVAW, which meant that most of the funds of £115,000 we had raised through CrowdJustice had to be paid to the CPS. We wrote to the CPS inviting them, as a publicly funded body, not to enforce the costs against a small women's charity, offering instead to use the money pledged to support rape victims pursuing justice. The CPS, however, insisted on taking their pound of flesh.

Although we were gutted that the case was thrown out, and dismayed to see people's donations going to pay the costs of a state body that was failing women, we took heart that, in terms of furthering our objectives, we were by no means the losers. Not only had we won in the court of public opinion but, in the wake of our challenge, the CPS did go on to introduce some improvements to their strategy around rape. We are now beginning to see some changes for the better in their decision-making and an increase in the number of rape prosecutions.

Another issue we were being told about in the handling of rape complaints was happening at the reporting stage. The police were, it seemed, requiring victims to consent to giving investigators access to all their 'digital data', ostensibly to ensure that it contained nothing that might undermine a prosecution case. But that blanket term would encompass all phone messages, emails and Facebook and other social media activity, some of which might be deeply private and personal. While limited disclosure of such communications might well be relevant to the case – any dialogue between the victim and the alleged rapist, for example – there would be a great deal that wasn't. The pursuit of such sweeping consent, particularly from women already intimately violated by the rape they were reporting, was profoundly intrusive and disproportionate.

We decided to bring a separate judicial review, on behalf of two women we had advised in relation to this issue, challenging the wholesale and excessive disclosure it represented. We argued that, as the majority of victims of rape were women, it amounted to sex discrimination. We teamed up with another legal charity, Big Brother Watch, who produced evidence, through a series of Freedom of Information requests, of the inconsistent approach taken by different police forces to digital downloads. The claim, funded by the Equality and Human Rights Commission, was brought against the National Police Chiefs Council and the CPS, the bodies responsible for producing an open-ended 'consent form' that rape victims were effectively obliged to sign if they wanted to see their case progress. Our claim was stayed to await the findings of an information commissioner's report on the same issue. Then a Court of Appeal judgment on a separate case helped decide the matter, and the NPCC caved in and withdrew the offending consent form.

This was one of several interventions that have seen improvements in procedures for the extraction of digital data, although problems are still encountered. CWJ subsequently joined forces with EVAW and Rape Crisis to press for amendments to the Victims and Prisoners Bill to ensure that requests by the police and the CPS for third-party data, whether digital or on paper, are reasonable or necessary.

Drawing on the evidence compiled for these judicial reviews, CWJ, EVAW and Rape Crisis also collaborated with Imkaan, an umbrella organization dedicated to addressing violence against black and minoritized women, to produce a report, *The Decriminalisation of Rape: Why the justice system is failing rape survivors and what needs to change*, which has attracted the attention of government and shadow ministers interested in tackling, or at least responding to, concerns raised about our defective legal process.

As well as letting down victims and survivors by failing to investigate or prosecute crimes against them, this same justice system, of course, lets down abused women who break the law by criminalizing them far too readily. It had always been clear to me, as it was to other lawyers involved with Justice for Women who had represented women driven by violence and cruelty to kill their abuser, that our criminal justice apparatus, steeped in centuries of sex discrimination, rarely delivered justice in such cases.

However, this picture was based only on our own experiences and anecdotal evidence. We needed reliable research to help demonstrate what happens in these cases, to raise awareness of the systemic patterns and to identify exactly what needed to change.

The opportunity to conduct some significant evidence-based research was provided by a member of the public moved by JFW's campaign work, and in particular by the case of Stacey Hyde, another damaged seventeen-year-old found guilty of the murder of a violent man. I had represented Stacey on appeal and, in 2014, her murder conviction had been quashed and a fresh trial ordered. At her retrial the following year, the jury found she had acted in self-defence and she was acquitted altogether. Our generous donor, a retired businessman, wanted to use some of the proceeds of the sale of his firm to help others like Stacey by supporting our ongoing work. With his blessing, CWJ channelled his gift into underwriting a four-year research study culminating in the publication in 2021 of our report *Women Who Kill: How the state criminalises women we might otherwise be burying.*

The report featured interviews with twenty women who had killed violent partners and observations from six trials taking place at the time. Other interviewees included journalists, academics, and lawyers who had defended and prosecuted such women. We provided data from twenty-three domestic homicide reviews, seventeen Criminal Cases Review Commission cases, Freedom of Information requests to police forces and detailed analyses of media reportage and of the specific intersectional experiences of black and minoritized women.

We found that, over a ten-year period, between 2008 and 2018, more than 800 men had killed their female partners, compared with approximately 100 women who had killed husbands or boyfriends. In 77 per cent of cases of women killing male partners, there was evidence that those partners had abused them. Yet 43 per cent were convicted of the most serious offence available: murder. There were acquittals on grounds of self-defence in only 7 per cent of cases.

Our report showed how a lack of understanding throughout the criminal justice system of the impact on victims of violence and abuse could put these female offenders at a disadvantage from the moment of their arrest, when decisions about legal representation and whether to speak in interview are taken. We recorded cases where the CPS chose not to accept manslaughter pleas when offered or lawyers opted not to advance appropriate and available partial defences. Bad tactical decisions by defence lawyers, such as advising the client 'not to speak ill of the dead', also contributed to poor outcomes. We found evidence of misreading of the demeanour of traumatized defendants by police, psychiatrists, judges and juries which impacted on judgments.

As we were concluding our study, we were joined by Katy Swaine Williams, a legal researcher who had been conducting an examination of the wider criminalization of domestic abuse victims on behalf of the Prison Reform Trust. Since the funding for that project had come to an end, I suggested that Katy continue her important work in this field with CWJ as we put together proposals for new statutory defences for women who offend due to abuse.

Nearly 60 per cent of women in prison are known to be DV victims and many have been prey earlier in their lives to other forms of male aggression, such as child sexual abuse. Sometimes the crime for which they have been convicted is the result of the use of violence in defending themselves; sometimes it may have its source in a coercive and controlling relationship, where women may be induced to hide drugs or weapons, or handle stolen goods, or commit fraud by signing papers. They may have broken the law only because they were more terrified of the consequences if they did not do as they were told. The only possible defence in such cases, duress, is so restricted in its applicability – it is limited to cases where the offender is under imminent threat of death or serious injury – that in practice it is unavailable to victims of CCB.

In January 2019, the government introduced the Domestic Abuse Bill with proposals to create a new statutory definition of domestic abuse, incorporating not just physical and sexual violence but also psychological and economic abuse, and to introduce a range of measures to provide more effective protections for DV victims. Alongside other women's charities, we lobbied for amendments to the bill on a range of issues. Katy and I proposed two new statutory defences for women who offend as a consequence of domestic abuse. The first was to extend the so-called 'householder's defence', brought in for situations where a householder might use disproportionate force against an intruder, to circumstances in which victims of domestic abuse have responded, apparently disproportionately, to attacks or threats from a violent partner.

The second proposal was modelled on Section 45 of the Modern Slavery Act 2015, which introduced a defence to victims of trafficking if they can show that the offence they have committed occurred only as a result of coercion by a trafficker. We argued that a similar provision could be added for victims of domestic abuse. These proposals were well received, debated in Parliament and passed by the House of Lords – but, while they had support from opposition parties, they were voted down in the Commons by the Tory majority on the front benches.

Nogah Ofer, working with a coalition of organizations, had more success in getting the government to accept and pass an amendment making non-fatal strangulation a new standalone criminal offence.

This was highly significant: we had learned from our work with front-line service providers that it is extremely common for abusive and controlling men to use near-strangulation as a means of terrorizing women by demonstrating how easy it would be to kill them if they step out of line. Despite the prevalence and sinister nature of non-fatal strangulation, before the new Domestic Abuse Act came into force in 2022, such assaults were often not prosecuted at all or, if they were, the charge could be no more severe than common assault – a low-level offence that might not even result in a custodial sentence.

Strangulation is recognized as a red flag for escalating violence in abusive relationships, and studies have shown that victims subjected to previous non-fatal strangulation are seven times more likely to be killed by their abusers. It is the second most common method used in murders of women by men, after knives and other sharp instruments.

In a climate where 'consensual strangulation' of women during sex is at risk of becoming normalized, we supported the campaign group We Can't Consent To This in their drive to amend the law around consent to extreme violence. A separate amendment to the Domestic Abuse Bill was passed, aimed at clarifying the law in this regard, although its impact seems to have been of limited value. One case in which CWJ tried to intervene was that of Sam Pybus, who strangled Sophie Moss to death in 2021 and pleaded guilty to manslaughter. The court accepted his account that she 'enjoyed erotic asphyxiation' and that he hadn't intended to kill her. Sadly, she was not in a position to contradict this assertion. His sentence of four years and eight months, which meant he would be released after just three years, was referred by the attorney general as unduly lenient to the Court of Appeal, where three judges declined to increase it.

While men often kill women with their bare hands, our study on women who kill abusive male partners found that most – 80 per cent – use a weapon, in the vast majority of cases a kitchen knife, in a domestic setting. This is usually going to be the only weapon capable of counteracting the superior physical strength of a man. The method used matters as it can have a bearing on sentencing. So can location, as was highlighted by the murders of twenty-four-year-old Poppy Devey Waterhouse in December 2018 and, just a few months later, Ellie Gould, seventeen, stabbed to death with kitchen knives in their own homes by their ex-boyfriends.

The mothers of the young women, Carole Gould and Julie Devey, launched a campaign against the relatively light sentences handed down to their daughters' killers. They were calling for an increase in the minimum sentence for a murder with a knife in the home from fifteen to twenty-five years, to bring it into line with the minimum tariff for homicides where a knife has been taken to a scene outside the home, which had been introduced following a separate campaign to combat knife crime more generally. While there was a logic to this argument, and these were dreadful cases, I strongly opposed this particular reform because it would have the unintended consequence of penalizing abused women who kill while trying to defend themselves by grabbing the nearest weapon in the house: a kitchen knife.

CWJ convenes a femicide working group, bringing together lawyers and practitioners involved in supporting the families of victims. One member organization, Advocacy After Fatal Abuse, holds an annual conference where relatives' accounts of the failures of state agencies to intervene to protect women from escalating violence are shared. Too often I receive requests for assistance with cases where women have been murdered by men supposedly under probation supervision after serving prison sentences for violent crimes against women and children. The protections and systems that do exist are often not implemented properly and those responsible for discharging them need to be aware of how they can be manipulated by abusive men to further entrap or silence women.

One case I took forward with a Birnberg Peirce colleague clearly illustrates the issues we raised in our first super-complaint concerning the failure of the police to use the powers they already possessed to protect women from domestic abuse: the double homicide in Solihull in 2018 of Khaola Saleem and Raneem Oudeh, a mother and daughter of Syrian descent. Janbaz Tarin, Raneem's partner, was convicted of both murders.

The inquest in November 2022 into the deaths of Khaola and Raneem revealed some of the most shocking police failures I had ever come across. West Midlands Police neglected to follow their own basic policies and guidance on dealing with repeated reports of domestic abuse. They had contact with twenty-two-year-old Raneem on eight occasions over a five-month period and, despite a sustained campaign of abuse and stalking by Tarin, and reports of intensifying violence, they failed even to identify, let alone investigate, any criminal offences, did not once arrest Tarin and merely advised Raneem that she could apply for a non-molestation order. Which, having no other avenue open to her, she duly did. It did nothing to deter Tarin, who had told her that 'the day you leave me is the day I will kill you'.

On the day he murdered Raneem and her mother, he had already assaulted Raneem in a shisha bar. Khaola and Raneem called the police to report that he was in breach of the order but the police failed to attend. They told the women to go home and said they would come round to take a statement the following day. When Raneem and Khaola eventually, and in some trepidation, returned to Khaola's house, Tarin was lying in wait. He stabbed them both multiple times and they died in front of their home, witnessed by Khaola's younger daughter, still in her teens. The verdict of the inquest jury highlighted multiple failures by West Midlands Police that had contributed to the deaths of both women.

This case features in an examination of domestic homicides involving women from black and minoritized communities, on which we have been collaborating with Imkaan, to evaluate the additional barriers to justice they face.

The campaign started by Carole Gould and Julie Devey led to the government inviting Clare Wade KC, with whom I worked on the Sally Challen case, to undertake a review of domestic homicide sentencing, which was published in 2023. It was Clare's report emphasizing the importance of understanding the underlying dynamics of domestic abuse that recommended taking coercive and controlling behaviour into account as an aggravating factor when the perpetrator is the controller, and a mitigating factor when, as in the Challen case, the offender is the victim of CCB.

Having accepted this recommendation, the government has asked the Law Commission to look again at defences to murder in domestic settings. This has, for me, a sense of Groundhog Day about it: I contributed to a Law Commission consultation on the same issue twenty years ago, resulting in law reform that has not really changed anything. That included the repeal of the provocation defence and its replacement with a defence of 'loss of control', which recognizes 'fear of serious violence' as a trigger point.

This reform, which was incorporated into the Coroners and Justice Act 2009, was designed to address concerns we had originally raised back in the 1990s in our campaigns against the convictions of Sara Thornton, Kiranjit Ahluwalia and Emma Humphreys. In practice, though, as CWJ's 2021 *Women Who Kill* report highlighted, it hasn't prevented many women who kill their abusers from being convicted of murder: loss of control, like its predecessor, remains a difficult defence to use in such cases.

However, the new Law Commission consultation will, I hope, give us an opportunity to consolidate the work we have done in this area and to push for more effective and meaningful reforms.

Until all those working in the criminal justice field are alert to the dynamics of violence against women, we will continue to see too many deaths, too many grave miscarriages of justice where a victim becomes a defendant and ends up with a criminal record or – in some cases, a life sentence – and too many serial abusers and rapists left free to continue offending. Sometimes the relentless stories of preventable suffering and injustice leave me in a blind rage and give me sleepless nights.

We have to find ways to improve and recalibrate the criminal justice system so that it can identify and tackle those in our society who present a real risk and stop expending resources on prosecuting those who are essentially victims. That includes those we jail. Some civil rights organizations are becoming increasingly opposed to the so-called 'carceral state', which undeniably disproportionately imprisons people in certain demographics, black men in particular. Prisons are terrible places and rarely help those sentenced to spend time there to move forward with their lives.

But despite the grotesque failures we see every day in policing, among prosecutors, in the courts and post-sentence, I could not sign up to the decarceration model. There are some perpetrators of violence and sexual abuse, overwhelmingly men, who are so dangerous that they need to be contained for the protection of the public, and many others who are emboldened by a weak criminal justice system to repeatedly offend and get away with it.

Despite the enormity of the task we face, I know the Centre for Women's Justice stands as a beacon of hope for victims of male violence who have been ill-served by the machinery of the state that is supposed to keep them safe. I know this because women tell us so all the time. I also know that those in government and opposition, as well as leaders in criminal justice agencies, are listening to us, aware that what we have to say has resonance and they can't ignore the expertise we have to offer.

Epilogue

THE WOMEN AND MEN I HAVE guided through the often painfully slow and sometimes brutal process of litigation in their quest for justice have usually chosen this path not just for themselves, but because they recognize that their experiences are part of a bigger picture. Almost invariably, when seeking my legal assistance, or at some stage along the way, my clients tell me: 'I am doing this because I don't want anyone else to go through what I have been through.' I am very proud to have been instrumental in the pursuit of their objectives and in securing the outcomes they have achieved, some of which have led to changes to the law, or to policy and practice, as a result of a court judgment or in response to the threat of further costly legal challenge.

As we have seen, the Emma Humphreys case helped to root the concept of cumulative provocation in the law. The action brought by the victims of John Worboys established an investigative duty under Article 3 ECHR and opened up a route for others to hold the police to account when they fail to deliver. The Sally Challen case raised awareness of the phenomenon of coercive and controlling behaviour and of how sometimes the impact of that abuse may be the primary cause of an offence committed by a person subjected to it.

The women who took action in relation to their deception by undercover police exposed a secret, sinister underbelly to our so-called democratic country that had remained hidden for decades, and an institutionalized misogyny within the police. The challenge to the parole process produced reforms that enable the public to be given reasons when a decision is made to release a prisoner formerly considered dangerous. And women trying to put a history of street prostitution behind them no longer have to disclose their convictions to employers.

But what happens when the litigation ceases? What has happened to the people whose struggles to overcome adversity are recounted in this book? Well, while some have opted to retreat into a peaceful existence as they try to recover from the damage that led to them taking legal action in the first place, for others the battle continues.

Some of the women abused by undercover police officers have written and published their stories and are now embroiled in the ongoing public inquiry and involved in helping other victims through their campaign and support group, Police Spies Out Of Lives. David de Freitas, who awaits a decision from CEDAW, remains determined to hold the CPS accountable for the cynical choice they made to continue the private prosecution that triggered his daughter's death.

Others who might prefer to be left to get on with their lives are prepared to re-enter the fray if the outcome of their hard work is threatened – Meena and Fiona, for instance, not only stepped up to oppose the release of John Worboys, they were also willing to lend their voices to the campaign against the repeal of the Human Rights Act when, in the summer of 2022, the incumbent justice secretary, Dominic Raab, introduced his Bill of Rights (better known to campaigners as the 'Rights Removal Bill').

The tragic death of Emma Humphreys in 1998 has been commemorated every year since through the Emma Humphreys Memorial Prize, a small charity I co-founded. At an event held annually, we recognize the contribution of women whose work has challenged violence against women and girls with an award and a cash prize. The inaugural winner was Fiona Broadfoot, who had met Emma and has campaigned tirelessly to end the exploitation of women and girls caught up in prostitution. Some of the other women for whom I have acted have also been prize-winners, including Sana, the former immigration detainee who exposed sexual abuse by staff at Yarl's Wood, and Amber, the Rochdale grooming gang survivor who spoke out about police failures and the criminalization of sexually exploited children.

The cousins of Jean Charles de Menezes remember him on 22 July every year at the beautiful memorial shrine created at Stockwell Underground station. His story, and that of the day the Metropolitan Police mounted a major operation to target a terrorist gang and instead shot an entirely innocent man, will not be forgotten: plans for a number of TV documentaries and a four-part drama series to coincide with the twentieth anniversary of Jean Charles's death are in the works.

Sally Challen, who remains in touch with some of the women with whom she was in prison, tells me she has at last found happiness after meeting up again with Richard's former best friend, Dellon. They have since married. Sally's son David has continued to campaign around wider issues of coercive control and prisoners' rights and is one of a growing number of men willing to call out male violence against women and to stand as true allies of survivors and the feminist project.

Most of the lawyers with whom I worked so closely on these cases are still fighting the good fight, including my colleagues Gareth and Marcia, who have maintained the legend that is Birnberg Peirce solicitors. Many of the barristers have taken silk, and some continue to offer their expertise to assist with CWJ cases. A number have gone on to become judges, some sitting in the High Court; several, like Vera Baird, went into politics. Vera was MP for Redcar and appointed solicitor general during Gordon Brown's premiership before becoming police and crime commissioner for Northumbria and, more recently, victims' commissioner for England and Wales.

One of the aims of the Centre for Women's Justice is to nurture the feminist lawyers of the future and it is exciting for me, and for our enthusiastic and expert board of trustees and staff, to see young paralegals who have worked with us go on to forge careers in the field, and lawyers in other firms and charities building on the bank of knowledge and the changes we have helped to mould.

I am constantly buoyed up by the work and passion of my colleagues at CWJ, of activist survivors and of so many others in the wider women's sector and the legal world who have collaborated with us on litigation, law and policy reform and a range of initiatives to improve criminal justice outcomes for women.

Ours is an ambitious project and change does not happen overnight. But when those sleepless nights strike, I remind myself of how important and rewarding this work is and how far we have come. And the sweet moments when we do win a legal battle, or expose wrongdoing, make it all worthwhile.

Acknowledgements

FIRST AND FOREMOST, HUGE THANKS must go to all the clients whose stories feature in this book. They are told in my words and from my perspective but I have endeavoured as best I can to reflect your experiences accurately. Thank you for trusting me with your cases and with these accounts. I have worked with many other clients over the years who made their mark and whose stories I would like to have told, had there been the space. Maybe one day I will.

Thank you to my legal teammates from all the solicitor firms I have worked with. To Winstanley Burgess, for recruiting me as a trainee and introducing me to the world of legal aid practice and, in particular, to 'actions against the police' and immigration and asylum law. To everyone at Birnberg Peirce, and, in particular, my civil department colleagues, especially Marcia Willis Stewart, my Birnberg Peirce 'sister in law', for her wisdom, solidarity and support – and Irène Nembhard from the original gang of three. To the many PAs, paralegal assistants and trainees who assisted in the casework by taking statements, chasing records, reviewing and organizing disclosure and preparing bundles – Sheila Burton, Cassie Laver, Leah Thomas, Alice, Paul Ham, Zizi and Hattie Bland, among others. To my colleagues who remained at Birnberg's while I set up the Centre for Women's Justice and helped out on the many important cases I could no longer continue to manage myself: the long-suffering Sarah Kellas, Kate Thomas and Tara Mulcair, and Sally Middleton, Gareth, Nigel and others across various departments.

To the team at CWJ, who have led on many of the exciting projects and litigation described here, mainly in the final chapter: Nogah Ofer, Kate Ellis, Debaleena Dasgupta, Katy Swaine Williams and, in particular, my right-hand woman, Nic Mainwood. To my immensely supportive trustees: Sasha Deepwell, Sarah Ricca, Davina James-Hanman, Heather Harvey, Sanchita Hosali, Samira Ahmed, Janice Turner, Fiona McKenzie, Esohe Agaste and Yasmin Rehman.

To all the barristers I have worked with whose expert legal advice and advocacy helped guide so many of the cases towards a satisfying and significant outcome.

To members of Justice for Women who met and brainstormed on cases, supported the women, created leaflets, placards and banners and stood stoically outside courts come rain, sun or snow . . . Jinny Keatinge, Cheryl Stafford, Sarah Maguire, Bridget Irving, Clare Wade, Claire Mawer, Lee Nurse, Julie Bindel and Nic Mainwood, other lawyers we worked with and our West Yorkshire comrades, especially Sandra McNeill and Lesley Semmens.

To the late great Jalna Hanmer for her inspired idea, and the trustees and judges of the Emma Humphreys Memorial Prize: Claire Lazarus, Karen Ingala Smith, Joan Scanlon, Rosa Bennathan, Julie Bindel, Rahila Gupta, Fiona Broadfoot, Jenni Murray, Comfort Momoh and Bea Campbell.

To colleagues at other firms and barristers' chambers who worked collegiately on cases, particularly those from the Police Action Lawyers group and Inquest Lawyers group. To the campaign groups: Justice for Women and Southall Black Sisters (big shout-out to Pragna Patel and Hannana Siddiqui); members of the Justice4Jean campaign, including Asad Rehman, Yasmin Khan and Estelle du Boulay; Medical Justice, Yarl's Wood Befrienders; to the great women's sector groups with whom I have collaborated: Eaves, Nia, EVAW, Rape Crisis and many more.

To the feminist academics whose research and thinking has

provided added gravitas and evidential value to the cases, among them Liz Kelly, Linda Regan, Marianne Hester, Betsy Stanko and Katrin Hohl, Jalna Hanmer, Evan Stark and Cassandra Wiener.

To all the whistle-blowers who risked their careers to expose wrongdoing, with special thanks to Maggie Oliver, formerly of Greater Manchester Police, and 'XX' at the CPS.

To the trauma-informed and compassionate psychiatrists, psychologists and other experts who went the extra mile to produce reports that laid bare the harms caused by domestic abuse, sexual violence and both under- and over-policing.

To the writers, journalists and broadcasters who amplified the voices of those who battled for justice.

To the politicians who helped push through legislation and changes in approach that improved the landscape and who challenged some of the more frightening ideas of government.

And, specifically in relation to the production of this book, to special agent Becky, to my publisher, Susanna Wadeson, for her wonderful enthusiasm and guidance (and to her team at Torva), and to Caroline North McIlvanney, my painstaking editor, for making it all flow and hang together with integrity.

I am grateful to my dear friend Sasha Deepwell, who spurred and cajoled me into establishing CWJ and graciously accepted the role of chair, which she performs conscientiously and with flair, for her further encouragement and support with this latest project.

And to my greatest cheerleader, confidence-booster and provider of endless ideas and challenges, wisdom, humour and sustenance: Julie Bindel.

Notes and Further Information

KEY LEGISLATION

Street Offences Act 1959
Immigration Act 1971
Health and Safety at Work Act 1974
Data Protection Act 1998
Human Rights Act 1998
Regulation of Investigatory Powers Act 2000
Detention Centre Rules 2001
Sexual Offences Act 2003
Coroners and Justice Act 2009
Equality Act 2010
Defamation Act 2013
Serious Crime Act 2015
Modern Slavery Act 2015
Domestic Abuse Act 2021
Covert Human Intelligence Sources (Criminal Conduct) Act 2021
Illegal Migration Act 2023

CASE REFERENCES AND NOTES

1 From Campaigner to Lawyer

R v. Ruth Ellis [2003] EWCA Crim 3556
Ruth Ellis's conviction for murder in 1955 was eventually re-examined, almost
half a century after she was hanged, and dismissed.

R v. Thornton [1992] 1 All ER 306
Sara Thornton's first appeal, in 1991, which was dismissed.

R v. Ahluwalia [1992] 4 All ER 889

R v. Emma Humphreys [1995] 4 All ER 1008

R v. Stewart [1995] 4 All ER 999, CA
This case was relied on when considering the second ground in the Emma Humphreys appeal – in particular the passage: 'Where the judge must, as a matter of law, leave the issue of provocation to the jury, he should indicate to them, unless it is obvious, what evidence might support the conclusion that the appellant lost his self-control.' The judgment in the Humphreys appeal stated: 'In the light of *Stewart*, we consider that guidance, in the form of a careful analysis of these strands [of provocative conduct], should have been given by the judge so that the jury could clearly understand their potential significance.'

R v. Thornton [1996] 1 WLR 1174
The successful appeal that led to Sara Thornton's retrial.

2 Jean Charles de Menezes and the Politics of Policing

Armani da Silva v United Kingdom [2016] Grand Chamber ECHR 5878/08
The case challenging the decision of the DPP not to prosecute any police officer in connection with the shooting of Jean Charles de Menezes, which eventually went all the way to the European Court in Strasbourg.

Stockwell 1: Investigation into the shooting of Jean Charles de Menezes at Stockwell Underground station on 22 July 2005, published by the IPCC.
http://policeauthority.org/metropolitan/downloads/scrutinites/stockwell/ipcc-one.pdf

Stockwell 2: Investigation into complaints about the Metropolitan Police Service's handling of public statements following the shooting of Jean Charles de Menezes.
https://www.jesip.org.uk/wp-content/uploads/2022/03/Stockwell-Shooting-Report-Jean-Charles-De-Menzes-Part-2.pdf

3 'Shut Down Yarl's Wood'

ID and Others v. The Home Office [2006] 1 All ER 183
The case in which we intervened to preserve the right to bring claims against the Home Office for unlawful immigration detention.

NAB v. Serco Ltd and Another [2014] EWHC 1225 (QB)
The action brought by the *Guardian* and *Observer* newspapers for disclosure of the Serco report on Sana's case referenced in the civil proceedings.

Lord Chancellor v. Detention Action [2015] EWCA Civ 840
In which the Court of Appeal ruled that the Detained Fast Track system for processing asylum applications was unlawful.

4 Challenging the Failure to Investigate

Hill v. The Chief Constable of West Yorkshire Police [1987] UKHL 12 [1989] AC
House of Lords case relating to the murder of Jacqueline Hill, the last victim of Peter Sutcliffe, the so-called Yorkshire Ripper, which established that the police were immune from an action in negligence relating to the investigation of crime.

DSD and NBV v. The Commissioner of Police of the Metropolis [2014] EWHC 436 (QB)
The judgment given by Mr Justice Green following the civil trial in the High Court which found in favour of Fiona and Meena.

The Commissioner of Police of the Metropolis v. DSD and Anor [2018] UKSC 11
The Supreme Court judgment that established the investigative duty of the police under Article 3 ECHR.

5 A Perversion of the Course of Public Justice

Alexander Economou v. David de Freitas [2016] EWHC 1853 (QB)
The unsuccessful libel claim brought by Economou against David de Freitas.

The Code for Crown Prosecutors can be found at
https://www.cps.gov.uk/publication/code-crown-prosecutors

The United Nations Convention on the Elimination of All Forms of Discrimination against Women (CEDAW) came into force in 1981. It was ratified by the UK in 1986.

6 Undercover Police: The Personal Is Political

McDonald's Corporation v. Steel & Morris [1997] EWHC 366 (QB)
Libel case brought by McDonald's against Helen Steel and Dave Morris of
   London Greenpeace.

AKJ and Others v. Commissioner of Police of the Metropolis & Others [2013]
   EWHC 32 (QB)
Challenge brought by Lisa, Naomi and Kate over whether the Investigatory
   Powers Tribunal had exclusive jurisdiction in their case.

DIL and Others v. Commissioner of Police [2014] 2184 (QB)
Case concerning whether police can rely on Neither Confirm Nor Deny to
   avoid pleading a defence.

Kate Wilson v. Commissioner of Police and NPCC [2021] IPT/11/167/H
Kate's case in the IPT which ultimately led to a judgment upholding her
   claim that her human rights, as protected by Articles, 3, 8 10, 11 and 14
   ECHR, had been violated.

R (Monica) v. Director of Public Prosecutions [2018] EWHC 3508 (QB)
Unsuccessful judicial review challenge of the decision of the Crown
   Prosecution Service not to prosecute Jim Boyling for any offence. The
   legal challenge was focused on the offences of misconduct in public office
   and rape. In respect of rape, the question to be determined was whether
   Monica's consent to sex was vitiated by Boyling's deceit.

The Home Affairs Select Committee report on undercover policing,
   5 February 2013.
   https://publications.parliament.uk/pa/cm201213/cmselect/
   cmhaff/837/83702.htm

More information on the Undercover Policing Inquiry can be found on its
   official website: https://www.ucpi.org.uk/

The inquiry's Tranche 1 interim report was published on 29 June 2023.
   https://www.ucpi.org.uk/2023/06/29/undercover-policing-inquirys-
   tranche-1-interim-report-published/

Sharp-eyed readers will have noticed that timings in the account of his activities given by Mark Kennedy to the *Daily Mail* do not quite tally with Lisa's recollections. I adhere to the *v* more precise timings provided by Lisa and other women in my records.

7 Women Who Kill: The Case of Sally Challen

The new offence of controlling and coercive behaviour in an intimate or family relationship is enshrined in Section 76 of the Serious Crime Act 2015.

R v. Challen [2019] EWCA Crim 916
Judgment of the Court of Appeal quashing the murder conviction of Sally Challen.

8 Releasing a Serial Rapist: A Risk to the Public?

Associated Provincial Picture Houses v. Wednesbury Corporation [1948] 1KB
The case that established the test for irrationality in judicial review.

The Queen (on an application by DSD and NBV and Others) v. The Parole Board of England and Wales and the Secretary of State for Justice [2018] EWHC 694 (Admin)
The judgment quashing the decision of the Parole Board to release John Worboys and requiring the justice secretary to reformulate Rule 25 in accordance with the principle of open justice.

9 Fighting the Legacy of the Sex Trade

The Palermo Protocol, also known as the Protocol to Prevent, Suppress and Punish Trafficking in Persons Especially Women and Children, supplements the United Nations Convention against Transnational Organized Crime adopted by the General Assembly in 2000.

The Modern Slavery Act 2015 provides, under Section 45, a defence for a range of criminal offences where it can be shown that the offence was committed because of modern slavery or human trafficking.

R (on an application of P, G and W) v. Secretary of State for the Home Department [2019] UKSC 3

The citation for the Supreme Court judgment that considered a number of cases together concerning the operation of the Disclosure and Barring Scheme and the circumstances in which historical convictions could be filtered from disclosure. These were conjoined cases but in respect of *R(P)*, the court held that the blanket operation of the 'multiple convictions rule' was disproportionate under Article 8 ECHR.

R (QSA & Ors) v. SSHD & Anor [2018] EWHC 407 (Admin)
The full title of this case is *The Queen on an application of (1) QSA (2) Fiona Broadfoot (3) ARB v Secretary of State for the Home Department and Secretary of State for Justice*
The case we brought which held that disclosure of our clients' criminal convictions was unlawful.

10 The Centre for Women's Justice

R (End Violence Against Women Coalition) v. The Director of Public Prosecutions [2021] EWCA Civ 350
The claim we brought on behalf of EVAW against the DPP in relation to the drastic drop in the prosecution of rape.

The Coroners and Justice Act 2009 reformed the defences to murder of provocation and diminished responsibility.

The Domestic Abuse Act 2021 included the introduction of the new offence of non-fatal strangulation (Section 70) and codified the law around consenting to ABH or above for sexual gratification (Section 71).

Full reports and super-complaints are available on the CWJ website: https://www.centreforwomensjustice.org.uk

RECOMMENDED FURTHER READING, VIEWING AND LISTENING

For more on Sharon Henderson's long battle for justice:

Julie Bindel's five-part podcast *Three Doors Down* (Tortoise Media, 2023)

Dani Garavelli's article 'All in Slow Motion' in the *London Review of Books* (Vol. 45, No. 12, 15 June 2023)

https://www.lrb.co.uk/the-paper/v45/n12/dani-garavelli/all-in-slow-motion

On the issues raised in Chapter 1, and for fuller accounts of the stories of the women whose cases are featured:

Provocation and Responsibility by Jeremy Horder (Oxford University Press, 1992)

Sara Thornton: The Story of a Woman Who Killed by Jennifer Nadel (Gollancz, 1993)

Circle of Light: The Autobiography of Kiranjit Ahluwalia by Kiranjit Ahluwalia and Rahila Gupta (HarperCollins, 1991). Later published under the title *Provoked*.

Kiranjit's story is also told in the film *Provoked* (2006), directed by Jag Mundhra, available on various streaming platforms.

The Map of My Life: The Story of Emma Humphreys: edited by Julie Bindel and Harriet Wistrich (Astraia Press, 2003)

Emma Humphreys: The Legacy (2009), a film directed by Pratibha Parmar, can be viewed on YouTube: https://www.youtube.com/watch?v=yS80a5OOoZA

Our report on the treatment of detainees, *Outsourcing abuse: the use and misuse of state-sanctioned force during the detention and removal of asylum-seekers* (Birnberg Pierce & Partners, Medical Justice, National Coalition of Anti-Deportation Campaigns), published in 2008, is available on the Medical Justice website: https://medicaljustice.org.uk/research/outsourcing-abuse

The investigative failures of the police in the Worboys case are explored in a 2021 Channel 5 documentary, *Predator: Catching the Black Cab Rapist*.

On the women deceived by undercover police officers:

Undercover: The True Story of Britain's Secret Police by Rob Evans and Paul Lewis (Guardian/Faber & Faber, 2014)

Deep Deception: The story of the spycops network by the women who uncovered the shocking truth (Ebury Press, 2022), co-authored by five of the women whose experiences are recounted in this book: Alison, Belinda Harvey, Helen Steel, Lisa and Naomi.

The Channel 4 *Dispatches* documentary in which Belinda and Helen participated, 'The Police's Dirty Secret' (24 June 2013), can be viewed at: https://vimeo.com/69093606

Bed of Lies, an award-winning seven-part podcast by Cara McCoogan for the *Daily Telegraph* (2020), features interviews with some of the women in the case and with me.

Small Town Girl: Love, Lies and the Undercover Police by Donna McLean (Hodder & Stoughton, 2022). I also represented Donna in proceedings arising from her experience.

On Sally Challen's case and coercive control:

Coercive Control: How Men Entrap Women in Personal Life by Professor Evan Stark (Oxford University Press, 2009) is the seminal work on coercive control. A second edition (2024) is now available.

Sally's case, and the implications of the judgment, are discussed in numerous articles and books around the subject of coercive control. It is also examined in a 2019 BBC documentary, *The Case of Sally Challen*. https://www.youtube.com/watch?v=PwVEsuFMUTo

For more information on the legacy of prostitution:

'I'm no Criminal' – Examining the Impact of Prostitution-Specific Criminal Records on Women Seeking to Exit Prostitution (report by the Nia Project, July 2017) https://niaendingviolence.org.uk/resources/

Exiting Prostitution: A Study in Female Desistance by Roger Matthews, Helen Easton, Lisa Young and Julie Bindel (Palgrave Macmillan, 2014)

The Pimping of Prostitution: Abolishing the Sex Work Myth by Julie Bindel (Macmillan, 2017)

On women and the justice system:

Coercive Control and the Criminal Law by Cassandra Wiener (Routledge, 2023)

Eve was Shamed: How British Justice Is Failing Women by Helena Kennedy (Chatto & Windus, 2018)

How Many More Women? The silencing of women by the law and how to stop it by Jennifer Robinson and Keina Yoshida (Endeavour, 2023)

'Misogyny in the Criminal Justice System' – article by the author in *The Political Quarterly* (January 2022)

Women Who Kill, Criminal Law and Domestic Abuse edited by Rachel M. McPherson (Routledge, 2023), to which the author has contributed.

CWJ Manifesto by Harriet Wistrich
My ten-part 'manifesto' sets out what needs to change to improve our justice system in relation to violence against women and girls. https://www.centreforwomensjustice.org.uk/cwj-manifesto

The following reports can be found on: https://www.centreforwomensjustice.org.uk

The Decriminalisation of Rape: Why the justice system is failing rape survivors and what needs to change (EVAW, Rape Crisis, Centre for Women's Justice)

Women Who Kill: How the state criminalises women we might otherwise be burying

Life or Death? Preventing Domestic Homicides and Suicides of Black and Minoritised Women (report based on partnership collaboration)

WEBSITES

For more information on the objectives of organizations involved in featured cases and projects, and about the resources, services and support they offer:

Centre for Women's Justice
https://www.centreforwomensjustice.org.uk

Justice for Women
https://www.justiceforwomen.org.uk

Advocacy After Fatal Domestic Abuse (AAFDA)
https://aafda.org.uk

Emma Humphreys Memorial Prize
https://emmahumphreys.org

End Violence Against Women coalition
https://www.endviolenceagainstwomen.org.uk

Imkaan
https://www.imkaan.org.uk

Inquest
https://www.inquest.org.uk

Medical Justice
https://medicaljustice.org.uk

Nia
https://niaendingviolence.org.uk

Police Spies Out Of Lives
https://policespiesoutoflives.org.uk

Rape Crisis England & Wales
https://rapecrisis.org.uk

Southall Black Sisters
https://southallblacksisters.org.uk

Women's Aid
https://womensaid.org.uk

Index